Soviet Strategy in Europe

Soviet Strategy IN Europe

EDITED BY

Richard Pipes

Crane, Russak & Company, Inc.

NEW YORK

Soviet Strategy in Europe

Published in the United States by

Crane, Russak & Company, Inc.

347 Madison Avenue
New York, New York 10017

Printed in the United States of America

The research on which this work is based was
supported by the Advanced Research Projects
Agency of the Department of Defense under
Contract No. DAHC15–73–0380. The views
and conclusions contained here are those of the
authors and should not be interpreted as necessarily representing the official policies, either
expressed or implied, of the Advanced Research Projects Agency of the U.S. Government.

Stanford Research Institute is an independent
nonprofit organization providing specialized research
services under contract to business, industry, the
U.S. government, and some foreign governments,
particularly those in the developing nations. The
Institute's basic aims have been to enhance economic,
political, and social development and to contribute
through objective research to the peace and prosperity
of mankind.

The Strategic Studies Center of SRI was organized
in 1954 by Richard B. Foster, Director. Based in
Washington, D.C., the Center conducts multidisciplinary research on foreign, defense,
and international economic policy.

With a client structure consisting of the key U.S.
government agencies charged with responsibility in
these areas, the Strategic Studies Center has
participated in the ongoing dialogue in both the
policymaking and research communities on the critical
choices facing the United States, particularly in the
field of national security.

To make the findings of the Center's research
available to a broader public, the Strategic Studies
Center is publishing a series of books and monographs.
The views expressed are those of the authors and do
not necessarily reflect the position of the Center.

Contents

Contributors

CHRISTOPHER CVIIC is a Member of the Editorial Board of *The Economist* (London) and is a lead writer and correspondent on East European affairs.

JOHN ERICKSON is Director, Defence Studies, University of Edinburgh, Scotland. He is a specialist on Soviet military history and military affairs. Professor Erickson is the author of *The Soviet High Command 1918–1941* and *The Road to Stalingrad (Volume I: Stalin's War with Germany 1941–1945)*.

PHILIP HANSON is on the faculty of the University of Birmingham, England. He is the author of *The Consumer in the Soviet Economy* and *Advertising and Socialism, A Study of the Nature and Extent of Consumer Advertising in the Soviet Union, Poland, Hungary and Yugoslavia*.

MICHAEL KASER is a Reader in Economics at Oxford University and is a Professorial Fellow at St. Antony's College, Oxford. He is the author of *Comecon, Integration Problems of the Planned Economies; Soviet Economics; Planning in East Europe* (with J. Zielinski); and *Health Care in Comecon*.

JOHN PINDER is the Director of Political and Economic Planning (PEP), London, and author of *Britain and the Common Market*. He is also editor and part author of *The Economics of Europe* and is co-author of *The European Community's Policy Towards Eastern Europe*.

PAULINE PINDER was Director of the International Division of the Economist Intelligence Unit and is the author of *The Foreign Trade of Communist China*. She is also the coauthor of *The European Community's Policy Towards Eastern Europe*.

RICHARD PIPES is Frank B. Baird, Jr., Professor of History at Harvard University and is Senior Research Consultant, Strategic Studies Center, Stanford Research Institute. He directed the Russian Research Center at Harvard University from 1968–1973. He is the author of numerous studies on Russian history including *The Formation of the Soviet Union* and *Russia Under the Old Regime*.

LOTHAR RUEHL is a Specialist on European Security Affairs and is Deputy Chief Editor of *Die Welt* in Hamburg, the Federal Republic of Germany. He is the author of *Israels Letzter Krieg* and *Vietnam*.

MICHEL TATU is Director of the Foreign Department of *Le Monde* in Paris and previously was correspondent of *Le Monde* in Moscow (1957–1964). He is the author of *Power in the Kremlin*.

THOMAS W. WOLFE is a Senior Staff Member of the Rand Corporation and a member of the faculty of the Institute for Sino-Soviet Studies, The George Washington University, Washington, D.C. He is a specialist on Soviet military affairs and the author of *Soviet Strategy at the Crossroads* and *Soviet Power and Europe: 1945–1970*.

Foreword

In 1974 the Strategic Studies Center of the Stanford Research Institute embarked on an in-depth multidisciplinary reexamination of the basic issues and contradictions characterizing the complex relationships among the Soviet Union, its allies of the Warsaw Pact, the United States, and the other countries of the industrial West. The emergence in the 1970s of a new spirit of détente had softened the hard outlines of the confrontation that marked the 1950s and 1960s, but many of the basic conflicts remained unresolved, and new sources of potential confrontation such as the worldwide energy crisis threatened the stability of Western Europe.

In this paradoxical context of relaxed tension and crisis, the Center invited a number of research colleagues in Western Europe and the United States to assess the role of détente in the evolving post-cold war relationships between East and West as seen from the point of view of their own areas of specialization. This volume, which is a product of the basic 1974 research effort, presents the findings of these men and women.

Professor Richard Pipes, of Harvard University and the Strategic Studies Center, provided the overall guidance for the study and is the editor of this book. The contributors, who represent a broad spectrum of expertise in the fields of political, military, and economic analysis, are from the European Continent, England, and the United States. In spite of their diverse backgrounds, they present evidence that leads, although without premeditation, to the conclusion that détente as currently incurred in the United States is not in itself a bridge that will span the chasm between the world views of East and West. If the grave issues outstanding between the great powers are to be resolved, an exhaustive dialogue between the two adversaries will have to take place in an environment of good faith and with candor and realism. The Center is publishing these papers in the hope that they may contribute to this essential dialogue.

RICHARD B. FOSTER
Director
Strategic Studies Center
Arlington, Virginia

Editor's Introduction

The student of Soviet foreign policy confronts a perplexing combination of day-to-day opportunism and long-term strategy. The opportunistic moves occur on the surface and catch the eye; the strategic ones are generally concealed. A comprehensive picture of Soviet Russia's international conduct requires both these elements to be taken into consideration.

This volume is the outgrowth of a study undertaken by the Strategic Studies Center of the Stanford Research Institute to analyze the strategic aspects of Soviet global policy—that is, the coordination of political, military, economic, and ideological instrumentalities toward predetermined long-term objectives. Its subject matter is what Soviet parlance defines as the "political line." The papers included here stress Russia's policies toward and within Europe. The authors, all but two of whom are themselves Europeans, seek to lay bare the persistent elements in Soviet Russia's European policy and to assess that policy's successes and failures.

The first four papers concern themselves directly with political issues: Russia's conception of détente with the West, the nature of the decision-making process in the USSR and its influence on the conduct of foreign affairs, and Russia's relations with both West and East European states. The remaining four papers approach the political problem obliquely. Two discussions focus on Soviet military activities in Europe, stressing the relationship between military power and political objectives. The final two papers address themselves to the question whether and to what extent the recent expansion of trade between the Common Market and the Comecon creates ties of mutual dependence.

No attempt has been made to impose on the authors preconceived conclusions. They have been asked to seek elements of strategic planning and coordination, but they have not been urged to find them. As the reader will note, each author tends to view the matter in his own way, and the two contributors on the military question actually arrive at somewhat divergent conclusions. Even so, from the reading of these eight papers it should be possible to obtain a much better sense of the underlying purposefulness of Soviet conduct vis-à-vis Europe than from a casual collection of essays on the subject of Soviet foreign policy.

I would like to express particular gratitude to Mr. L. Labedz, the Editor of *Survey*, who has been most helpful in the preparation of this volume.

RICHARD PIPES

Soviet Strategy in Europe

Part I
THE
POLITICAL
DIMENSION

Détente: Moscow's View

RICHARD PIPES

Today, there is no question of any significance which can be decided without the Soviet Union or in opposition to it.... Moreover, it is precisely our proposals . . . that are at the center of political discussions. –*A. A. Gromyko at the XXIVth Party Congress (1971)*[1]

SOVIET HISTORICAL BACKGROUND

In the accounts they left behind, travelers who had visited Russia between the seventeenth and nineteenth centuries liked to stress the unusually low business ethics of the native population. What struck them was not only that Russian merchants, shopkeepers, peddlers, and ordinary *muzhiks* engaged in the most impudent cheating, but that once they were found out they showed no remorse. Rather than apologize, they shrugged the matter off by quoting a proverb which from frequent repetition became very familiar to resident Westerners: "It is the pike's job to keep the carps awake." This version of *caveat emptor*—"let the buyer beware"—not only enjoins the customer to look out for his interests but it also implies that if he is hoodwinked, the fault is entirely his, insofar as the pike (in this case the seller) has a nature-given right to gobble up unwary fish. It is a distillation of centuries of experience, a kind of folkish anticipation of Social Darwinism, to which a large majority of the Russian population (with the notable exception of the intelligentsia) has learned to adhere, whether placed by fortune in the role of pike or of its potential victim.

[1] *XXIV S"ezd KPSS–Stenograficheskii Otchet*, vol. 1 (Moscow, 1971), p. 482.

3

All people tend to some extent to base their understanding of foreign civilizations on personal experience and self-image and to assume that underneath the cloak of even the most exotic exterior there thinks the same mind and beats the same heart. But no one is more prone to work on this assumption than a person whose occupation is commerce and whose political creed is liberalism. The idea of human equality, the noblest achievement of "bourgeois" culture, is also the source of great political weakness because it denies a priori any meaningful distinctions among human beings, whether genetic, ethnic, racial, or other, and therefore blinds those who espouse it to a great deal of human motivation. Those differences that cannot be ignored, the commercial-liberal mind likes to ascribe to uneven economic opportunity and the resulting cultural lag. The most probable cause of this outlook, and the reason for its prevalence, lies in the contradiction between the "bourgeois" ideal of equality and the undeniable fact of widespread inequality. Such an outlook enables the "bourgeois" to enjoy his advantages without guilt, because as long as all men are presumed to be the same, those who happen to be better off may be said to owe their superior status to personal merit. In the United States, a country whose underlying culture is permeated with the commercial ethos and liberal ideology, this way of thinking is very common. Among the mass of the people it expresses itself in a spontaneous and rather endearing goodwill toward foreigners, accompanied by an unconscious and (to foreigners) irritating assumption that the American way is *the* way. Among the more learned, it conceals itself behind theoretical façades that appear to be supremely sophisticated but on closer inspection turn out to be not all that different from the ideas held by the man on the street. The various theories of "modernization" that have acquired vogue among American sociologists and political scientists since World War II, once they are stripped of their academic vocabulary, say little more than that when all the people of the globe have attained the same level of industrial development as in the United States, they will become like Americans.

This outlook is so deeply ingrained in the American psyche and is so instinctively and tenaciously held that it produces among U.S. legislators, diplomats, and other politicians a strong distaste for any sustained analysis of foreign civilizations, because such analysis might (indeed, almost certainly would) demand recognition of permanent cultural pluralities and thus call for an effort at learning and imagination not required by its more comforting alternative. It is probably true that only those theories of international relations that postulate a fundamental convergence of all human aspirations with the American ideal have any chance of acceptance in the United States. It is probably equally true that no major power can conduct a successful foreign policy if such policy refuses to recognize that there exist in the world the most fundamental differences in the psychology and aspirations of its diverse inhabitants.

The current policy of "détente," as practiced in Washington, is no exception to these rules. To me at least, it appears to be without theoretical underpinnings and to repose on nothing more substantial than a vaguely felt and poorly articulated faith that the march of human events follows the script written by the Founding Fathers, and that if one can only avoid general war long enough all will be well. We are told that détente is vital because the only alternative to it is a nuclear holocaust. This, however, is an appeal to fear, not to reason. When pressed further, the proponents of détente justify it with offhand allusions to the "web of interests" that allegedly enmeshes the Soviet Union with the rest of the world and gradually forces it to behave like any other responsible member of the international community—as if a metaphor were a substitute for evidence or analysis. A convincing argument in favor of the present détente policy would require a close investigation of the internal situation in the Soviet Union, as it was, is, and becomes, insofar as a basic postulate of this policy holds that its pursuit will exert a lasting influence on the mind and behavior of the men who rule the USSR. It would demand, at the very least, an inquiry into the social structure of the USSR, its various "interest groups," the Communist party apparatus, the internal agitation and propaganda as they relate to détente, Soviet public opinion, and the Soviet government's ability to maintain its internal controls. It would seek to explain the apparent contradictions between the Soviet government's professions of détente and certain contrary actions such as incitement of its population to the "ideological struggle" against the West, the pursuit of an unabated pace of armaments, and the appeals made to the Arabs in 1973 to persevere with their oil embargo. Furthermore, it would analyze the probable effects of détente on the Western alliance system, on the morale of the dissidents and the non-Russian inhabitants of the Soviet Union, and on U.S.-Chinese relations. It would try to do this and much more that is clearly relevant. But in fact little analysis of this type has been attempted, and virtually none of it has been made public.

What makes such failure inexcusable is that the other party to détente certainly has done its homework. Whatever the limitations of their understanding of the United States (and they are considerable), the leaders of the Soviet Union at least have made the mental effort to place themselves in the position of the U.S. government and public. With the help of the expertise available at such of their international research institutes as IMEMO (The Institute of World Economy and International Relations) and IShA (Institute of the U.S.A.), they have devised a policy of détente which serves their immediate interests without jeopardizing their long-term aspirations. *They* at least know what it is they want and how to try to go about getting it, by objectively analyzing Western strengths and weaknesses. And although the results of détente to date probably have not justified the Politburo's most sanguine expectations, thanks to an effort to understand the rival power it at least has managed to extract more than it has had to concede.

The purpose of this paper is to try to show how détente is viewed by Moscow. Much attention is given to internal factors, it being my conviction that in Russia, as elsewhere, political thinking and behavior are shaped largely by the experience gained in the arena of domestic politics. The argument in favor of this postulate is that politicians make their careers within a domestic power apparatus and, as a rule, gain the right to conduct their country's international affairs only after having successfully fought their way to the top of an internal power structure. (At any rate, the contrary almost never happens.) Foreign policy is thus an extension of domestic politics: It involves the application to other countries of habits acquired at home, in dealing with one's own subjects. The approach is also historical. Experience indicates that a country's internal politics evolve more gradually and prove more resistant to change than its foreign politics. It should be apparent that this approach differs fundamentally from that underlying the present administration's approach to the Soviet Union. The administration appears to assume the primacy of international politics (that is, the decisive impact of international relations on a country's domestic politics) and to ignore historical experience in favor of a "behavioral" response to the immediately given situation.

The first historical fact to be taken into account when dealing with the political life of Russia is that country's peculiar governmental tradition. For economic and geopolitical reasons that cannot be gone into here, during the nearly seven centuries that have elapsed since the founding of the Moscow monarchy the Russian state has claimed and, to the extent permitted by its limited means, actually exercised a kind of "proprietary" or "patrimonial" authority over the land and its inhabitants.[2] In a regime of this type, the government and its bureaucratic-military service elite feel that the country literally belongs to them and that in their capacity as its administrators and defenders they have the right to live at its expense without owing an accounting to anyone. Although Russian history has known several "liberal" interludes—notably the reigns of Catherine II and Alexander II—when attempts were undertaken to depart from this patrimonial tradition, these proved short-lived and without lasting effects. By expropriating all the "productive wealth" and much private property besides, the Soviet regime has dramatically reverted to this tradition (even though this had not been its founders' intention). In Communist Russia, as in Muscovite *Rus'*, the government as represented by the bureaucratic and military elites owns the country. No comforts or privileges in the USSR can be acquired save by favor of the state; and none are likely to be retained unless that state remains internally frozen and externally isolated.

This basic fact of Russian history has had many consequences for the *modus operandi* of Russian politicians, whatever the regime and its formal ideology. One of them of special relevance to détente is the intrinsically illiberal, antidemocratic spirit of Russian ruling elites. In

[2]The historical evolution of this type of state authority is the theme of my book *Russia Under the Old Regime* (New York: Scribner's, 1975).

"capitalist" countries it is in the interest of the elite composed of
property owners to restrain the powers of the state, because the state is
an adversary who, by means of taxes, regulations, and the threat of
nationalization, prevents it from freely enjoying its property. By contrast, in the USSR or any other state where "property" is merely
conditional possession dispensed by, and held at the grace of, the state,
the elite has an interest in preventing the diminution of the state's
power because this would inevitably result in the mass of the population demanding its rightful share of goods. The Soviet elite instinctively dislikes democratic processes, social initiative, and private property at home as well as abroad. In its relations with foreign powers it
prefers to deal on a state-to-state basis, preferably on a "summit" level,
bypassing as much as possible unpredictable legislatures that represent the citizenry. Because it fears emboldening its own population, it
rejects people-to-people contacts, unless suitably chaperoned. Nor is
the Soviet elite averse to corrupting democratic processes in foreign
countries. In its relations with the Nixon Administration, the Soviet
government placed its authority squarely behind the president during
his various contests with Congress. Thus, in violation of accepted
international practices, during President Nixon's June 1974 visit to
Moscow, Brezhnev publicly sided with him against congressional critics of his foreign policy. The Soviet government has also openly
encouraged private lobbies (for example, the National Association of
Manufacturers) to apply pressure on Congress on its behalf and has
urged the administration in various unsubtle ways to bypass Congress
in concluding various agreements with it. Entering into business arrangements with European governments and private enterprises, the
Soviet government has been known to insist on secrecy, which, in the
long run, also tends to subvert democratic procedures.[3] In countries of
the so-called Third World, representatives of the USSR openly exhort
local governments to strengthen the "public" sector of the economy at

---

[3]It is reported, for instance, that the Finnish government, which owing to Soviet
pressures must pay nearly double the prevailing world price for the oil it imports from
the USSR, is pressured not to reveal this unpalatable act to its citizenry (Neue Zürcher
Zeitung, 19 June 1974). Similarly, in their dealings with private West European banks,
Russia and the "Peoples' Democracies" are insisting, with apparent success, on a high
degree of secrecy. See Christopher Wilkins in The Times (London), 17 December
1973.

the expense of the private.[4] Just as the capitalist entrepreneur feels most comfortable in an environment where everybody pursues his private profit, so the Soviet elite prefers to be surrounded by regimes of the "patrimonial" type, run by elites like itself.

Second, attention must be called to the persistent tradition of Russian expansion. Its causes are to be sought not in racial or cultural propensities (as a matter of fact, Russians are not noted for imperialist fantasies and dislike leaving their homeland), but rather in the same economic and geopolitical factors that account for Russia's peculiar tradition of government. Climate and topography conspire to make Russia a poor country, unable to support a population of high density: Among such causes are an exceedingly short agricultural season, abundant rainfall where the soil is of low quality and unreliable rainfall where it happens to be fertile, and great difficulties of transport (long distances, severe winters, and so on). The result has been unusually high population mobility, a steady outflow of the inhabitants in all directions, away from the historic center of Great Russia in the taiga, a process that, to judge by the censuses of 1959 and 1970, continues unabated to this very day. The movement is partly spontaneous, partly government sponsored. It is probably true that no country in recorded history has expanded so persistently and held on so tenaciously to every inch of conquered land. It is estimated, for example, that between the middle of the sixteenth century and the end of the seventeenth, Russia conquered territory the size of the modern Netherlands *every year* for *150 years* running. Not surprisingly, it has been the one imperial power after World War II not only to refuse to give up the colonial acquisitions made by its "feudal" and "bourgeois" predecessors, but to increase them by the addition of new dependencies acquired during the war in Eastern Europe and the Far East. Nothing can be further from the truth than the often heard argument that Russia's expansion is due to its sense of insecurity and need for buffers. Thanks to its topography (immense depth of defense, low population density, and poor transport) Russia has always been and continues to be the world's most difficult country to conquer, as Charles XII, Napoleon, and Hitler each in turn found out. As for buffers, it is no secret

---

[4]Much evidence to this effect can be found on the pages of *USSR and Third World* published in London by the Central Asian Research Centre.

that today's buffers have a way of becoming tomorrow's homeland, which requires new buffers to protect it. Indeed, a great deal of Soviet military activity in Western Europe in recent years has been justified by the alleged need to defend Russia's interests in Eastern Europe, which interests Russia had originally acquired with the tacit acquiescence of the West as a buffer zone. It is far better to seek the causes of Russian expansionism in internal impulses springing from primarily economic conditions and the habits that they breed.

In this connection it deserves note that the population movement, which initially took the form of spontaneous colonization and in time became increasingly dependent on conquest, has from the earliest times brought Russians into intimate contact with a great variety of nations and races. It has taught them how to handle "natives" and how to exploit to their advantage "contradictions" present in neighboring countries for the purpose of weakening and subverting them preparatory to annexation. To understand some of the techniques presently employed on a global scale by Soviet diplomacy one can do no better than study the history of Moscow's conquest of Novgorod (fifteenth century), the Golden Horde (sixteenth century), and the Polish-Lithuanian Commonwealth (eighteenth century), as well as the efforts of Imperial Russia in the nineteenth century (largely frustrated by Western countermeasures) to partition the Ottoman Empire and China. No other country has a comparable wealth of accumulated experience in the application of external and internal pressures on neighbors for the purpose of softening them prior to conquest.

The third historical factor to which attention must be called in assessing Soviet attitudes to détente is the personal background of the elite that at the present time happens to govern the Soviet Union. This group rose to positions of power in the 1930s, in the turmoil of Stalin's purges and massacres—that is, under conditions of the most ruthless political infighting known in modern history. No ruling elite in the world has had to learn survival under more difficult and brutal circumstances. This elite is the product of a process of natural selection under which the fittest proved to be those who knew best how to suppress within themselves everything normally regarded as human—where indeed the "dictator of genius" treated any expression of human qualities as personal disloyalty and usually punished it with deportation or death. No one dealing with Brezhnev and his colleagues ought to forget this fact. [5]

The fourth historical fact bearing on détente is that the elite currently ruling the Soviet Union is for all practical purposes directly descended from a peasantry. This holds true also of those of its members whose parents were industrial workers or urban petty bourgeois (*meshchane*) because a large part of Russian industry was traditionally located in the countryside, and much of the so-called urban population consisted of peasants temporarily licensed to reside in cities. Now the Russian *muzhik* is a very complicated being: The mysteries of his character form a puzzle that has engrossed some of Russia's finest literary minds. Certainly no quick characterization can hope to succeed where some of the greatest writers have tried their talents. However, as far as his social and political attitudes are concerned (and these alone matter where détente is concerned) it must be borne in mind that during the past four centuries (the brief interlude 1861–1928 apart) the majority of Russian peasants have been serfs—that is, they had few if any legally recognized rights, were tied to the soil, and did not own the land they cultivated. They managed to survive under these conditions not by entrusting themselves to the protection of laws and customs, but by exercising extreme cunning and single-mindedly pursuing their private interests. This experience has left deep marks on the psyche of ordinary Russians. The world view of such people, including those running the Communist party apparatus, is better studied from Russian proverbs (for example, Dal's *Poslovitsy russkogo naroda*) than from the collected works of the "coryphaei" of Marxism-Leninism. The basic thrust of these proverbs is that life is hard and that to survive one must learn to take care of oneself and one's own, without wasting much thought on others ("the tears of others are water"). Force is one of the surest means of getting one's way ("*bei Russkogo, chasy sdelaet*"—"beat a Russian and he will make you a watch"). In personal relations, the Russian peasant always was and probably still remains one of the kindest creatures on earth, and nowhere can a stranger in need feel more certain of finding sympathy and help than in a Russian village.

[5]Nor should it be forgotten that the officers who command Soviet Russia's military establishment are veterans of the most brutal war of modern history in which defeat would have spelled enslavement and eventual mass annihilation of their people.

But these qualities of decency and empathy (unfortunately, much corrupted by the trauma of Stalinism) have never been successfully institutionalized: They tend to vanish the instant the Russian peasant leaves the familiar environment of personal contacts and becomes a stranger among strangers. When this happens, he is likely to view the world as a ruthless fighting ground, where one either eats others or is eaten by them, where one plays either the pike or the carp.

These various elements of historical experience blend to create a very special kind of mentality, which stresses slyness, self-interest, reliance on force, skill in exploiting others, and, by inference, contempt for those unable to fend for themselves. Marxism-Leninism, which in its theoretical aspects exerts minor influence on Soviet conduct, through its ideology of "class warfare" reinforces these existing predispositions.

Admittedly, history does not stand still. There are examples on hand to indicate that deep national experiences or vastly changed conditions can indeed alter a people's psychology. The consciousness of a people and the mentality of its elite are constantly affected by life around them. But in the case of Russia, all the great national experiences, especially since 1917, happened to reinforce the illiberal and antidemocratic impulses. It is surely unreasonable to expect that the increase of U.S.-USSR trade from $1 billion to, say, $5 billion a year, or agreements on joint medical research, or broadened (but fully controlled) cultural exchanges will wipe the slate clean of centuries of accumulated and dearly bought experience. Nothing short of a major cataclysm that would demonstrate beyond doubt that impulses rooted in its history have lost their validity is likely to affect the collective outlook of the Russian nation and change it, as defeat has caused the Germans or Japanese to turn away from dictatorships, and the Nazi massacres have caused the Jews to abandon their traditional pacifism. Unless and until that happens, one can ignore Russia's historical tradition only at great risk.

DÉTENTE AND SOVIET POLICY
In order to understand how, in view of what has just been said of its outlook on life, the Soviet government initiated a policy of détente with

the West, one must consider the situation in which the Soviet Union found itself after the death of Stalin.

Genealogically, détente is an offset from the "peaceful coexistence" inaugurated by the Khrushchev administration nearly twenty years ago. But "peaceful coexistence" itself was much less of an innovation in Soviet foreign policy than world opinion, anxious to have the burden of the cold war lifted from its shoulders, liked to believe. It had been an essential ingredient of Lenin's political strategy both before and after 1917 that when operating from a position of weakness one had to exploit "contradictions" in the enemy camp, and this entailed a readiness to make compacts with any government or political grouping, whatever its ideology. "Direct action" ran very much against Lenin's grain. In 1920, when he expelled the Anarchists from the Third International, the charge that he leveled against them (and that his successors of the 1950s and 1960s revived against the Chinese communists) was a dogmatic rejection of the *divide et impera* principle. Both he and Stalin made no secret of the fact that in their foreign policy dealings expediency was always the principal consideration. Hitler was barely one year in power (into which he had been carried by a viciously anticommunist campaign) when Stalin approached him in a public overture. At the XVIIth Party Congress, held in 1934, he announced his willingness to establish with Nazi Germany a relationship that today would be characterized as one of détente. Stalin declared on this occasion:

Of course, we are far from being enthusiastic about [Hitler's] fascist regime in Germany. But it is not a question of fascism here, if only for the reason that fascism in Italy, for example, has not prevented the U.S.S.R. from establishing the best relations with that country.[6]

Inaugurating détentes (as well as calling them off) is for the USSR a relatively easy matter: There exist for such action ample historic precedent and more than adequate theoretical justification. A "soft" foreign line must, therefore, under no conditions be interpreted as prima facie

[6]J. V. Stalin, *Works*, vol. 13 (Moscow, 1955), pp. 308–309.

evidence of a change in the basic political orientation of the Soviet Union.

Behind the "peaceful coexistence" drive inaugurated in the mid-1950s and reinforced by decisions made in the early 1970s lay several considerations. Some of these had to do with the need to overcome the disastrous consequences of Stalin's rule; others, with changes in the world situation.

The most immediate task facing Stalin's successors was the need to give the country a chance to lick its wounds after twenty years of privations, terror, and bloodletting of unprecedented dimensions. Stalin had assured himself that no opposition could endanger his dictatorship, but he did so at the cost of draining the citizenry of all vitality. In the mid-1950s the population of the Soviet Union was spiritually exhausted, as can be confirmed by those who had a chance then to visit the country.

Looking beyond these most pressing exigencies, it was thought imperative to extricate the USSR from the diplomatic-military predicament in which Stalin's postwar policies had placed it. Every attempt by Stalin to bully the West had caused the West to close ranks and build up its military potential. The net effect of Stalin's intransigent aggressiveness had been to enhance the role of the United States as leader of the noncommunist majority of humanity and, correspondingly, to isolate the Soviet Union. A different, more pliable and indirect strategy seemed to promise much better results. One had to initiate friendly relations with the freshly liberated colonies of the West, which Stalin had rudely alienated on the grounds that they were dominated by a "national bourgeoisie" allegedly tied to the apron strings of its departed colonial masters. Further, one had to establish contacts with all kinds of political groupings and movements of public opinion in the United States and Western Europe that, without being friendly to the Soviet cause, could nevertheless serve its purposes. In short, instead of following Stalin's (and Lenin's) dictum "who is not with us is against us," it was thought preferable to adopt for an indeterminate time the principle "who is not against us is with us"—a more sophisticated political strategy first devised by the Russian Social Democrats in the 1880s in their struggle against the imperial regime.

The third problem confronting Stalin's successors derived from the development of strategic nuclear weapons. Stalin had ordered his military to provide him with a nuclear arsenal, but it is doubtful whether he fully appreciated the implications and uses of nuclear weapons. His successors seem to have realized that after Hiroshima nothing would ever be the same again. War with such weapons was suicidal, and this meant that one could no longer count on mere quantitative and qualitative superiority in weapons to assure hegemony. This realization must have strengthened the resolve of the new leadership to depart from the strategy of confrontations with the West, pursued by Stalin in emulation of Hitler.

Such appear to have been the principal considerations behind the decision, taken in 1954–1955, to reverse the "hard" line pursued by Stalin since the end of the war and adopt in its place a "soft" strategy. The plan was simple and attractive: By means of a reasonably long period of relaxation of internal and international tensions to energize the Soviet population and reinfuse it with the enthusiasm of the early years of communism; to break the ring of alliances forged by the United States around the Soviet Union; to gain support of the Third World and public opinion in the West; and in this manner to initiate a gradual shift of the international balance of power in favor of the USSR. One of the implicit assumptions of this strategy was that during the era of "peaceful coexistence" the Soviet Union would greatly improve its economic potential and, by devoting a goodly share of the growing national product to defense, would expand its military power so as to attain parity or even superiority vis-à-vis the United States. The end goal of this policy was to turn the tables on the United States and, by containing the would-be container, drive him into the corner into which he had driven the USSR during the cold war.

The Khrushchev policy succeeded up to a point. The Third World responded enthusiastically to Soviet diplomatic overtures and offers of economic and military aid. Western opinion appeared more than ready to put Stalin out of mind and accept at face value professions of the Soviet government that it had no wish to export revolutions. America's leadership remained suspicious, the more so that every now and then détente was tested by means of strong-arm methods reminiscent of the

coldest cold war.[7] But by persuading President Eisenhower to ac-
knowledge in principle the necessity of renouncing war between their
two countries, Khrushchev scored a major success. He planted an idea
that, once adopted, would have caused the West to give up its strongest
weapon against the Soviet Union—superiority in strategic
weapons—without the Soviet Union being compelled in return to
forfeit political and ideological warfare, at which it excelled.

This policy's principal failure was economic. In his exuberance, a
kind of throwback to the early 1930s and First Five-Year Plan when his
own political career got underway, Khrushchev seems to have believed
that, given a fair chance, the Soviet economy, thanks to the advantages
inherent in planning, would catch up and overtake the U.S. economy.
He also thought that this economic progress would accelerate the shift
in the international balance of power on which he counted to achieve an
ultimate isolation of the United States. But being a rather primitive,
commonsensical man (judging by his memoirs), Khrushchev had little
idea how much the world economy had changed since the days when
he had helped Stalin with his Five-Year Plans. While he kept his eyes
riveted on statistics of steel production, a technological revolution
was reshaping the economies of the capitalist countries. After Khrushchev's removal, it became apparent to the new Soviet leadership
that, notwithstanding the upward movement of their productive
indices, Russia and its bloc were steadily falling behind the United
States, Western Europe, and Japan.[8] One symptom of this fact was the
decline in the Eastern bloc's participation in world trade. Between
1966 and 1973 the share of world exports of the USSR and the six

[7]Malcolm Mackintosh, in E. L. Dulles and R. D. Crane, *Détente: Cold War
Strategies in Transition* (New York: Praeger, 1965), pp. 103–120.

[8]See Brezhnev's views: "A scientific and technical revolution unprecedented in its
rate and scope is now taking place in the world. And it is the communists, [those] who
carried out the greatest social revolution, that should be in the front rank of the
revolutionary transformations in science and technology. The CPSU believes that one
of our most important tasks now is to accelerate scientific and technical progress, to
equip the working people with modern scientific and technical knowledge, and to
introduce as quickly as possible the results of scientific discoveries." L. I. Brezhnev,
Pravda, 13 November 1968, cited in Foy D. Kohler et al., *Soviet Strategy for the
Seventies: From Cold War to Peaceful Coexistence* (Coral Gables, Florida: Center for
Advanced International Studies, University of Miami, 1973), p. 168.

"People's Democracies" declined from 11.4 to 9.0 percent; the Soviet Union's share dropped from 4.3 to 3.4 percent.[9] These figures suggested that owing to some basic flaws—technological backwardness, poor management, bad planning—the communist countries not only were not catching up with the capitalist countries but were failing to keep pace with them; and this, in turn, meant that the automatic shift in the balance of power postulated by "peaceful coexistence" would not take place either.

Tackling this matter presented formidable difficulties; and it is testimony to the courage and capacity at objective analysis of the post-Khrushchev Soviet leadership that its members acknowledged the problem and boldly set themselves to deal with it. They had two basic alternatives open to them. One was to carry out major economic reforms of the kind that had been discussed and even halfheartedly attempted in the late 1950s. This course, however, posed certain political dangers. All proposals of economic reform current in the communist bloc called for a certain degree of decentralization of economic decision making. But decentralization of the communist economy always threatens to end up in decentralization of the political process, for where the state owns the economy there can be no firm line separating economics from politics, and no effective way of ensuring that reform stays within safe limits. If there was any chance of the Politburo adopting the path of internal reform it was eliminated by the experience of Czechoslovakia in 1968, which showed how quickly and irreversibly economic reform led to a breakdown of communist controls.

So there was only the other alternative left—instead of economic reform, economic aid from abroad. It was easier to swallow the idea that all the Soviet economy needed to put it right was Western technical know-how than to concede that the fault lay with bureaucratic centralism, easier because to concede the latter point meant to put in question the Soviet system as a whole. The decision, formally ratified at the XXIVth Party Congress in 1971, must have been accompanied by anxious soul-searching. It marked one of the major turning points in

[9]*Frankfurter Allgemeine Zeitung,* 24 May 1974.

the history of the Soviet Union, and only the widespread contempt for, and ignorance of, history among people who occupy themselves with Soviet affairs explains why Western opinion has not been made aware of this fact. It had been one of the principal claims of the Bolsheviks before coming to power that Russia was an economic colony of the imperialist West, and one of their proudest boasts upon assuming power was that they had freed Russia from this degrading dependence. The fact that fifty-odd years after the Revolution, the Soviet Union, in the words of Chou En-lai, has to go "begging for loans" and put "its resources for sale"[10] is a tacit admission of stupendous failure. It signifies that notwithstanding all the human sacrifices and privations of the past half century, the Soviet system has not been able to generate the resources, skills, and enterprise necessary to keep the pace set by the allegedly wasteful, crisis-ridden free economies. The humiliation is extreme. To convey what it would mean in terms of American history one would have to imagine the United States in the 1850s, threatened by Civil War, concluding that it was, after all, incapable of governing itself and requesting Britain temporarily to assume charge of its administration. The point needs emphasis because only if one realizes how agonizing the decision to seek Western economic assistance must have been for Soviet leaders can one appreciate how desperate was the need that drove them to it and gain an idea of the price the West could demand for its help. It makes one much less anxious than the present U.S. administration seems to be lest too hard bargaining on our part should cause the USSR to abandon détente.

MAJOR SOVIET STRATEGIC OBJECTIVES OF DÉTENTE

The national policy of the Soviet Union is distinguished by a high degree of strategic and tactical coordination. Because it is the same group of people—the Politburo—who bear ultimate responsibility for the totality of domestic and foreign decisions, they have no choice but to package their policies, as it were, into neat bundles, without loose ends. The kind of situation that exists in the United States where

[10]Speech of 18 February 1974 welcoming the President of Zambia, *USSR and Third World*, vol. 4, no. 2, p. 108.

authority over people and objects is widely distributed—with the administration pulling one way and Congress another, with industry looking out for its own interests and the media for theirs—such a situation is, of course, unthinkable in the Soviet Union. Even the most sanguine believer in the "interest group" approach to Soviet politics would not go so far as to see in them an arena of untrammeled competition.

Lest the use of the terms "strategy" and "tactics" in the Soviet context arouse in the reader the suspicion that we are employing cold war terminology, it must be said at the outset that Soviet theoreticians insist that they are, in fact, thinking in strategic and tactical terms when making political decisions. The following passage, taken from a standard Soviet party manual, makes this point without equivocation:

The measures which make up the activity of the Marxist-Leninist Party are not the result of improvisations of the party leadership. They represent the concrete expression of the *political line*, which is worked out by the party on the basis of scientific analysis of a given phase of the struggle and a given situation. In the political language to describe this line one also uses the concepts of *tactics* and *strategy*. . . .

At the present time, Communists talk of strategy or the strategic line when referring to the party's general line, which aims at the fulfillment of the principal tasks of the given historical phase, proceeding from the existing correlation of forces among the classes. In this respect strategy differs from tactics, which defines the *current policy* and which is worked out on the basis of the party's general line for a briefer period (e.g., tactics in an electoral campaign, the attitude toward the maneuvers of right-wing socialist leaders, the approach to left socialists, etc.).[11]

One can, of course, dismiss such claims as meaningless pretense on the grounds that in the end all politics must be improvisation and that no country, the Soviet Union least of all, operates in accord with preconceived "scientific analysis." This argument is correct, but only up to a point. After all, in military affairs, where no one would deny the applicability of the concepts of strategy and tactics, it is improvisation,

[11]Gosudarstvennoe Izdatel'stvo Politicheskoi Literatury, *Osnovy Marksizma-Leninizma: Uchebnoe Posobie*, 2nd ed. (Moscow: 1962), pp. 359–360. Emphasis in the original.

too, and not "science" that wins battles. Yet who would argue that one can wage war successfully without some strategic concept and tactical skill? In the end, the terms "strategy" and "tactics" always mean economy of force, whether we speak of warfare, of politics, of investment, or of athletic contests; he who seeks to attain any objective with insufficient means must employ some kind of strategic and tactical concept lest he hopelessly scatter his resources. In this sense, any strategy and any improvisation carried out within some strategic design are better than no strategy at all.

The Soviet effort at coordination of policy facilitates the task of the observer. Here we shall attempt to delineate in their broad outlines the principal tasks of the strategy and tactics of détente as they may be perceived by Moscow.

Inside the Soviet Union
Internally in the USSR the highest priority is attached to political security—that is, to preventing the idea of relaxation of tensions with the "capitalist" world from leading Soviet citizens to question the necessity of preserving the dictatorial regime. To this end, the Party's leadership has emphatically committed itself to the line that détente does not mean an end to the conflict between capitalism and socialism or any convergence between the two systems.[12]

One of the major tasks of the whole vast agitprop machinery in the USSR is to keep up the "ideological struggle" against hostile or alien ideologies and to forestall any blurring of the lines separating the two systems. Increased internal controls, symbolized by the recent promotion of the head of the KGB to the Politburo and, even more so, by the dismissal of P. N. Demichev as Secretary for Agitation and Propaganda (see below, p. 41) are manifestations of that effort.

Related is the drive to enhance Soviet Russia's military posture. We shall revert to this subject later on. Here we must merely point out that the military effort is in no small measure inspired by the fear that détente could lead to internal relaxation and thus to a dissolution of the system. It is as if Soviet leaders felt that by keeping up a steady tempo

[12]Numerous citations to this effect can be found in Kohler et al., *Soviet Strategy for the Seventies.*

of armaments they were helping to maintain that state of tension that is required to keep the system intact.

The failure, promises notwithstanding, to give the population more consumer goods probably stems from the same motive. Consumerism, as Russian leaders had the opportunity to observe in the West, leads to a decline in public spirit and an addiction to comfort that significantly diminishes the state's ability to mobilize the citizenry.

Toward the United States

One of the highest priorities of the Soviet Union in dealing with the United States has been to gain recognition as an equal, that is, as one of two world "superpowers," and hence a country with a legitimate claim to have its say in the solution of all international problems, even those without immediate bearing on its national interests. Recognition of this status is essential because only by establishing itself in the eyes of the world as an alternate pole to that represented by the United States can the Soviet Union hope to set in motion the shift in the world balance of power that is the long-term aim of its foreign policy. To achieve and maintain this status, the USSR requires an immense up-to-date military establishment with a devastating destructive capability, for in Moscow's eyes to be a "superpower" means nothing more or less than to have the capacity to face the United States down in a nuclear confrontation.

It is very much in the interest of the USSR to induce the United States to renounce or at least limit (regulate) the use of those instruments of power politics at which it enjoys a pronounced advantage, and to do so without offering reciprocal concessions. This means, in the first place, reducing to the maximum extent possible the threat posed by the American strategic nuclear arsenal. The various agreements into which the United States has entered with the USSR for the purpose of controlling and limiting the use of nuclear weapons certainly have not been accompanied by concessions on the part of the Soviet Union to restrain those instruments of power politics at which it is superior, namely, subversion and ideological warfare—and in this sense, such agreements are inherently inequitable.

Because of its planned and coordinated character, and because of its unwillingness to relegate authority farther down its bureaucratic hierarchy, the Soviet system is intrinsically offensive-minded: It always prefers to take the initiative, inasmuch as he who initiates an action has better control of his forces than he who responds to the actions of others. Time and again, when it has been forced to respond to firm initiatives (for example, the U.S. blockade of Cuba in 1962 or Israel's preemptive strike against the Arabs in 1967) the Soviet government has reacted in a manner that suggested a mental state bordering on panic. For this reason it is very valuable for the Soviet Union to be aware at all times of its rivals' intentions. The practice of regular U.S.-USSR consultations, instituted in the past decade, works greatly to the advantage of the Soviet leadership. The fact that the Soviet ambassador in Washington has virtually free access to the president, and indeed has been known to travel to Moscow on the same plane with the American secretary of state, assures the Politburo that it is reasonably well informed of major American initiatives before they occur. By terms of the U.S.-USSR agreement of 1973, each party is required to inform the other of any actions endangering the other's security or that of its allies. It is far from clear that the Soviet Union kept its part of the bargain in early October 1973 having learned at least a few days ahead of time of the impending Egyptian-Syrian attack on Israel. At any rate, it was neither commended nor criticized publicly by the U.S. administration for its behavior on this occasion. Yet it is reasonably certain that the Soviet Union would secure from the United States the relevant information should the roles be reversed.

Although it sometimes threatens to seek the capital and technology it requires in Western Europe and Japan, the Soviet Union has no viable alternative to the United States because it is only here that the capital and productivity it needs are available in sufficient quantities. Furthermore, U.S. corporations control worldwide rights to the most advanced technology. Part of the strategy of détente is to exploit the need of the U.S. economy for raw materials and markets so as to induce it to help with a fundamental modernization of the economy of the Soviet Union. Last but not least, because the United States is the only country able to deal with the USSR as an equal in any contest of wills, other potential investors (most notably Japan) have been reluctant to commit large sums in the USSR without U.S. participation for fear of ultimate expropriation—a fact which makes American economic cooperation doubly valuable to the Russians.

Toward Western Europe

It seems probable that the long-term objective of Soviet foreign policy is to detach Western Europe from its dependence on the United States, especially where defense is concerned, and to make it dependent on the USSR. It is difficult to conceive of any event that would more dramatically enhance Soviet power and tilt the "correlation of forces," so dear to its theorists, to its advantage. Russian military power resting on a West European economic base would give the USSR indisputable world hegemony—the sort of thing that Hitler was dreaming of when, having conquered continental Europe, he attempted to annex to it Soviet Russia's natural resources and manpower. However, the separation of Western Europe from the United States must not be hurried. The Soviet leadership has taken a measure of U.S. politics and knows (whatever its propagandists may say) that it faces no danger from that side. After all, if the United States had any aggressive intentions toward the USSR it would have made its moves in the late 1940s or early 1950s when its monopoly on nuclear weapons allowed it to do so with impunity. The U.S. forces in Western Europe present no offensive threat to the Soviet Union. Their ultimate removal is essential if the USSR is to control Western Europe, but their purely defensive character does not seriously inhibit Russia's freedom to maneuver. What the Soviet Union fears more is a German-French-English military alliance that might spring into existence should U.S. troops withdraw precipitately from Western Europe. The Russians are well aware that close to the surface of what appears to be a "neutralist" Western Europe there lurk powerful nationalist sentiments that could easily assume militant forms. Nor do they forget that England and France have nuclear deterrents that they could place at West Germany's disposal. Hasty action on their part, therefore, could cause the emergence on their western flank of a nuclear threat probably much greater than that which they face in the east, from China, let alone from the United States. As long as the United States is in control of European defenses, this development is not likely to occur. Hence Soviet strategy is to hurry slowly.

If realized, the European security system for which the Russians have been pressing with moderate success for many years would give them a kind of veto power over West European politics, military affairs included. It would make them arbiters of West European defense and thus preclude the emergence of an effective West European military force equipped with nuclear weapons.

The Soviet Union is seeking to make the West European countries maximally dependent on the Eastern bloc, without, however, losing its own freedom of action. It tries to achieve this end by the following means: promoting heavy indebtedness of the Comecon countries; gaining maximum control of West European energy supplies (oil, natural gas, fuel for nuclear reactors); and promoting "cooperative" arrangements with West European business firms. For its part, the USSR (the other Comecon countries to a lesser extent) seeks to confine Western economic aid to "turnkey operations" and similar devices that minimize dependence on foreign sources. In their dealings with Western Europe, the Russians like to insist on very long-term arrangements, which would have the effect of tying Western economies to the Soviet economic plans. In some cases they even propose deals that would run for up to fifty years.[13] The effect of such economic relations would be increasingly to link the economies of Western Europe with those of Eastern Europe.

Toward the Third World

The Third World that interests the Soviet Union the most is that which adjoins its long and strategically vulnerable southern frontier. This perimeter is an area of primary importance and the theater of its most determined political, economic, and military activity. Suffice it to say that two-thirds of all foreign military and economic aid extended by the USSR between 1954 and 1972 went to six countries located in this region (India, Egypt, Iran, Afghanistan, Iraq, and Turkey). Africa and Latin America are of much smaller concern, and the same holds true of Southeast Asia.

[13]D. Lascelles, *The Financial Times* (London), 6 February 1974.

On no political subject have Soviet theoreticians spilled more ink than on what strategy and tactics to adopt toward the underdeveloped countries. Analyzing Soviet behavior in this vast region, one can discern three consecutive strategic lines:

1. In the late 1950s, in the first flush of enthusiasm, the Soviet Union scattered its limited resources far and wide, helping any and all regimes that seemed ready to collaborate with it against the United States and the rest of the "imperialist camp." Much of this "water can" aid strategy ended badly, and a great deal of the investment went down the drain, in large part because the Russians were unfamiliar with the infinite variety of local situations, each calling for fine political and economic nuances.

2. To overcome this squandering of resources, in the early 1960s the theory of "national democracy" was pushed to the fore. This theory viewed the underdeveloped countries as in varying degrees of transition from feudal to socialist society and maintained that it was possible as well as desirable for them to bypass the capitalist phase. Soviet aid went to those countries which were prepared to expand the "public sector" at the expense of the "private," thereby eliminating Western influence, undermining the native bourgeoisie, and creating cadres of socialist functionaries hostile to capitalism. A prerequisite was political "democracy," by which was meant allowing Communist parties in these countries to surface and gradually to assume leadership of the "progressive" forces moving toward socialism. This policy too proved unsuccessful, in part because of the chronic instability of the governments of the "national democracies," and in part because most of these countries remained adamantly hostile toward their native Communist parties. By the late 1960s it became apparent that the Chinese, who had criticized this strategy from the beginning on the grounds that its net effect would be to promote in the Third World sturdy state capitalisms, may well have been correct.

3. Around 1970 the Soviet government began to adopt another strategy toward underdeveloped countries, one based less on political or military and more on economic considerations. Aid at present is extended as part of a broadly conceived Soviet "complex" plan intended gradually to mesh the economies of the underdeveloped coun-

tries with those of the Comecon. Its hoped for result is a double effect of complementing Comecon economies (for example, with raw materials) and creating deep ties of economic (and ultimately, political) interdependence.

The common aim of the three consecutive Soviet strategies toward the Third World has been to cut off the capitalist countries from sources of raw materials and cheap labor, to deprive them of military bases, and ultimately to isolate them. The undertaking, however, is complicated and exacerbated by Russia's conflict with China. The Chinese are threatening the USSR from a flank which they had been always accustomed to regard as secure—namely, the political Left. They are trying to wean away the radical and nationalist constituency in the underdeveloped countries that since 1917 had been viewed from Moscow as a safe preserve. The Soviet Union cannot allow China to do this, least of all in regions adjacent to its own territory, and this fact compels it to take vigorous counteraction. From East Africa to Southeast Asia a bitter fight is being waged between Russia and China for hegemony over the local governments. Though little discussed in the press, it may well be the most significant political struggle in the world at large today. By means of military and economic aid programs, the cost of which must represent a heavy burden to their economies, the two powers contend for allies as each seeks to expel the influence of its rival.

Toward Communist China

Having tried every means at its disposal from appeals to sentiment to officially leaked rumors of a preemptive nuclear strike to bring China back into the fold, the Soviet Union appears to have settled on a patient strategy of containment. The immense military force concentrated on China's border (apparently defensive in posture) assures that China will not lightheartedly encroach on Soviet territory. The Soviet effort in the rest of Asia, and among the left-wing, nationalist movements elsewhere, alluded to earlier has so far been successful in preventing the Chinese from seizing control of major territorial or political bases of potential use against the USSR. One of the greatest benefits of détente for the Soviet Union has been the unwillingness of the United States to exploit the Sino-Soviet conflict to its own advantage by pursuing more vigorously a "détente" with China. If détente with the United States had no other justification, this alone would suffice to keep it alive, as far as the Soviet Union is concerned.

The Soviet Union appears to have decided not to exacerbate further its relations with China, but to await opportunities for intervention in internal Chinese affairs, which are likely to open up after Mao's death. In the long run the USSR will probably strive for a breakup of China into several independent territorial entities. After the experience with Mao, even the emergence of a pro-Moscow successor government in Peking would not still Russia's long-term fears of China. A China separated by spacious buffer states (Sinkiang, Inner Mongolia, Manchuria) would be a far more comfortable neighbor to live with.

The political strategy we have outlined suffers from obvious contradictions. It seems odd, for instance, to urge multinational corporations to invest in the USSR while seeking to expel them from the Third World. Or to ask for economic assistance from the United States while building up a military machine directed against the same United States. Or to intervene in the internal affairs of other countries while denying anyone the right to interfere in its own. But each of the adversaries of this global policy tends to see only one of its facets at a time and to remain unaware of the whole picture, which facilitates the execution of what otherwise might have become an impractical line of conduct.

Soviet Tactics for Implementing Détente

At the very beginning of any discussion of Soviet methods of implementing détente, attention must be called to prudence as a feature common to all Soviet tactics. A certain paradox inheres in the Soviet Union: It is at the same time immensely strong and fatally weak. Its strength derives from the ability to marshal all its national resources in the service of any chosen cause; its weakness, from the necessity always to succeed or at least to appear to do so. The Soviet government lacks a legitimate mandate to rule and can never risk putting its credentials (that is, force) in question. Failure effectively to apply power abroad would at once raise doubts in the minds of Soviet citizens about the regime's ability to cope with internal opposition; and any loss of public faith in the omnipotence of the regime (and hence in the futility of resistance to it) might prove the beginning of the end. Thus the Soviet regime finds itself in the extremely difficult situation of having to create the impression of a relentless advance forward as it in fact moves very cautiously and slowly. It can act decisively only when it has a near 100 percent assurance of success, which, of course, occurs rarely.

Related is the habit of overinsuring by keeping open all options. The Soviet leadership by ingrained habit never places its eggs in one basket. It maintains some form of contact with all foreign political parties, from extreme Right to extreme Left; it builds up conventional forces as well as nuclear ones and simultaneously expands its naval arm—in all the service branches it accumulates masses of weapons, old and new, just to be on the safe side; in its economic drive, once the decision to seek help abroad had been taken, it sought to deal with everybody—the United States, Western Europe, Japan, and even such powers of second rank as Brazil. The lack of selectivity indicates insecurity lurking very close behind the airs of supreme self-confidence that Soviet leaders like to exude in public.

In our discussion of tactics we shall deal, successively, with political, military, and economic measures, concentrating on Soviet operations vis-à-vis Western Europe.

Some Political Tactics

The basic political tactic employed by the USSR on a global scale since its acquisition of nuclear weapons has been to try to reduce all politics to the issue of preserving the peace. The line it advocates holds that the principal danger facing humanity today is the threat of a nuclear holocaust, for which reason anything that in any way risks exacerbating relations between the powers, and above all between the United States and the Soviet Union, is evil. This line (which happens to have been adopted by President Nixon and Secretary of State Kissinger) has two advantages from the Soviet point of view:

1. It offers it an opportunity to silence external criticism of the Soviet Union, for no matter what the Soviet Union may do or fail to do, good relations with it must never be jeopardized. A crass example of this tactic is to be found in arguments advanced by the USSR and

echoed by certain Western politicians and commentators that the West should not support dissident movements inside the USSR, lest this exacerbate relations between the superpowers and thereby heighten the risk of war.

2. It allows the Soviet Union to avoid questions touching on the nature of the peace that is to result from détente. Peace becomes an end in itself. The issue of freedom is relegated to the margin, for once survival is at stake, who is going to haggle over the conditions?

As has been suggested earlier, the Soviet strategy for Europe is gradually to detach the Western half from the United States and bring it within the Soviet orbit. To achieve this end, the Soviet government works intensively to promote and make dependent on its goodwill parties and movements in the West that, whatever their motivation and attitude toward communism, happen at a particular time to further this end. Soviet support of de Gaulle represents a clear example of this tactic. Once the French leader had set himself earnestly to reduce American influence on the Continent, the USSR extended to him the hand of friendship, even though behind him stood the anticommunist Right. Very instructive, too, has been Soviet behavior in the 1974 French presidential election. Although Mitterand ran on a common ticket with the Communist party and in the event of victory was committed to put ministerial posts at its disposal, the Soviet government treated him with reserve. The reason behind this coolness seems to have been, not the fear of embarrassing the left-wing ticket and thus handing useful campaign ammunition to his opponent, but uncertainty about Mitterand's foreign policy views.[14] The same holds true of Moscow's behavior in the U.S. presidential election of 1972. On the face of it, Russia could have been expected to support Senator McGovern, because he advocated drastic cuts in the defense budget and reductions in American military commitments abroad, Europe included. But the Democratic candidate seemed to appeal to isolationist sentiments that at this juncture are not in Soviet Russia's interest. The policy of détente postulates a U.S. administration willing to assume certain global responsibilities (at any rate, in the immediate future); any other administration would be unlikely to favor the huge

[14]H. Hamm, *Frankfurter Allgemeine Zeitung*, 4 May 1974.

loans, investments, and sharing of technical knowledge that the Soviet Union seeks from the United States. Further, as noted, Moscow fears a precipitate withdrawal of U.S. troops from Europe, as advocated by McGovern, preferring such a withdrawal to proceed piecemeal and in the context of a European "security pact." For all these reasons Moscow preferred to back President Nixon.

Such tactics require Moscow to have friendly access to all kinds of political groupings, no matter what their ideology. It could well happen that an European party committed to anticommunism should also turn out to be very anti-American, in which case its attitudes toward the USSR could be temporarily overlooked. On the other hand, a Communist party in power might choose to pursue an independent foreign policy that was harmful to Soviet interests. It is not inconceivable, for instance, that in view of its advocacy of a "European" policy line, the Italian Communist party may appear in Moscow's eyes a less palatable alternative to the present Christian Democratic government than a fascist one. In general, Moscow does not seem all that anxious to promote at this time Communist parties in Europe, apparently preferring to deal with parties of the center and to the right of it. Direct cooperation with the West European "establishment" has proved very profitable. It is undoubtedly safer to exploit the "bourgeois" desire for profits and peace than to incite the Left and risk a backlash and possibly even open the door to Chinese penetration.

A persistent feature of Soviet policy toward Western Europe has been the effort to break up all political, economic, and military alliances, the very existence of which obstructs Soviet objectives. Originally, the Soviet Union did whatever it could to frustrate the creation of the Common Market (EEC). Later, it reconciled itself to the EEC's existence, although it continues to refuse to treat it as a juridical entity and by various means tries to bypass it. (For example, anticipating the establishment of EEC control over all foreign trade of its member states as of 1 January 1973, the Soviet Union has promoted bilateral "cooperative" arrangements with West European countries, which so far have remained exempt from central EEC management.) The difficulties that the EEC has experienced in recent years, including the breakdown of its unity during the October 1973 war, has certainly not been lost on Moscow.[15] There is also some reason to expect that the Soviet Union may ultimately succeed, as a result of the European "security pact" that it has avidly sponsored, in emasculating NATO.

The pursuit of Soviet strategy in the West entails a steady increase of Soviet intervention in the West's internal life. This effort, so far, has had very limited success, but it represents a development deserving greater attention than it ordinarily receives. In the United States, the Soviet Union has established a lobby that can reveal on occasion an astonishing degree of activity. Represented by diplomats, journalists, and occasional delegates from Eastern Europe, it operates on Capitol Hill, in business organizations, at universities, and in learned societies, and its purpose is the promotion of legislation favorable to the Soviet Union. Perhaps the lobby's most ambitious effort has been mounted against the amendment introduced by Senator Jackson to the Trade Bill which would deny the USSR and other nonmarket economies Most Favored Nation status until they accord their citizens the right of unrestricted emigration. Great pressures have been brought to bear upon Senator Jackson and the co-sponsors of his amendment to have it withdrawn in which, at various stages, the National Association of Manufacturers and some leaders of the Jewish community in the United States, acting in what they considered their constituents' best interests, were involved.

In the United States, these pressures to interfere with domestic politics have so far had little success. In Western Europe the Russians have been more fortunate. The idea is gaining acceptance in Western Europe that nothing must be done that could be interpreted in the USSR as endangering its security or challenging its prestige. An outstanding example of this is the willingness of Norway to prohibit international companies from exploring oil deposits under the waters along its northern seacoast, where the Soviet Union is anxious to keep NATO away from the sea-lanes used by its naval units stationed at Murmansk. Negotiations in progress between the two governments seem to point to the recognition by Norway that oil exploration in this

---

[15]See Brezhnev's speech of 26 October 1973, in which, in evident reaction to the EEC's gasoline shortages, he urged integrating its economy with that of the USSR.

area will be carried out either by itself alone or in cooperation with the Soviet government.[16]

Pressures are being exerted on European governments and private enterprises to prevent the spread of literary works unfavorable to the Soviet Union and to isolate individuals and groups whom the Soviet government dislikes. (A telling instance is the report that the Czech Chess Master Ludek Pachman, who had been a political prisoner in Czechoslovakia following the Soviet invasion, has been unable after his recent emigration to Western Europe to gain admission to internal tournaments; the Icelandic government has rejected a German offer to have him play as a member of the West German team on the grounds that this might annoy the Russians and prevent their participation.)[17]

In all, the results of these internal pressures leave much to be desired from the Soviet point of view, and one wonders whether they are worth the effort (and bad publicity) that they cost. The unexpectedly firm behavior of certain European delegations at the Geneva Security Conference in discussions connected with "Basket Three" and involving human cultural exchanges between East and West indicates that powerful sectors of Western opinion not only will not tolerate Soviet repression but insist on the right to bypass the Soviet government and establish contact with its citizenry. Still, the matter deserves close watch; certain forces in the West prefer conciliation at all costs and, willingly or not, help the Soviet government gain acceptance of the principle—from which it alone can benefit—that because of its awesome military arsenal it must always be placated.[18]

Military Policies

It is fair to say that the West has consistently underestimated the Soviet willingness and ability to pay for a large and up-to-date military estab-

[16]C. Genrich, *Frankfurter Allgemeine Zeitung*, 21 March 1974, and H. Kamer, *Neue Zürcher Zeitung*, 9 June 1974. The USSR sees nothing wrong, however, in asking the very same international oil companies to help it conduct drilling off the coast of Soviet Sakhalin—*New York Times*, 22 February 1975.

[17]*Frankfurter Allgemeine Zeitung*, 31 January 1974. There also exist reports that the movie *One Day in the Life of Ivan Denisovich* will not be shown in Japan, because the film distributor, Toho, fears Soviet objections.

[18]An important subject in its own right is Soviet subversion in Western Europe (and elsewhere), the breadth and sophistication of which is depicted in *The Peacetime Strategy of the Soviet Union* (London: Institute for the Study of Conflict, 1973).

lishment.[19] Western policymakers have always hoped that sooner or later their Soviet counterparts would conclude that they have enough weapons and decide to devote a growing share of their "national product" to peaceful purposes. This has not happened. The mistaken expectation rests in part on a misunderstanding of Soviet attitudes to military instrumentalities (the belief that they are primarily inspired by a sense of fear and insecurity) and partly from a stubborn faith in Soviet promises to raise Russia's living standards.

The most likely explanation for the relentless Soviet military drive is that nearly all communist expectations—except the reliance on the mailed fist—have been disappointed. The worldwide revolution that the Bolsheviks had expected to follow their seizure of power in Russia did not take place and, as early as the 1920s, had to be given up as a realistic objective. The economic crisis of the West on which they had counted did occur a decade later, but it failed to bring capitalism down. Communist ideology, having attained the apogee of its influence in the 1930s, has since lost much of its appeal and today attracts youth less than it had done before, the more so because it has to compete with anarchism and the Chinese variety of revolutionary doctrine. After its giant achievements in the 1930s, the Soviet economy has not been able to keep up with the pace set by the free economies; the Soviet economic model can hardly attract emulators after the USSR itself has had to seek help outside. In other words, had the Soviet government chosen to rely on the appeal of its ideology or the accomplishments of its economy, it would have consistently found itself on the losing side. Military might alone has never disappointed it. It won the Bolsheviks—in 1917, a tiny party—the Civil War that ensconced them in power. It saved the country from the Nazi invaders. It made it possible for Russia to occupy and retain Eastern Europe. Reinforced with a strategic nuclear arsenal, it has enabled the Soviet government to stand up to the United States and exact recognition as an equal. In short, military power has been the instrument by which a party once composed of a small band of émigré radicals gathered around Lenin had managed first to capture power in Russia, then to defeat the greatest war machine of modern times, and finally to rise from the

[19]See Albert Wohlstetter, "Is There a Strategic Arms Race?" *Foreign Policy*, no. 15 (Summer 1974), especially p. 5.

status of a pariah nation to become one of the world's two superpowers. Merely to list these achievements is to gain an insight into the reason behind the single-minded obsession of Soviet leadership with military power. Anyone who counts on a deceleration of the Soviet military effort must be able to come up with some alternate instruments of international policy on which the Soviet leadership could rely with equal assurance of success.

The buildup of Soviet military forces in the 1960s and early 1970s has been phenomenal and, notwithstanding certain international agreements on arms limitations, shows no signs of abating. There is some disagreement among experts whether this buildup bears a measurable relationship to legitimate Soviet defense interests or has become an end in itself, a search for power for power's sake.[20] There is no dispute, however, about the intensity of this effort, of the willingness of the government to allocate talent and money, of the dedication with which the armed forces maintain the martial spirit among the people. The Soviet leadership seems to strive to obtain a marked superiority in all branches of the military, in order to secure powerful forward-moving shields behind which the politicians could do their work. To reach this objective, the Soviet Union must have open to it all the options—to be able to fight general and limited conventional wars near its borders and away from them, as well as nuclear wars employing tactical and/or strategic weapons. The probability of this aim being given up is very low. Only effective pressure from below by a population fed up with seeing so much of the national wealth disappearing in the military budget could do so, but for this to happen, something very close to a revolution would have to occur in Russia. So far, the Soviet government has shown itself willing to limit the production or employment mainly of those weapons in respect to which it was bound to remain inferior to the United States or the further spread of which seemed counterproductive. A good test of its intentions would be to attempt negotiating limitations in the field of naval construction where the USSR is trying to attain parity with the United States. It is a safe prediction that should the U.S. government try to initiate such negotiations at this time it would run into a stone wall.

[20]See Thomas W. Wolfe and John Erickson, pp. 129–209, below.

An interesting feature of Soviet military activity in recent years has been the practice of quietly establishing a presence in areas where, should hostilities break out, Soviet forces would already be in place and able to deploy for action. A case in point are Soviet incursions by air and naval units of NATO territories in the North Sea. Potentially even more dangerous are large Warsaw Pact maneuvers held in areas near major NATO troop concentrations.[21] As is known, prior to the invasion of Czechoslovakia, Warsaw Pact troops had been put into a state of readiness in this manner. Something of the same tactic seems also to have been followed, possibly under Soviet guidance, by the Egyptians and Syrians in 1973 preparatory to their combined assault on Israel. The unwillingness of the USSR to agree to an exchange of warnings of such exercises more than a short time in advance indicates that its military leaders contemplate the possibility of using maneuvers as cover for preparing offensive operations against NATO.

Finally, mention must be made of the tactic of "war by proxy." Détente cramps Soviet freedom to engage in military action, for it is a sine qua non of this policy that there must be no direct military confrontations between the United States and the USSR. To get around this limitation, the Soviet leadership seems to be systematically developing a technique of indirect military involvement. In regions where it has a strong need to expel hostile foreign influence (Western or Chinese), and yet fears direct involvement, it seeks to achieve its purpose by employing third parties. It provides its allies with arms and with diplomatic protection; in the event of disaster it undertakes an all-out effort on their behalf, but it does not commit to any appreciable extent its own forces. The use of this technique is especially evident in the Middle East, where the Soviet Union seems to have decided that the expulsion of Western political, economic, and military influence and the reduction of Israel to the status of an impotent minor power transcend its day-to-day relations with the Arab states. In an article written upon his return from an extended tour of the Middle East, the editor-in-chief of *Izvestiia*, Lev Tolkunov, has hinted that the Soviet Union had given the Arab countries in their conflict with Israel a blank check. The Arabs could be certain of Soviet backing regardless of the

[21]See the essay by John Erickson in this volume, pp. 169–209.

state of their relations with the USSR or the outcome of their initiatives:

The last war [October 1973] showed that the Soviet stand in the Arab-Israeli conflict is not connected with the current state of affairs in relations between the USSR and certain Arab countries. It was not possible for this principled position to be affected by the artificially created negative factors which manifested themselves in respect to Soviet military experts in some Arab countries. To put it more directly, they know in the Arab capitals that when the threat of war hung over the Arab world, the Soviet Union proved in deed the constancy of its policy of active support of the Arab states, by sending arms both to Syria and Egypt.[22]

Those acquainted with the diplomatic history of Europe will find in this policy a striking echo of the *carte blanche* given by Imperial Germany to Austria-Hungary in July 1914, promising unconditional support in its quarrel with Serbia, an assurance generally regarded as a prime immediate cause of World War I.

The first major "war by proxy" was the Indian-Pakistani war; the second, the October War, alluded to above. It seems entirely possible that the USSR may attempt similar action in the future (for example, Iraq and Afghanistan versus Iran, or India and Afghanistan versus Pakistan).

Economic Policies

The main objective of Soviet economic policy abroad during the era of détente is to modernize the Soviet industrial establishment. But, as noted, under the communist system economics is never considered in isolation from politics, and every economic policy is measured in terms of its likely political consequences. Indeed, in recent years the economic weapon has been increasingly used to secure political benefits.

The principal political result desired is increased dependence of the Western and Third World economies—and therefore, as a corol-

---

[22]*Izvestiia*, 25 July 1974. Lest these words be misread to apply only to defensive actions, Mr. Tolkunov insists in the same article that the October war had discredited the story that the USSR was supplying the Arabs only with "defensive" weapons, and preventing the Arabs from attacking Israel, arguing that the distinction between defensive and offensive weapons was quite arbitrary.

lary, of Western and Third World governments—on the Soviet Union. We may single out three means by which this dependence can be accomplished: control of energy supplies, indebtedness, and manipulation of West European labor.

The Soviet government seems to have realized earlier than its Western counterparts how great had become the dependence of modern economies on energy, especially oil, and to have initiated steps to obtain control of this resource. The single-minded persistence with which the USSR, its failures notwithstanding, has advanced its influence in the Middle East has had (and continues to have) as one of its prime motives the desire to establish control over the oil supplies of that region. Should the Soviet Union succeed in filling the military vacuum created by the British withdrawal from the Persian Gulf and sustained by American reluctance to commit forces there, it would be in a superb position to exercise a stranglehold on European and Japanese fuel supplies. The October 1973 war unmistakably demonstrated how low Europe would stoop to ensure the flow of its oil.

The Soviet Union has also been very active in seeking to establish itself as a major fuel supplier to the West. It already furnishes respectable amounts of oil and natural gas to Germany and Italy, and everything points to the further expansion of these deliveries. The recently concluded deal involving supplies of natural gas from Iran to the USSR to be matched by Soviet deliveries to Germany will further enhance Soviet control over West European energy requirements. The same applies to bids (consistently below those made by U.S. firms) to furnish enriched uranium to West European nuclear reactors. All this creates conditions of dependence that the USSR could exploit, should the need arise, much in the manner the Arab oil producers had done in the fall of 1973. It goes without saying that the ambitious plans for U.S.-USSR cooperation in developing Siberian oil and gas fields would give the USSR similar leverage vis-à-vis the United States.

In monetary matters, the Soviet Union has traditionally pursued a very conservative policy. Its patient accumulation of gold reserves, at the time when the world offered more remunerative forms of investment, was part and parcel of the "bourgeois" approach to fiscal matters characteristic of Communists. In recent years, however, the Soviet government appears to have thrown its traditional caution overboard and gone all out for foreign borrowing. The same applies to the "People's Democracies." The obligations assumed are onerous, because before long the Soviet Union will have to set aside a good part (perhaps one-half) of its precious hard currency earnings for debt servicing.[23] In part, this untypically risky policy may be influenced by the belief that inflation will cause a disastrous depreciation of Western currencies while enhancing the value of the raw materials that the Soviet Union is in a position to supply. (If this is indeed the case, this calculation leaves out of account the possibility that inflation could lead to a depression that would, in turn, severely curtail the demand for primary materials; but then, perhaps, the Soviet leaders assume that this time a worldwide depression would be followed by a collapse of the capitalist system, an event that would wipe out their debts altogether.) Another consideration may have to do with the psychology of the debtor-creditor relationship. Heavy Soviet indebtedness to Western governments and banks produces among the latter a vested interest in the preservation and well-being of the Soviet Union and improves the chances of the flow of credits continuing unimpeded.

Studies carried out by specialists in the field of East-West relations[24] indicate that the degree of economic interdependence so far achieved is not significant. But the danger is there; and should Moscow succeed in realizing its more ambitious plans for economic "cooperation" involving capitalist economies, the interdependence would attain a level at which political consequences of the most serious nature would be bound to ensue.

The steady growth of advanced modern economies and the difficulties of rationalizing production beyond a certain maximal point have resulted in a growing labor shortage; and that, in turn, has enhanced the power of organized labor. In some advanced industrial countries the trade unions have acquired a virtual veto power over government

[23]M. Kaser estimates (quoted in *Sowjetunion 1973*, Munich, 1973, p. 126, from *International Currency Review*, July–August 1973) Soviet foreign indebtedness for goods and services alone (that is, exclusive of capital borrowings) at $8.5 billion in late 1973. In his estimation, should Russia continue to accumulate obligations abroad at the same rate as recently, its external debt in 1980 would rise to $31 billion.

[24]P. Hanson and M. Kaser, "Soviet Economic Relations with Western Europe," and J. and P. Pinder, "West European Economic Relations with the Soviet Union," pp. 213–267 and 269–303, in this volume.

policies. It may be expected that (barring a depression) this power will continue to grow. This development induces the Soviet Union to try to heal the breach between those foreign trade unions that are communist-controlled, and therefore in some measure manipulable by it, and the free trade unions that either are directed by socialists, Catholics, or some other group or lack political affiliation entirely. One of the by-products of the American-Soviet détente has been to make communism respectable in labor circles and to weaken the resistance of democratic trade unionists to pressures for closer contacts and joint action with communist and communist-dominated trade union organizations. In the past two years, the Soviet Union has succeeded in partly healing the breach created in 1949 when the Communist World Federation of Trade Unions broke up due to the secession from it of democratic labor organizations. The quarantine on communist trade unionism, in effect during the past quarter of a century, seems to have broken down. With the active support of the British Trade Union Congress and the West German Federation of Labor, the recent head of the Central Soviet Trade Union Organization, A. N. Shelepin (a one-time KGB head!) has persuaded European labor leaders to agree to a joint conference. That meeting could well presage an era of collaboration and end up with free trade unionism falling under the sway of the better financed and centrally directed communist movements.[25] Further penetration of European labor, of course, would give Soviet leadership a superb weapon for influencing or even blackmailing West European industry.

CURRENT SOVIET ASSESSMENT OF DÉTENTE

What, from Moscow's vantage point, has been the balance sheet of "peaceful coexistence" and détente to date?

On the *debit* side of the ledger two results deserve emphasis:

1. The dispute with China. The foreign policy pursued by the post-Stalinist leadership has served primarily the national interests of the Soviet Union, not those of the communist community at large. This had been the case even before 1953. As Stalin's words, cited above,

[25]A. Beichman, *International Herald-Tribune*, 26–27 January 1974.

assert, and as the historical record demonstrates, the guiding principle of Soviet foreign policy has always been national self-interest. But before Stalin's death, Soviet Russia had been the only major power with a communist regime, and until then one could argue with a certain logic that what was good for the USSR was good for communism. After all, the small East European regimes, put in power by the Red Army, hardly counted (except for Yugoslavia, which quickly fell out with Moscow). China, however, was a great power in its own right, and it would not tolerate a policy among whose primary objectives was an arrangement with the United States intended to elevate the USSR to the status of a superpower. Neither references to Lenin's lessons on strategy and tactics, nor arguments based on expediency, nor threats achieved their desired result. The Chinese remained stubbornly convinced that the ultimate winner from détente would be either the Soviet Union or the United States, or both, but never China, and they reacted with the fury of the betrayed.

2. A certain degree of loss of internal control. For this, détente is only partly responsible. The abolition of indiscriminate terror and the intellectual "thaw" of the mid-1950s were principally inspired by the wish to reinvigorate the country and reinfuse it with enthusiasm for the communist cause. Détente, however, undoubtedly accelerated the process by which society in the USSR began to resist totalitarian controls. An authoritarian-demotic regime must have a threat with which to frighten the population into granting it unlimited powers: Napoleon had his "Jacobins," Lenin and Stalin their "counter-revolutionaries" and "interventionists," Hitler his "Jews" and "Communists." Détente in some measure de-Satanizes the external threat and thereby undermines the Soviet regime's claim to unquestioned obedience. To proclaim the cold war over—even while repeating *ad nauseam* that the struggle between the two systems must go on to the bitter end—is to put in question the need in Russia for a repressive regime. It makes it that much more difficult to justify tight controls over foreign travel and over access to information. Implicit in détente is also a certain respect for foreign opinion. To project the image of a country worthy of being a partner of the Western democracies, the Soviet regime cannot simply shoot people for holding seditious ideas. The presence of Western correspondents in the USSR has given Soviet

dissenters a powerful weapon with which to neutralize the KGB—at any rate, where better-known public figures are concerned. All this is not without long-term dangers for the regime.[26]

On the *credit* side of the ledger there are the following achievements:

1. The USSR has indubitably achieved the status of an equal partner of the United States. As Gromyko publicly boasts in the passage cited at the beginning of this paper, all major international decisions are now acknowledged to require Soviet participation and acquiescence; no actions that seriously threaten Soviet interests are likely to be taken. The Soviet Union has at long last become a world power. Russia's international prestige is greater than it has ever been in the country's history.

2. The USSR has succeeded in smashing the ring of alliances forged around it by the United States during the late Stalin era. NATO is in disarray; the other alliance systems lead only a paper existence. For its own part, the USSR has succeeded in establishing a strong political and military presence in the Middle East, where its good relations with the Arab countries and India have helped her in considerable measure to eject Western influence and establish the position of a regional patron. Countries that at one time had been solidly wedded to the United States—Germany, Japan, and the states of Southeast Asia, for example—find it increasingly necessary to conduct an "even-handed" foreign policy.[27]

3. On the terms of détente, as laid down by the Brezhnev administration and tacitly accepted by President Nixon, the Soviet Union has

---

[26]It is in this light that one may interpret the dismissal of P. N. Demichev from the post of Secretary of the Central Committee for Agitation and Propaganda in November 1974. Demichev, who had held his post since 1965, was responsible for the relatively "liberal" handling of dissidents. His dismissal has been immediately followed by repressive actions. See A. Solzhenitsyn in *Neue Zürcher Zeitung*, 15 January 1975.

[27]In this connection it is interesting to note that polls conducted in recent years in West Germany and Japan have revealed a significant shift in the public's attitude toward the USSR. While Russia's popularity remains very low, a large part of the inhabitants of both countries have come to regard "good relations" with the USSR as essential to their security. In Germany some 19 percent of the persons polled thought good relations with the USSR to be more important than good relations with any other country, the United States included.

not been seriously inhibited in carrying on its assault on the capitalist system. It has remained free to support national liberation movements (without risking similar actions against territories lying within its own orbit); it has been able to encourage "wars by proxy"; and it has been able to lobby and exert pressure abroad, without being obliged to grant the West corresponding rights in the communist bloc.

4. Détente has helped secure for the Soviet Union recognition, by West Germany, of its conquests in East Germany: It has legitimized the existence of two Germanys. The recently held Security Conference legitimized Russia's conquests of the rest of Eastern Europe. Such recognition is of great importance to Russia because it helps undermine whatever hope the peoples of Eastern Europe may still entertain of some day being freed of Soviet occupation armies and the regimes that these armies keep in power. It also makes it possible to begin to think of some day incorporating Eastern Europe into the Soviet Union.

5. Détente has already led to a considerable growth of Western investments in the Soviet economy and, if continued, should help the Russians overcome some of the most glaring deficiencies plaguing it. Especially attractive are long-term "cooperation" plans that tie the Western economies to the Soviet, without creating undue Soviet dependence on the West.

It is thus fair to say that, on balance, détente has proved a profitable political strategy for the Soviet Union. It has vastly enhanced the international position of the Soviet Union and enlarged its room for maneuver, while, at the same time, legitimizing its conquests and strengthening its economy. The cost—alienation of China and internal restlessness—has been high, but apparently the Soviet leadership feels that it can prevent both dangers from getting out of hand. This explains why the Soviet leadership is vigorously pressing for détente to continue. There is every reason to expect that it will persist in so doing, no matter what the obstacles and frustrations, because as now defined and practiced, détente primarily benefits the Soviet Union.

SUGGESTED U.S. POLICY IN THE AGE OF DÉTENTE

There was a time in the United States when to question the country's policy of "containment" and the cold war exposed a person to the charge of disloyalty. Today, to question the readiness of the USSR to enter into a genuine détente with the West, or to criticize the manner in which relations with the Soviet Union are carried out, is to run the risk of being labeled a "cold warrior." Such labels are meaningless. The problem lies in finding not labels but policies. That can be achieved only if the motives of the critics of the present U.S. policy toward the Soviet Union are considered to be no less honorable than those of its supporters.

A sound policy toward the Soviet Union requires that the following objectives not be lost sight of:

1. *Its effect on the internal situation in the USSR.* Our policies must be so designed that they discourage those tendencies that make the Soviet government think and act in the traditional pike-carp fashion. This means, above all, doing everything within our ability to enhance the participation of the population in political and economic processes. A détente policy that relies exclusively on government-to-government relationships and therefore is subject to the slightest political vicissitudes is not only inherently unstable, but reinforces the centralist, authoritarian tendencies of the Soviet regime. To some extent such a policy entails "intervention" in the internal affairs of the USSR; but then insofar as détente postulates that the world has become too small a place for countries to engage in classical nationalist policies, intervention—as long as it is not pursued by violent means—is right and proper, and in the fullest sense progressive.

2. *Its effect on the national interest of the United States.* Concessions to the Soviet Union, whatever forms they take (for example, recognition of East Germany, sale of wheat at subsidized prices, access to U.S. guarantees of foreign investments) should always be accompanied by a commensurate *quid pro quo:*—not pledges redeemable in an unspecified future, but instant political, military, or economic repayment. This practice is always sound because of the difficulty of foreseeing the future, especially in a country like the USSR, which lacks legitimate succession procedures and which can renege on its commitments with comparative ease. Instantaneous reciprocity or barter of concessions ought to lie at the heart of peaceful U.S.-USSR relations at all times.

It is also important in negotiating détente with the Russians to make certain that détente is not confined to those fields where an easing of tensions happens to suit the Russians, while allowing in all other realms of U.S.-USSR relations for war, both of the "cold" and "hot" variety, to rage unabated.

1. *Détente ought to be global and all-inclusive.* One should not tolerate the Soviet Union, while ostensibly engaging in "peaceful coexistence" with us, inciting its own population to "ideological struggles" against us, exhorting the underdeveloped countries to expropriate U.S. firms, or arming the Arabs to wage war against a small country to the survival of which we have a deep commitment. Either détente embraces all areas of U.S.-USSR relations, or it is a sham.

2. *In particular, détente is not compatible with an unabated Soviet military effort* for which no reasonable defense justification exists. As long as the USSR keeps on multiplying its arsenal and increasing the variety of military options open to it, its professions of peaceful intent must be viewed with skepticism. For as the Chinese strategist Sun Tzu warned in the fourth century B.C.: "When the enemy's envoys speak in humble terms, but he continues his preparations, he will advance."[28]

[28]Sun Tzu, *The Art of War* (London: Oxford University Press, 1963), p. 119.

Decision Making in the USSR

MICHEL TATU

Of all the great countries of the world, the Soviet Union (along with China) is the one that least lends itself to an examination of the mechanics of decision making. "An enigma wrapped up in a mystery," said Churchill of Russia at a time when, entirely owing to the personality of Stalin, it was, in fact, less of a mystery. Today things are even more complicated—partly because international life and the more modern level of Soviet society present problems of a more technical kind that cannot be solved by a single person or by a small group, and partly because for that very reason as well as on account of inevitable political evolution, the USSR has undergone some decentralization of power. The subject cannot therefore be studied with the same precision as in the case of a Western democracy. The "microkremlinology" of the press, for example, provides some indications about tensions at the summit and about the varying fortunes of this or that leader; but it is a very unreliable source of information that can sometimes mislead the reader about matters under discussion and about what policy has been decided upon. (It should never be forgotten that the function of the press is propaganda, and often camouflage.) "Macrokremlinology" can provide a key—that is to say, a broad approximation based on a general understanding of the system, on isolated experiences, and on a great deal of guesswork.

CONSTANT FACTORS UNDERLYING SOVIET DECISION MAKING

Monolithism

The first thing to grasp is the image that the Soviet system ideally wishes to present of itself, the object at which it aims and which it has attained during long periods of its history. Soviet society must be, or at least appear to be, *monolithic*. There are not, nor may there be, any social groups defending particular interests. There exist only servants of the state and of the Communist party—they are identical—united by the same ideology. Social conflicts are therefore unthinkable; bureaucratic conflicts, if they take place at all, are an aberration of the system and must be carefully screened from the public.

At the summit, this monolithic quality results in the virtual extinction of all policy and decision making as we understand them in the West. There are no institutional conflicts, no warring tendencies, and, of course, no controversial or overt debates. Secrecy pervades the whole Soviet Union, but the secrecy that surrounds the discussions held in the Politburo is the most closely guarded of all. Even Khrushchev, chatting apparently without inhibition before his death about events which had taken place ten or fifteen years previously, either would not or could not provide a single detail about the deliberations of his colleagues.[1] First established as a dogma by Lenin in 1921, the prohibition against "fractionism," a corollary of monolithism in the political field, has been extended to its ultimate limits. Not only is a leader precluded from identifying himself with a "tendency" (if he does, he is almost instantly demoted), but political leaders are supposed not even to deliberate outside the appropriate precincts. If two or three members of the Politburo meet apart from the others, Brezhnev must as a matter of course be informed. Exceptions do occur (Khrushchev had such an experience in 1964), but the results are disastrous in the event of failure.

The primary object of this practice and of this secrecy is, of course, to avoid any division in the directing apparatus, but it is also designed to make policy conform to the image that doctrine intends to present to the public, that is, that perfect harmony reigns at the summit; the leaders think for the people; their decisions are the product of their collective "wisdom," a wisdom enlightened by the "science of leadership" of which the Party is the purveyor. This concept of "scientific leadership" is the only explanation—and a very modest one, at that—that the regime is ready to give of its process of decision making. The

[1]See *Khrushchev Remembers*, 2 vols. (Boston: Little, Brown, 1970, 1974).

Party receives the opinion of experts, it weighs the pros and cons; but it alone, or more precisely, its Politburo,[2] can and should make the necessary synthesis, for it alone knows the "laws" of social development thanks to its mastery of "scientific Marxism." Imperceptibly, a new legitimacy based on "science" has replaced the original one founded on the concept of the "party of the working class," which is less practicable now that the ideologists have found it necessary to announce the end of the class war in the USSR and the emergence of a state embodying the whole people. This legitimization is not firmly grounded and carries, as we shall see, great dangers for the system. But in the existing circumstances the Party is hardly in a position to find another one.

Concentration of Means

This situation has had certain general consequences that can be observed in Soviet political action and particularly in the conduct of foreign policy. The first of these results is the almost complete coordination of the various instruments of power. Throughout the various developments that have taken place during the past fifty years and in spite of the suppression of methods of terror in order to obtain political consensus at the summit, the regime has remained totalitarian in the true sense of the term. The Party, and in consequence its Politburo, controls and directs almost all human activity in the country insofar as it affects policy, the economy, and culture, including science and information. No other system concentrates to such an extent all power in a few hands, and consequently no other system is in a better position to practice totalitarian diplomacy. Not only are the armed forces, the police, and the diplomatic corps capable of being instantly mobilized in

[2]Officially, the term "Central Committee" is preferred to Politburo. This is because the Politburo emanates from the Central Committee and has legal status only between the Committee's sessions. These take place only twice a year and are too brief to enable the average member of the Central Committee to take any real part in its business. It should also be noted that the Politburo and the Party Secretariat depend on an apparatus consisting in the main of a type of ministries known as "departments [otdely] of the Central Committee." Finally and most importantly, to speak of the Central Committee rather than of the fifteen men who make up the Politburo reinforces the impression of a great "collective," which the leadership wishes to convey.

support of this or that external action, but also the whole economy and all the information media—the press, the foreign language broadcasts, not to speak of the special services of "disinformation" at the disposal of the KGB. An operation of intimidation or enticement can set in motion one or more of these instruments as required by the central direction. In certain instances the press performs the role of an advance guard by revealing the displeasure of the government toward a given state before this is translated into diplomatic action. In other cases practical steps are taken in secret, while the press continues the fiction of "eternal friendship" with the intended victim of these steps.

The system has therefore at its disposal great flexibility, a distillation of expedients unknown to many other governments. On the other hand, it has the disadvantage of obliging the leadership to declare itself on occasions when it does not wish to do so. Because nothing in the media is neutral, the way in which the press reports a given event will justifiably be interpreted as conveying the positive or negative attitude of the authorities, or simply their embarrassment. Because all information stems from them, "no comment" is impossible, or at least more difficult than elsewhere.

Greater Aptitude for Attack

The second result is less favorable. This concentration of means and their excellent coordination are more effective in attack than in defense. The regime is better adapted to conducting operations in which it has taken the initiative than to coping with crises.

All governments are, of course, in the same situation, but it is somewhat surprising that such a situation prevails in a system that has concentrated all power in a few hands and should in principle be better equipped than any other to react to the unexpected. But even Stalin, who was not embarrassed by any collective leadership and was thus able to take decisions without delay, was subject to the same rule. His alliance with Hitler in 1939 was negotiated and implemented in a masterly fashion; but it took him weeks, if not months, to organize his defenses after the invasion of 1941. It is true that his "subjective" errors—the refusal to believe reports about the preparations for the German attack—explain in great part this dilatoriness; but there were other more fundamental reasons. Because no autonomy was accorded to subordinate formations, the supreme command had to fill a vacuum that was quite beyond its capacity. Instinctive mistrust of headquarters and the consequent refusal to take any spontaneous initiative result in procedures for the transmission of information and orders that are too ponderous and therefore too slow. Inertia becomes all the greater if the Party directorate, regarding itself as the sole depository of "the science of leadership," is supposed to be thinking for everyone.

Added to this dilatoriness are the difficulties inherent in periods of collective leadership. When this collectivity is really complete in the Politburo, when no single member has raised himself above the rest, the regime seems to be less well equipped to conduct an active foreign policy, whether offensive or defensive. The first few years immediately following the death of Stalin might have given a contrary although illusory impression in the sense that the armistice in Korea and Indochina and the Geneva conference of 1955 marked a revitalization of Soviet diplomacy after the dreary stagnation of 1951–1953. In fact, however, Khrushchev was unable to move a step without his associates and rivals, Molotov, Malenkov, and Kaganovich, and it was only after he had got rid of them in 1957 that he was able to conduct his own diplomacy, with varying success, in Berlin and Cuba, for example.

After Khrushchev's fall, the years 1964–1969 were once more marked by a narrow collective leadership at the summit, more particularly by the omnipresence of the troika of Brezhnev, Podgornyi, and Kosygin working together and almost on an equal footing in matters relating to foreign policy. These, too, were years of passivity and torpor even in the diplomatic field. The Soviet leadership hesitated in opening the talks proposed to them by the West, on strategic armaments with Johnson and McNamara and on the normalization of relations with Brandt, then the foreign minister of the coalition government in Germany. They confined themselves to concluding negotiations of secondary importance (for example, the Nuclear Nonproliferation Treaty) or to the conduct of interesting but minor operations, such as Kosygin's successful mediation between India and Pakistan in Tashkent in 1966. Whenever something unexpected happened, however, the collective leadership was much slower in its reactions and more confused in its actions. It took many years for it to overcome the consequences of the errors that it had made during the Middle East crisis of 1967. The intervention in Czechoslovakia, although apparently offensive in character, can be included in this same category of tardy reaction to unforeseen situations. It was decided upon only after long and painful hesitation and after insufficient political preparation, and it only attained its objective several months later.

In 1969, however, there ensued a more active diplomacy marked by the beginning of SALT, the opening of talks with Chancellor Brandt and later with the three Western powers on Berlin, and the return to the "offensive" for the conference on European security. The "policy of peace" dates from this period, and all these moves were feelers toward the détente that emerged in 1972 and 1973. This policy does not inhibit large strategic operations of an offensive character such as the encouragement given to India in her war with Pakistan, the support for creation of Bangladesh in 1971, the massive arms deliveries to Vietnam in the same year and, in 1975, the involvement in Angola. Pressure on China continues by means of military encirclement combined with diplomatic overtures to Japan and the campaign for "a system of Asian security." In all these fields the deployment of Soviet efforts has been much better planned and coordinated than previously.

What is the reason for this revival of Soviet activity after 1969? There are a number of objective reasons, the most important being that it was in 1969 that the USSR caught up with and overtook the United States in ICBMs, which gave it a new confidence and enabled it to gather the first fruits of the great parallel military effort that it had made in the conventional sector. The second reason was the expansion of the Soviet merchant marine, which enabled the Soviet arms industry to pursue a much more active policy in respect to arms deliveries. At the same time, the Czechoslovakian affair had been brought under control, and this made possible the convening in 1969 of the world conference of Communist parties for which Moscow had been pressing since 1963. Finally, the accession to power of President Nixon in Washington and of Chancellor Brandt in Bonn simultaneously brought on the scene more active and better disposed interlocutors.

Trend Toward "Personalization"

These reasons for the change in the tone of Soviet foreign policy after 1969 counted for much, but it is necessary to add a further, more subjective one. It was also in 1969 that Brezhnev emerged as if by chance from the dark shadow enshrouding the collective leadership and embarked, specifically in the field of foreign policy, on the "personal diplomacy" that was destined to symbolize the renewed activity and to reap the advantages it offered. What was the why and wherefore of this emergence? We can only see the tip of the iceberg represented by foreign policy, and we can only guess at the delicate internal maneuvers that had led up to this situation—the shunting off to honorary posts of the potential rivals, Podgornyi and Shelepin, the curtailment of Kosygin's authority, the reaffirmation of the primacy of the Party and its *apparat*, confederacy with, and flattery of, the armed forces, manipulation of the provincial machine, and so forth. But it is unquestionably true that it is in the field of foreign contacts that the primacy of the leader is manifesting itself.

Prestige is an integral part of the function of leadership. If Brezhnev has become somewhat more than *primus inter pares*, he must convince not only the intimate circle of his colleagues but also (and more importantly) the Soviet public and the outside world. What better way of doing this than to monopolize the work of diplomacy and, like Khrushchev before him, to embark on the practice of "summits"? At all events, it was when Brezhnev received Brandt alone in the Crimea and was photographed with him in sporting attire and when he went alone for his first "summit" in a Western country without being flanked by another member of the Politburo (Paris, October 1971), that he brought home to everyone, to the Soviet as well as to the foreign public, that he was now indeed "the boss." Khrushchev reached this stage only in 1958–1959, and we have now seen a repetition of the same process.

Let us take note of the following coincidence, without, once again, being able to distinguish with precision between cause and effect: The leader who emerges from the collective leadership tends to manifest his primacy mainly in the domain of foreign affairs (thereby reinforcing his primacy), while at the same time, the quest for effectiveness in foreign affairs postulates the necessity for "personalization."

NEW FACTORS UNDERLYING SOVIET DECISION MAKING

What we have observed so far is related to the constant factors in Soviet policy—monolithism, the concentration of means, greater aptitude for the offensive, and a tendency toward "personalization" have been apparent since the early 1920s. But in recent years there have emerged some new phenomena that, when added to the constant factors, may lead to new developments.

Increased Stature of the Military

The most important of these is without a doubt the increased stature of the military hierarchy. One cause of this is the great armament drive in progress since the middle 1960s; another is the increasing part played by the military in peacetime diplomacy, in particular through the expedient of supplying arms. The notably good relations that have long existed between Brezhnev and the military have favored this process; but it may be asked whether these good relations are becoming almost a matter of necessity, for in the Soviet Union of today the supreme leader is no longer in a position to take any important decision that runs counter to the opinion of the military.

The last case in point occurred in Khrushchev's time. In 1960, an important reduction in the strength of the armed forces was decided upon with the formal support, given in principle, of the then minister of defense, Marshal Malinovskii, but not without grumbling and reservations. The next tussle came in 1967 when, after the death of Malinovskii, the political leaders had the idea—all the evidence agrees on this subject—of naming as Malinovskii's successor a civilian, Dmitri Ustinov. The military opposed this action and secured the nomination of their own man, Marshal Grechko. This trial of strength seems to have been decisive, and it explains in large part the "leap forward" taken in 1973, when Grechko made his entrée into the Politburo as a full member in the company of Gromyko and Andropov, the minister of foreign affairs and the director of the KGB, respectively.

It is tempting, but a little naïve, to equate the role of the military in the USSR with that which it assumes in other countries, for example in the United States. It is true that there exists in the Soviet Union as in the United States what Eisenhower called "a military-industrial complex," a vast organization embodying high officials of the Ministry of Defense and the directors of large firms working for defense. But whereas in the United States this "complex" comprises two quite distinct pillars, the great armaments firms representing a power in themselves, a power capable of acting and of making their views known like responsible civilians independent of the military, in the USSR the armaments industry does not seem to constitute a power really distinct from its principal customers, the military. At the summit of the hierarchy there are, it is true, some important civilian officials belonging to this branch of activity (Dmitri Ustinov, Party Secretary and acting member of the Politburo, L. V. Smirnov, vice-president of the Council of Ministers, the ministers S. A. Zverev, E. P. Slavskii, P. V. Dementiev, A. I. Shokin, and others), but their sole function is to satisfy the military and to serve as a link between them and the political leaders; they are broadly speaking the equivalent of civilian officials in the Pentagon. It would, therefore, be more accurate to speak of "a military complex" standing by itself.

Besides, the principal discussions and the power of decision are on a higher level in the USSR and are much more closely restricted than in other countries. Because there is no legislative control, there is evidently no need for lobbying in the Supreme Soviet. It is in the Politburo that things happen, and there are many indications that the head of the Party himself is closely associated with all important and even minor decisions affecting defense.[3] This is the penalty exacted by a general rule observable in other fields: In a hierarchical system the supreme leader has to concern himself with everything, even with

[3]Thus, according to *Khrushchev Remembers*, it is the head of the Party who goes to see Tupolev when he has an idea for a new aircraft project. Khrushchev also arbitrated the various projects of the military for the ICBM program, and it was he, so he boasts, who first had the idea of concealing them in silos. It is, however, not known if there is a special organization for the coordination of military and civil activities on the lines of the wartime *Stavka* or of the State Committee for Defense (GKO) which existed under Stalin. The *Spravochnik Ofitsera* published in Moscow in 1971—and quoted by

details. This factor enhances the exercise of authority, but also delays the taking of decisions.

Some people refuse to attach special importance to the rise of the military insofar as the internal structure of the regime and its future are concerned. The military are Communists, it is said (in fact, more than 90 percent of the officers are members of the Party or of the Komsomol), and their preoccupations and their world outlook are the same as those of the whole Soviet elite. Besides, it is agreed, the presence in every military headquarters of a political directing body and the fact that at the summit the political direction of the armed forces is just as much a function of the Central Committee of the Party as an annex and a "watchdog" of the Ministry of Defense are enough to keep up the interpenetration of the Party and the army, and to prevent any dissidence.

There is some truth in these arguments, but it is precisely the massive nature of the structure set up to prevent dissidence and the constant propaganda designed to underline the cohesion of the Party and the army that bear witness to the permanence of the danger of such a program. In the first place, it is not always certain whether, if he could choose, the inner sympathies of the average *politruk* (political officer) would be on the side of the Party rather than of the army. In their careers and in their everyday life these men, particularly in the middle and lower formations, are attached primarily to the military family. In the second place, it must never be forgotten that there are two sorts of Communists in the USSR: (1) members of the *apparat*, that is, those who exercise responsibility inside the Party system and dedicate themselves exclusively to this task, and (2) the simple Party members who, even if they work in a high echelon of the Party, in the Central Committee, for example, actually work elsewhere, as a cog of the state machine other than the Party. The military belong to the second

---

C. G. Jacobsen in *Soviet Strategy–Soviet Foreign Policy* (Glasgow: Maclehose & Co., 1972)—speaks, it is true, of a *Stavka*, but in conditions that seem to be those of a past or future war. On the other hand, the "higher military council" mentioned by the same author is, by all accounts, an internal organism of the Ministry of Defense, which can play the part of commander-in-chief in time of war or of a supreme instrument of civil and military coordination in time of peace.

category; they are professionals whose vested interests are not the same as those of the *apparatchiki*.

It is here that the promotion of Marshal Grechko to the Politburo takes on a fresh significance. It is not the first time that a minister of defense has sat in the highest branch of the Party directorate. Voroshilov, for example, who was minister of defense for a very long time, was its member for many decades, as was Beria, minister of security, and Molotov, minister of foreign affairs. But these three men were as much—and even more so—"veterans" of the Party as professional members of the army, the police, and the diplomatic service. In the case of Voroshilov, it was not the soldier who sat in the Politburo (he was in fact a poor exponent of the soldier's art), but the veteran of the Civil War, the faithful supporter of Stalin. The technology of modern warfare has brought about a rise in the level of military expertise, and no professional military had sat in the Politburo since World War II except Zhukov for a few months in 1957.

The fact that the conqueror of Berlin had to be expelled on account of "Bonapartist tendencies" shows that this rule was not fortuitous. Now, Marshal Grechko, if he is politically more prudent than his unfortunate predecessor, belongs no less to the category of professionals of the new army, and he has very little in common with the Party machine.

The Party thus has had to agree to share its power while at the same time drawing dangerous attention to itself. In the USSR of the 1970s, the Party no longer plays such a fundamental role as it had in the past; while taking refuge in a rigid ideology and holding up necessary reforms in the administration and the economy, it presents the appearance of a parasite in the bosom of a system of which the three pillars are the armed forces, the diplomatic service, and the police. They alone constitute the sole bastions of a state which has become a classic great power.

Under these conditions, the Party—or more precisely, its *apparat*—now plays an ambiguous part, fatal for the management of the economy but positive as a bond between the various cogs of the administration, as an internal instrument of coercion (although, as is well known, this latter role has been in the past effectively played by the police), and finally, as presenting a well-tried framework for the concentration of authority, thanks to the Politburo and the Secretariat. But this positive role retains its value only so long as unity reigns at the top. It cannot be excluded that should a division occur at the top—and this is always possible—the Party would forfeit even more of its *raison d'être*. In such an eventuality, the more concrete forces that the Party has begun to introduce into its sanctuary, of which the army is the principal, will naturally be tempted to usurp its waning authority.

More Sophisticated World View

The second change that has come to light during the past few years is the tendency toward a greater sophistication, a more realistic and occasionally more cynical view of the world. We are here entering on subjective ground and the writer must have recourse to his personal impressions. Fifteen years or so ago, any conversation that a journalist might have had with someone close to the seat of power would have been either largely of an emotional type, more or less sincere, but always elementary in character, or it would have been propaganda pure and simple. "We are out for peace, the Soviet Union has suffered too much from war not to long for peace, the imperialists are preparing to attack us, the malignant tumor of Berlin must be cut out, let us strive toward general and complete disarmament. . . ." Khrushchev's speeches used to reflect this mixture of good feeling and aggressiveness, of gratuitous accusations and good wishes. Today, analyses are colder and tactical considerations at once more subtle and less disguised. There is now no hesitation in saying that it is "in our interest" to play this card rather than another, that there is an international "game" in which the USSR must play its part, that it is more worthwhile dealing with "an intelligent reactionary" than with a statesman who is well-disposed but not very dependable, and so on. There are fewer threats, but more calculation.

Twelve years ago, Soviet power, then too weak, had to be proclaimed to the accompaniment of rocket rattling and threats. Today it is no longer necessary to exhibit what everyone knows. Still, the Soviet Union and its leaders, conscious of the fact that now at last their military exertions have indisputably conferred on them the role of a world power almost equal to that of the United States, have acquired a much greater confidence in themselves and are discovering with delight the joys of playing on the world's chessboard.

It is true that this change has its roots deep in the origin of the Soviet regime. Lenin and Stalin were great calculators also, and Stalin, making the maximum use of the strong position of the USSR just after World War II, had already practiced great power politics with consummate art. All the same, the change now in progress has introduced some new elements.

The USSR of thirty years ago was operating in a more limited field in Europe, in Iran, and to a relatively small extent in the Far East, that is to say, on the periphery of its empire. The absence of a navy worthy of the name and the inadequacy of its air force did not permit it to go any further afield. This resulted in an oversimplified and dualistic conception of the rest of the world and in particular of the Third World, which was judged to be of no interest and was therefore largely ignored. (Stalin's attacks on Nehru are a case in point.) Today, the means of action at the disposal of the Soviet Union enable it to make itself felt far beyond its continental confines, particularly in the Mediterranean and in the Atlantic and Indian oceans, and to pursue a very much more sophisticated policy toward the Third World. Its policy has not, however, become entirely worldwide, partly owing to a still inadequate radius of action (Latin America is still almost completely out of range, in spite of the Cuban bridgehead) and partly owing to a choice more or less dictated by circumstances. (In Africa, for example, until the Angolan conflict, Soviet influence was in partial retreat compared with what it was in the 1960s.)

Stalin projected his influence at a lesser distance, but he had more shots in his locker; he exercised military and diplomatic pressure, but also exerted a very strong psychological presence and long-range manipulation of internal political factors in the target countries thanks to the Communist parties in the countries of Western Europe. We should recall not only the subversive strikes of 1947 and 1948 launched by the Communist parties, but also the Stockholm appeal and the great "peace movement" against the atomic weapon, the last a masterpiece of what a state can do to compensate for its material and technical inferiority.

Today, the Communist parties have not entirely lost their function as the spearheads of Soviet diplomacy, but this function is much attenuated. It is now more negative or passive (for example, as in France and Italy by dissuading the governments from taking action judged by Moscow to be "provocative") than active. The USSR no longer seeks to overturn established governments and has less need to encourage for this purpose social unrest, which in any event takes place on its own. It may also be noted that, perhaps as a matter of routine, Moscow continues to spend vast sums on foreign propaganda; but it no longer makes the same effort as formerly to convince the masses of the West that the Soviet Union is "a red paradise." Ten years ago the refusal of the authorities to allow any emigration was still motivated largely by the desire to prevent the tales of malcontents from tarnishing still further the image of Soviet socialism abroad. Today, by contrast, the Brezhnev team does not hesitate to let its detractors leave, or even to expel them by force, because it prefers to have them outside its frontiers. This is an admission of weakness, but it also marks less reliance on an ideology that was once a determining factor.

However, other, nonideological expedients are being given priority today, even if they are more a result of the dialogue with foreign countries than a leverage exercised on Western governments. The taste for economic exchanges responds, if not to a need (in spite of its economic weakness, it is unlikely that the USSR will give up its major strategic plans simply in order to obtain credits from the West) at least to a desire to bolster up the weak points of the Soviet system, for example, its economic backwardness, with advantages which may accrue from its strong points—the army, the police, and the diplomatic service. There may here be a question of a "relapse" into the policy of coexistence, sought after all the more naturally because it is not, contrary to current belief, an innovation of the Brezhnev group. During the early stages of industrialization in the 1930s, the Soviet Union had already had considerable recourse to foreign technology, and the contribution made by the allies to the Soviet war effort after 1941 is well known. In other words, an active policy of dialogue may intensify the commercial and technological exchanges with the West, but their relation with foreign policy is not so close as is sometimes thought. It is only during periods of serious tension that these exchanges come to an end, as happened during the cold war of 1947–1955.

Another new feature is that this sophistication has spread among the ruling class. Stalin was for many people pragmatic and cynical, but most of the time he made his decisions alone, sharing his secrets at most with one or two of his old comrades-in-arms (Molotov?). Khrushchev, even though a member of the Politburo, indicates throughout his memoirs that he was not *au courant*, except fortuitously and very indirectly, with foreign policy decisions. As often as not, he knew even less about them than a professional foreign observer. He did not know, for example, what Mao Tse-tung was doing in Moscow in the winter of 1949–1950, whether he came once or several times to the Soviet capital. Today, not only is the whole Politburo associated with major decisions, but information, expert advice, and perhaps even discussion are extended over a much wider field, for example, among the military. It is reasonable to suppose that the traditional caution of military men and their tendency to evaluate without wishful thinking the forces involved and to respect those of the enemy have contributed to the raising of the level of sophistication in political thinking to the detriment of the doctrinaire outlook of ideological politicians. Bringing in civilians, too, has had the same effect, thanks to the appearance of brain trusts, which are now more active and up to date than in the past.

Role of Think Tanks and Study Groups
It is in Brezhnev's time that these brain trusts have made notable progress. Without himself being particularly modern either in his style or in his philosophy, the Party chief seems to have understood that in modern times the more technical nature of decision making demands a much wider recourse to the advice of experts recruited from outside the traditional hierarchy. (It is also possible that this has been seen as a means of reducing the all-embracing powers of this hierarchy by short-circuiting leaders who are too old or too doctrinaire.) Besides, the example of the American "think tanks" has set a fashion: IMEMO (The Institute of World Economy and International Relations) and the Institute of the U.S.A., two organizations well known to American visitors, have become important, relatively open centers that are well informed and staffed by highly competent personnel. On demand, they carry out studies for the government and advise the Ministry of Foreign Affairs even on matters outside their original purview (IM-EMO also deals with strategic matters).

It may be noted also that over the years a number of close personal contacts have grown up between political leaders of the traditional type and study groups concerned with international affairs, both of which make up the upper crust of "the new class." The most sought after careers in the Soviet system are those that relate to foreign affairs and require frequent journeys abroad, and particularly to the West—that is to say, the diplomatic service, the press, or, more indirectly, the KGB. It is therefore not surprising that the sons of very many leaders are to be found in the Institute of Foreign Languages, even more in the Institute of International Relations, and more recently in the corridors of power. Because, for their part, the "fathers" have done not a little traveling during the past twenty years, everything has contributed toward a wider knowledge of the outside world.

These phenomena have not, however, driven out everything of the old. The regime remains so hidebound that certain of its aspects must clash with its superficial modernization, and thus give rise to contradictions.

The first of these contradictions is that the sophistication of the ruling circles is getting increasingly out of step with the tenor of the primitive propaganda conducted internally. The more sober and closely argued analyses that one encounters in private conversations are hardly reflected in the Soviet press, which is still largely Manichaean, simplistic, standardized, and at bottom very unenterprising. In brief, "serious matters" are discussed and decided in small gatherings on the basis of realistic arguments shorn of all ideological considerations; but the public at large continues to be served the same good old propaganda, with explanations that are all the more invariable because everyone knows that they will never be contradicted.

The absence of free public discussion does harm to the press itself, which becomes a kind of artificial superstructure in which no one believes, the journalists least of all; but it also probably has an adverse effect on the real discussions that take place behind closed doors because it cuts them off from a wider public and deprives them of the valuable support furnished by the printed word. In the United States, for example, discussions on strategic subjects would not be what they are if they had to take place exclusively between responsible officials of the Pentagon and other government departments without the added contribution of the academic community, the press, and a fairly wide section of public opinion. The important discussion which took place in 1969 on the antiballistic missile (ABM) question both in Congress and in the press certainly induced the Pentagon and the White House to make their analyses and explanations more specific and thereby helped them to adopt a more rational course. (Let us say, rather, that the final choice would probably have been less rational had this discussion not taken place.)

Nothing of this sort exists in the USSR. Free discussion having been replaced there by propaganda incantations, it would even be surprising if this storehouse of dogmatism did not have a negative, even destructive effect on the genuine discussion that takes place between responsible officials. Besides, in relation to strategic matters the obsession with military secrecy restricts to a remarkable extent the number of participants in discussion and thus sets limits on its quality. This was seen at the beginning of the SALT talks when it became apparent that the Soviet negotiators did not know how many rockets their country had at its disposal. It seems that since that time some barriers have been lifted; yet even now the average Soviet citizen does not know these numbers and various other items of information accessible to everyone in the West.

One can, of course, reply to this with the Soviet leaders that decisions are taken by those who "have the necessary knowledge," and that such persons are neither more nor less intelligent than their counterparts in the West. However, the ABM affair was in this respect just as illuminating in the USSR as in the United States, although in a different sense. The decision to create an antimissile system around Moscow was probably taken at the end of Khrushchev's reign. Taking into account the secrecy regulations that prevailed at the time, which were stricter and therefore less sophisticated, the decision had to be taken by a very small committee. Most probably the marshals responsible for air defense had been demanding such a system for a long time (they had induced Khrushchev to announce that the problem of missile interception had been "solved"); and they attained their wish in the name of the elementary principle traditional in Russia that everything that strengthens the defense of the homeland is "good," an argument that Kosygin used publicly in 1967. This decision was a mistake, not only because it called in question the principle of dissuasion by massive reprisals, which was, and apparently still is, the basis of Soviet doctrine, but also because it prompted the United States to enter the race.

The result was that in 1970–1971, the Russians found themselves confronted by an American ABM system much more advanced than their own, and of much wider scope, because, had the program been carried to its conclusion, it would have covered the greater part of U.S. territory. It was necessary, therefore, for them to beat a retreat and, relinquishing the position taken up two years previously, to conclude in 1972 a treaty limiting ABM. It probably would be an exaggeration to assume that the American ABM would never have come into existence without the Soviet ABM, but at least the USSR had provided the advocates of such a system in the United States with their most powerful argument, and extensive measures were set in motion.

The second contradiction that results in conflict between the old and the new is that which sets what we call the "hawks" and the "doves" at each other's throats. It should be made clear at once that it is not here a question of the well-worn picture of "Brezhnev the peacemaker wants to salvage his policy of détente" opposed by "Grechko and his marshals, the advocates of a hard line." It seems to me that Brezhnev is just as much a militarist as Grechko and that the military are the ones less addicted to adventures. They are cautious and careful men who act only when they are sure of success and not without weighting the scales on their side, that is, by making certain of their superiority in men and armaments. Most probably Brezhnev and the marshals share the same view of the role of armed force, that is, that it should influence the course of world affairs by its presence alone and from that presence derive political advantage.

The cleavage is largely institutional, but it brings those who are responsible for policy into conflict with those who are not. A governing body aware of the pressures and limitations imposed by world politics finds itself opposed to a mass of lower grades (cadres) who are prisoners of the dogmas and of the primitive view of the world imposed upon them by that same governing body. In other words, the cleavage is the sequel to that lack of rapport described above between the sophisticated realism cultivated by the elite and the crude Manichaeism im-

posed by the propaganda machine. All those who "are not concerned
with" the subtleties of *Realpolitik* are invited to be "on the lookout
for imperialist intrigues," to believe in the "worldwide crisis of capitalism," and so forth. How can they avoid being more "hawkish" than their
leaders?

To this must be added a contradiction even more specific in
nature. Seen from the summit, the dialogue with the outside world is
inevitable and necessary, not only because in the thermonuclear age
war is impossible, but also because it is through diplomacy that the
advantages obtainable from military strength can be realized, and it is
by means of diplomacy that the USSR can play the role of a world
power. But at the same time, the internal system of the USSR must
disapprove of the "ideological contamination" and the too frequent
contacts with foreigners that a policy of dialogue brings in its train,
particularly when détente is in the air. Thus, the dividing line normally
passes between the upper and middle echelons of society (cadres), and
disapproval is expressed mainly by provincial Party officials, by those
who are more in touch with the "base" and are more aware of the
dangers inherent in a general ideological relaxation in the cohesion of
the system. These provincial cadres make up the bulk of the active
membership of the Central Committee, and they also have some
spokesmen within the Politburo.

In any event, it is almost always in this way that dispute with the
policy of the leadership takes place, that is, when it finds expression. If
free discussion on foreign policy existed, there is no doubt that many
"doves" would show up, people anxious to release more of the country's resources for the economy or to express the "liberal" point of view.
But because those who hold the latter view are isolated from public life,
"authorized" discussion can take place only between "the orthodox"
and "the extremists," between responsible officials generally observ-
ing some degree of moderation by reason of their broad and practical
outlook and the fierce defenders of the ideological purity of the Party or
of an exaggerated patriotism. Everything that happens can be compared with a hypothetical situation in the United States were the
president required to govern with a Congress in which southern ul-
traconservatives constituted the vast majority.

This "opposition" is occasionally penalized—as indicated by the affairs of Shelest and Voronov in 1973 and of Iegorychev in 1967[4]—but Brezhnev is up against this kind of pressure almost all the time. It could affect the policy of détente in the short term, but not in the middle term. As has been shown in the past, it is often for having overstepped the mark in the matter of dialogue with the "imperialists" that supreme leaders have been punished or downgraded. First Beria, then Malenkov, and finally Khrushchev were taken to task for having attempted to cold-shoulder East Germany in order to get on better terms with West Germany. Nor can there be any doubt that if one day Brezhnev finds himself taken to task, it will be for having put too much hope in détente and having been too patient with the "imperialists." But it is equally clear that his successor would follow a similar policy after allowing it to remain for a while in cold storage. This is what all his predecessors have done, not only because no other policy is possible but also because, as we have mentioned, it is through dialogue with the outside world, through "summits," that the supreme leader asserts his authority and acquires a reputation.

[4]Iegorychev, first secretary of the Party for the city of Moscow, apparently criticized the leadership for want of vigor during the Six-Day War. He was downgraded a few days later. Shelest, first secretary of the Party in the Ukraine, was demoted in 1972 and dismissed in 1973, most probably for having raised objections to the rapprochement with the United States.

Soviet Policy and the Domestic Politics of Western Europe

LOTHAR RUEHL

The foreign policy of the Soviet state has never been "classical" in the coventional sense in which one country conducts normal relations with another in peace and war. One expert Western diplomat, the former American ambassador to Mosow, Charles Bohlen, expressed this peculiarity of Soviet foreign policy in a phrase: He wished, he once said, that after World War II the Soviet Union would cease acting "like a cause" and start acting like a country.

Much has been written since then to prove that the "cause" is losing its hold over the Soviet state and that Soviet Russia is at long last changing from an embodiment of permanent revolution into a national political body possessing a conventional character and incorporating the Russian people, together with their traditions and feelings, into a modern industrial society.

However real this metamorphosis may be, the Soviet state is still unlike any other in Europe, even when compared with its affiliates in Eastern Europe, where the socialist order has been more or less successfully established by ruling Communist parties after the Russian example. In the field of foreign policy the Soviet state still seeks, on the one hand, to consolidate the status quo on the continent and, on the other hand, to provide political support for forces striving to bring about the downfall of capitalist society. No other country in Europe pursues such a paradoxical policy, and no other power maintains direct and organized relations with political parties within other countries.

The exercise of political influence by one country over the internal affairs of another country is as ancient as the state system itself. The history of Europe right into the twentieth century can well be written as a history not only of war and intervention by force but also of indirect action by means of political supporters and through the exercise of intellectual influence on other societies. Ideological conflicts played an important part in European power politics long before the Russian Revolution of 1917. The three outstanding examples are the century-long medieval contest between the pope and the emperor over supreme authority, followed by the conflict between the Roman church and the kings of Catholic Europe; the Protestant Reformation that led to the religious wars of the sixteenth and seventeenth centuries; and finally the French Revolution and its aftermath. The French republic and Imperial France were the two successive forms of a revolutionary power that challenged not only the peace and the balance of power of Europe but also its political and social order. The War of Coalition against Napoleon was waged by the old powers and their vassals both in defense of the old order and for the protection of their territories and the maintenance of the balance of power. Revolutionary France had attacked the foundations of all European states by challenging the legitimacy of their governments and their very existence. The creation of the popular republics after the French example showed this revolutionary intent as far as the French republic was concerned. Napoleon sought to maintain his own postrevolutionary order among the vassal states of France. Later in the nineteenth century, the growing conflict between the ideas and ethical concepts of European democracy and those of autocracy became the major reason for the isolation of Imperial Russia. Bismarck warned the tsar a century after 1789 that an alliance with republican France would endanger his throne because it would force him to admit French democratic republicanism into his capital and hence into Russian society. The French for their part were openly opposed to the Russian alliance because of their antipathy to the orthodox autocracy of the tsar. It took some time and great efforts to wear this resistance down.

Although tension and ideological conflict have long existed between Western Europe and Russia, the creation of the Soviet state has changed the substance and scope of the issues. The conquest of Eastern Europe was not in itself the decisive fact, because Poland and the Baltic countries had been under Imperial Russian rule for long periods before the Russian Revolution of 1917. It was the unique political character of the Soviet state that imposed a new type of tension upon the relations between Russia and its neighbors. This tension also dominates relations between the Soviet Union and Europe.

The Soviet state demands political security in addition to the military security provided by its own strength. This political requirement goes beyond the Soviet borders. Security to the Soviet Union means unchallenged political control over Eastern Europe and the absence of any foreign influence on the communist countries that would run counter to Soviet interests. The established internal order of these countries and the special links to the USSR must be maintained at all cost. This extensive and demanding security requirement makes the Soviet Union extremely sensitive to internal and international change in Europe, because the communist system and the relations of these countries with the hegemonial Soviet power are in a state of latent tension. Crisis, as in Hungary and Poland in 1956 and in Czechoslovakia in 1968, is therefore a real and permanent risk. This situation has led to an excessive security demand on the part of the Soviet Union that equates domination of other countries with its own national security. This concept limits and endangers the security of other nations. It also complicates Soviet relations with Western Europe and even with the Communist parties of Western Europe.

Stalin told Tito in 1945 that in modern times conquest meant the extension of the social order of the conqueror to the conquered. The Soviet Union has tried to do this as effectively as possible in Eastern and Central Europe, and by so doing has divided Europe and brought about a state of tension between opposing ways of life. "Peaceful coexistence" is possible, but only when arms, secret police, and high walls are used to preserve the internal order imposed on otherwise unruly societies by a minority in power. In the Soviet Union, "peaceful coexistence" is not considered to be synonymous with free and open competition. Instead, it is seen as a projection of the class struggle into international politics by all means short of war and the use of armed force beyond international borders. It is a concept of limited ideological and political conflict, involving competition for political power between "socialism" and "capitalism." As formulated by authoritative communist spokesmen, political aggressiveness with the intention of destroying the political opponent is the fundamental law of "peaceful coexistence." Furthermore, this aggressiveness can be employed with little risk of encountering armed resistance or provoking international war because the military power and political achievements of the "socialist camp of peace" are superior to those of the "capitalist" and "imperialist" adversary.

Within this context, a major element of Soviet policy is the exertion of influence on the domestic politics of European countries. As long as the political constituencies favoring the Soviet Union consisted exclusively or predominantly of Communist organizations, the relationship was a relatively simple one: Communist parties and trade unions (as in France and Italy) were considered vehicles of Soviet policies and were treated as such in the context of national politics. Similarly, the Communist party in West Germany and the Communist cells in the West German labor organizations were sharply set apart from the body politic at large. Soviet influence on the domestic politics of these countries was limited to the influence of the local communists and dependent on their success in producing propaganda, winning seats in national elections, and employing effective parliamentary tactics. From 1945 onwards the Soviet Union found little comfort in this restricted relationship. The only real success in this respect was the change of regime forced upon democratic Czechoslovakia in 1948. The events of 1968 demonstrated, however, that even this success had been fragile; consolidation of Soviet rule in Czechoslovakia required isolation and the imposition of iron discipline, even after twenty years of building socialism in the communist sense. All the other revolutionary changes in Eastern Europe were carried out under the direct supervision and with the decisive assistance of the Soviet army and political police.

GERMANY

Soviet influence in Germany and Austria differed from Soviet influence in the East European countries, where the pattern was one of complete conquest. The Western Allied powers occupied major parts of both Austria and Germany and participated in the international control and administration of the two countries. The Austrian Communist party and trade union forces had tried to usurp political power by means of a revolutionary coup about the time of the takeover in Prague in 1948 but were defeated by the passive resistance of Vienna's workers. Their failure to seize power or to throw the country into a general strike was the beginning of the decline of postwar Communism in Austria. In Germany, the attempt to extend Communist influence beyond the Soviet Zone of Occupation failed decisively when the campaign for the integration of the West German labor movement into the Socialist Unity Party (*Sozialistische Einheitspartei Deutschlands* or SED) ended in defeat at the internal party polls of the Social Democratic Party (*Sozialdemokratische Partei Deutschlands* or SPD).

The construction of socialism under Communist party rule was successful only in the Soviet Zone, where it was forced upon the people by Soviet power. The ensuing partition of Germany (and later, of Berlin) not only severely restricted Soviet influence and the political activities of the Communist party but also discredited those political groups that hoped to overcome the division of Germany by a policy of accommodation with the Soviet Union. The All-German People's Party (*Gesamtdeutsche Volkspartei* or GVP), founded after 1950 by Gustav Heinemann, the former minister of the interior in the first Adenauer cabinet and future president of the Federal Republic, was a complete failure. The same fate befell the short-lived association of politicians and trade union leaders within the West German Christian Democratic Union (*Christlich Demokratische Union* or CDU), which entertained the ambition of building political bridges to the CDU in the Soviet Zone by participating in a Communist-led campaign which called for "all-German" political alliances, opposing the creation of the Federal Republic, and later its rearmament. At about the same time (1949) the only attempt to form a national-conservative opposition in West Germany to the Western alignment policies failed when Konrad Adenauer denounced it as a naïve conspiracy in the service of the Soviet Union. The persons involved, including a former German ambassador to Moscow, were soon removed from the political scene.

Communism never emerged as a viable political force either in

West Germany or in West Berlin, and the old Communist party (*Kommunistische Partei Deutschlands* or KPD) lost much of its electoral support between 1949 and 1953 before being finally outlawed. The Soviet Union therefore had no official ally on the political scene in West Germany until the formation in 1967–1970 of a new German Communist party (*Deutsche Kommunistische Partei* or DKP), which is a reincarnation of the outlawed party. There is some argument about this new party's legal status in light of the rule laid down by the Constitutional Court, which had dissolved the KPD on the grounds that it was an anticonstitutional organization. Politically, however, the DKP is accepted as preferable to a secret Communist party, and its emergence demonstrates that freedom of political opinion really does exist in West Germany. Allowing the DKP to participate freely in the electoral process provides also a convenient means of demonstrating that communism enjoys little popular support and gives a yardstick for measuring the electoral strength of the regular Communist forces. Last but not least, it represents a concession to the Soviet Union and the East European countries, who have always insisted that the legal ban on the Communist party in West Germany was incompatible with détente.

At this point the question arises as to what the Soviet government has to gain by the existence of a Communist party in West Germany. The problem is more complex than may appear at first glance. Indigenous Communist parties have shown themselves to be liabilities as well as assets when the Soviet Union seeks to exercise indirect political influence in Western Europe. This obviously has been true in the past of the Italian and French Communist parties. The role of communism in the area that was formerly Germany, however, is fundamentally different from its role in any other European country, inasmuch as the area is politically divided into two states and the very existence of one of them—the German Democratic Republic (GDR)—depends upon the rejection of national unity or even the concept of a single German nation. This sets German Communism sharply apart from all other bodies of political opinion in Germany and at the same time from communism in all the other European countries. It is open to question, however, whether this official doctrine is to be taken seriously— that is, whether the German Communists in the GDR have really renounced all hopes for national unification of the two parts of Germany under Communist rule. On the other hand it would seem extremely difficult for the GDR and the SED to absorb about sixty million people into their political system and keep their identity as well as control of Germany without a major catastrophe in Western Europe, such as war or revolution.

Soviet policy in the German question has been ambivalent, although the creation of a separate Communist state was the logical consequence of an incomplete conquest and the consolidation of Soviet rule in Eastern Europe. As long as Germany remains partitioned, the Communist party of West Germany will have little political influence, and if relations between Moscow and Bonn should again become frozen in confrontation, this party would exert even less influence and would indeed find itself viewed as a foreign agent, as was the case from the beginnings of the cold war until the commencement of détente in the mid-1960s.

Even if, on the contrary, relations between Bonn and Moscow were to be governed by a spirit of cooperation or, at any rate, by a willingness to recognize each other's mutual interests, this party would not be allowed to participate in national governmental business. It could greet with applause actions that contribute to more cordial official relations between the two countries, press for still more détente or greater accommodation with the Soviet Union, criticize any policies that did not accord with this priority, and attack all opponents of cooperation with the USSR. In its electoral competition with other parties, however, it would be handicapped by its obvious link with the Soviet Union, and this constraint would limit its effectiveness.

The same applies to the more complex and contradictory relations between Bonn and East Berlin and between the SPD in West Germany and the SED in the GRD. The DKP is considered by West German officials to be an affiliate of the SED, drawing on financial resources in East Berlin and controlled by the SED. This raises several interesting questions, the most important of which concerns the allegiance of the DKP: Is it fully dependent on the SED and will it execute orders from East Berlin, or does it report directly to Moscow via the Soviet Embassy in Bonn? The Soviet government is known to keep a separate channel of political communications to the DKP headquarters, and the Soviet Embassy in Bonn maintains an official relationship with this party, if for no other reason than to lend it political support and give it visibility on ceremonial occasions, such as the visit of Brezhnev to the Federal Republic.

The DKP has not as yet made any impact on the electorate or on public opinion generally, nor has it had any electoral success, notwithstanding some small gains in trade union and factory committee elections and in a few municipal elections in industrial areas. It has offered weaker electoral competition to the SPD than the former KPD, and its propaganda has been overshadowed by that of the SPD and the extremist groups to the left of them. Its youth and student organizations, however, have made visible inroads in public high schools, universities, and trade union youth groups, and at the present time, Communist influence in these institutions is growing. Contacts with the left wing of the SPD and the trade unions, especially at the universities, are being established and maintained despite the resistance of the SPD party leadership. This is particularly true of relations with the Young Socialists (*Jungsozialisten*), an official party organization of the SPD, and the Federation of Social Democratic Students (*Sozialdemokratischer Hochschulbund* or SHB), and even some local and regional party organizations of the SPD itself. Such collaboration is generally justified on the grounds of common interests in the promotion of détente, social justice, and a fundamental change of the capitalist society as well as the need to struggle against "reactionary forces," "imperialism," "international trusts," and so on. The new Communist organizations have associated themselves prominently with the propaganda campaigns against military service, the armed forces, NATO, national defense expenditures, and the European Economic Community (EEC). They are in favor of neutralism, unilateral disarmament, and all-European cooperation as alternatives to alliance policies and military security. They support the agitation of conscientious objectors against military service, and they have attempted to effect covert penetration of the conscripts serving in the armed forces. In all these activities they maintain a competitive-cooperative relationship with radical socialist and liberal groups.

Knowledgeable officials in West Germany believe that Soviet agencies exploit all of these organizations in the promotion of Soviet policy goals. This Soviet activity became evident in the call for a Conference on Security and Cooperation in Europe (CSCE) following the Warsaw Pact Declaration at Karlovy Vary (Carlsbad). The statement issued on this occasion urged popular support for the conference and for détente policies in general, including the dissolution of the "military groupings." "Peace forces" in all European countries were asked to join their efforts with those of the Communists and other "progressive forces" in order to overcome the resistance of the "reactionary" and "imperialist" or "militarist" elements arrayed against détente and the CSCE. This appeal led to several Communist-sponsored conferences in Germany (as well as in Belgium, Holland, Denmark, France, and Italy) but they did not kindle much of a public response. The campaign consistently failed to generate enthusiasm and drive, and one widely heralded international convention held at Brussels in 1973 amounted to little more than a gathering of familiar neutralist and pacifist groups, with few new recruits to the cause in evidence. This does not mean that the Soviet government had no great interest in this campaign. Brezhnev made prominent use of the international congress of the "world peace forces" held in Moscow at the end of October 1973 as a forum to promote the image of the Soviet Union as a power for peace. There is no evidence, however, that this campaign has served the interest of the Soviet Union in extending its political influence beyond the realm of its direct control.

According to the best available intelligence, most radical socialist groups in Western Europe may be assumed to be infiltrated by Soviet agents, even though these groups have not proven to be very effective vehicles for the promotion of Soviet influence. Soviet agencies in this field of activity still depend largely on regular Communist organizations and Communist cells. In West Germany these activities include the penetration of all trade unions and political parties, particularly the SPD, using an undercover network of agents that is believed to have numbered 30,000 persons in 1973–1974, according to an official estimate of the West German government. The "Guillaume affair," which caused the resignation of Chancellor Brandt and led to an extensive restructuring of the federal government at Bonn in 1974, revealed that this infiltration of covert agents in West Germany is widespread and its influence far-reaching. Guillaume had been sent to West Germany

some fifteen years before he had made his way into the Bonn administration. He had joined the SPD and posed as a conservative in the
party. He served as an assistant to Georg Leber, the future minister of
defense, who was a leader of the moderate-conservative wing of the
SPD. Guillaume was a typical East German Communist agent whose
mission included the collection of political intelligence in addition to
conventional espionage, which is primarily concerned with ferreting
out military or technological secrets.

The main question that arises from the Guillaume affair concerns
the policy of the Soviet government and its relations with the government of East Berlin. Did the Soviet leadership know and approve of the
secret political espionage of this East German agent who was a member
of the immediate entourage of Chancellor Brandt? If it did, which is
quite probable and by no means unnatural, it would show that the
Soviet government was exploiting the situation in West Germany for
all it was worth. As far as one can determine at this point, however,
Guillaume did not attempt to exert any improper influence on the
person of the West German chancellor, which would have been much
more serious.

If the Soviet leadership did not in fact know of Guillaume's role as
an agent or if it knew but was unable to have him removed, the East
German regime would have a higher degree of autonomy in its relations with Moscow than is generally believed to be the case. This
speculative question is introduced for the sole purpose of illustrating
the complex set of relations existing among the Soviet Union, its East
German vassal state, and the Federal Republic. It is generally assumed
in Bonn that after Guillaume's arrest an explanation was given to Soviet
leaders in Moscow by the head of the SED party in the GDR and that
criticism and concern were expressed by Brezhnev and Kosygin. Information on this point, however, is sketchy, and there is no conclusive
evidence to substantiate this assumption. It is only natural, of course,
that the Soviet government would prefer to appear uninformed, sur-
prised, and outraged than be identified as an accomplice to the intrigue.

The Guillaume affair also raises a further question—that of the
overriding interest of the Soviet Union in maintaining and promoting
its influence in West Germany. Logically, this interest should demand

good relations with the governing SPD as long as this party is the principal proponent of socialism in West Germany and as long as it advocates rapprochement with the Soviet Union and respects Soviet control over Eastern Europe. Why then put such good relations, which constitute a prerequisite for the continuous exercise of political influence, in jeopardy for the sake of gathering political intelligence by placing an agent in the entourage of the SPD's chairman and chancellor, thereby running the risk of discrediting him, his party, and his policy? To ask this question is to point to a more fundamental one: What is the nature of Soviet policy toward West European countries? Is it predominantly conspiratorial and subversive? Or does it merely use whatever means happen to be at its command to promote its interests—indirectly and covertly or officially and openly—as other powers have done in the past and still do at present?

WEST EUROPE
It is evident that Soviet foreign policy is governed by ideological conviction as well as by normal self-interest and the classical drive toward hegemony. It is leaning on its neighbors in Europe, and its power exercises a certain attraction as much as it inspires awe and fear. The declared policy of the Soviet government toward Western Europe since the mid-1960s, however, has been to reassure and placate in order to establish the credibility of the USSR as a peaceful power and a reliable partner in the search for common security. In this particular context it is irrelevant whether this policy of reassurance and cooperation represents the real interest and intent of the present Soviet leadership or not. Even if it did not, the policy could be an effective maneuver only if the deception worked. Influence on the governing parties in Western Europe is essential for the promotion of Soviet interests, but these parties must, of course, continue to command the support of electoral majorities and govern their countries. It should therefore be the main concern of Soviet policy to impress Western governments and their constituencies favorably and not to create domestic or international difficulties if it can be helped—that is, as long as there are no superior or pressing Soviet contrary interests at stake, such as in the Middle East in October 1973.

Through its diplomatic and political activities, the Soviet Union has consistently tried to develop its image as a champion of peace, especially among politicians and political groups as well as among intellectuals, academicians, journalists, writers, and their various associations. This campaign to establish a peaceful identity is necessary in order to dissipate Western distrust of the Soviet Union and diminish support for more conservative policies that emphasize strength, alliances, and defense. In West Germany, as in most of Western Europe, the success of the campaign has contributed to the emergence of détente. Its main targets are political parties, primarily those left of center. Invitations to members of parliament to visit the USSR, exchanges of cultural and scientific delegations, and assistance to conventions of trade unions and other professional associations are standard procedures in this pursuit of goodwill and influence. The concerns of academicians in scientific research, environmental protection, education, health, and social security schemes are used to focus attention on cooperation between East and West rather than on the underlying confrontation between the two systems. The latter, of course, belongs to the province of political propaganda and doctrinal rhetoric.

In 1970, during the election campaign in Hesse, Foreign Minister Gromyko visited his West German colleague, Walter Scheel, in Frankfurt to demonstrate the existence of good relations between the two countries and to underscore his personal interest in a successful outcome of the difficult negotiations then in progress. Since 1969, Soviet ambassadors have been seen as guests at all SPD party conventions, at all trade union conventions, and at all meetings of industrial federations. The fact that there is no strong Communist party in West Germany makes these gestures of courtesy and contacts with members of these socialist parties and groups easier to arrange than would be the case in Italy and France. Forming political constituencies in the major parties and in trade unions, industry, and banking is a recognized goal of Soviet foreign policy, which is aimed at effecting a more favorable attitude toward the USSR in Western politics.

In West Germany this process was accompanied by a massive propaganda campaign against those who opposed Brandt's *Ostpolitik*, in particular against the CDU and the Christian Social Union (*Christlich Soziale Union* or CSU) and their leading politicians, who were described as exponents or instruments of "revanchism and revisionism." The political intervention in the electoral campaign of 1972 by the Soviet press left no doubt whom Moscow wanted to see as the winner of that election. The stakes were high, because the coalition government of the SPD and the Free Democratic Party (*Freie De-mokratische Partei* or FDP) seemed in grave danger of losing office after having lost control of the Bundestag and having suffered a stunning election defeat in the state of Baden-Württemberg. The *Ostpolitik* seemed to be at stake, even though the treaties of Moscow and Warsaw had been ratified. It was therefore understandable that the Soviet government should not only indicate its preference in the current election but also remind the West Germans of past hostilities and the possible danger of a future catastrophe. Soviet interest in keeping a particular party in office in order to maintain the policy inaugurated by that party was openly revealed. The anxieties of the West German electorate were openly exploited with menacing oratory in the official press releases disseminated by the Soviet radio and newswires.

FRANCE

Soviet preferences in the various French elections were revealed more discreetly. The relationship between the USSR and France during the administrations of presidents de Gaulle and Pompidou (from 1958 to the spring of 1974) was complicated by the existence of the French Communist party (PCF) and by the dominant role of the Communist-led association of trade unions (CGT) in the French labor movement. Both stood in firm and aggressive opposition to the Gaullist regime on domestic grounds, but both supported de Gaulle's policies toward NATO and the United States, as well as the Soviet Union. Both also backed the claims of the USSR and its East European allies against West Germany and generally assailed France's policy toward Germany since 1947 as being inconsistent with the security of Europe and the real interests of France.

The Gaullist movement had similarly opposed the European policies of the Fourth Republic, particularly the proposal to establish a European Defense Community (EDC) which was voted down in the National Assembly by a coalition of Gaullists, Communists, and a group of opponents within the government's majority. De Gaulle's attitude toward West European unification and the Atlantic Alliance was ambivalent, but his provocative and intransigent methods of operation served to reinforce Soviet efforts to weaken the Alliance. His pressure on the Bonn government to recognize the territorial status quo was regarded by the Soviets as valuable, while his rhetorical insistence on the right of the German people to self-determination and national unification was clearly a nuisance. On balance, his policies were considered by the Soviets to be as good as could be expected from France.

The Soviet accommodation with de Gaulle at the same time that French Communists were bitterly opposed to the Gaullist regime presented Soviet policymakers with a difficult problem to which there was no really satisfactory solution. To make matters worse, the French Communists had no prospects of exercising any real influence in French public affairs in the foreseeable future. During the cold war they had been one of the major political propaganda assets for the Soviet Union. Their opposition to official French policy had also been useful in 1951–1954 when the EDC was proposed, but they had not been able to prevent either the admission of West Germany to NATO or West German rearmament. Their agitation against French colonial rule and the French war efforts in Indochina and Algeria had been fruitful from the Soviet point of view, but these actions had also contributed to the return of de Gaulle to power—a fundamental change in French politics that resulted in a stronger conservative regime than ever before. Under de Gaulle, France became a major power in international politics, a development that caused the Soviet Union concern, particularly with respect to West Germany.

It was only toward the end of 1964, after de Gaulle had come out openly against any kind of West German participation in the nuclear defense of Western Europe, that Soviet policymakers could feel less anxious about a possible combination of French-German military power. After 1966, when France had separated itself from the military system of NATO, blocked the unification of Western Europe, and embarked on the road to all-European rapprochement under de Gaulle's motto "détente-entente-coopération," the Gaullist Fifth Republic became the Soviet Union's favorite partner in Western Europe. If the new relationship with France was to continue, however, domestic stability in France was a necessity. Because Soviet foreign policy was closely identified with the Gaullist conservative regime, the Soviet Union developed a vested interest in the distribution of political power in France. This preference became clear in the 1967 election, when Soviet commentary on the relative electoral chances of the incumbent government compared with those of the Communist-socialist electoral alliance—the first since the Popular Front of 1936—showed bias in favor of the Gaullist-Conservative coalition.

The upheaval of May 1968—when de Gaulle's power was seriously challenged and the prospect of a "popular front" emerged from the general strike and the anarchy in the streets of Paris—again prompted Soviet preference for the political status quo in France. The French Communist party itself did not seem to want to assume any political responsibility, and the leaders of the CGT needed time to regain control over the labor movement that had slipped away to their leftist socialist rival, the French Democratic Confederation of Workers (CFDT). Neither the Russian nor the French Communists wished to bring down the Fifth Republic, with the PCF avoiding participation in government in order to forestall a revolutionary situation. In 1969, after de Gaulle's resignation, the Soviet government clearly favored Pompidou over any other candidate in the presidential election. There was, however, at that time no electoral alliance between Communists and socialists. The Communist candidate, who had no chance of being elected, ran only to show that his party was an uncompromising and vital force in French politics and the only real alternative to the Gaullist regime. Communist propaganda was radical and aggressive, but the PCF was resigned to the role of a minority party after the heavy electoral defeat of the Communist-socialist alliance in the June election of 1968, which had given the Gaullist regime the strongest majority ever as well as absolute control of the National Assembly.

The problem for both the PCF and the Soviet government became more complicated after 1972. President Pompidou had inaugurated a new European policy; Britain had joined the EEC after an understanding between the two conservative governments in Paris and London; and the prospect had emerged for a new Anglo-French joint leadership in Western Europe that would include cooperation in the field of nuclear armaments and military policies and perhaps lead to an integrated West European defense effort in conjunction with West Germany. However slim this prospect may have been, there was the potential for a power concentration in Western Europe hostile to the Soviet Union. The new mood in French policy toward the Russians was revealed in the French positions taken at the CSCE negotiations at Helsinki and Geneva. These were much more reserved in regard to the Soviet demands for the definition of European security and broad statements of intent. The French also publicly denounced American-Soviet global arrangements on the grounds that they contained the risk of a superpower "condominium" over Europe or "neutralization."

The presidential election in France in the spring of 1974 offered the possibility of change and the probability that Gaullist rule had come to an end. For the first time the Communist-socialist alliance had a real chance of winning, and the effect of such a victory would have been incalculable. Nevertheless, Soviet policymakers still seemed to prefer stability over change, at least as long as the future seemed to be uncertain. The Soviet tactic, therefore, was to invest in both sides. Press commentary, which was reserved, featured the powerful surge of popular forces in the coalition of the progressive parties of the Left and the popularity of the Communists, and the firmness of the alliance between Communists and socialists was emphasized. However, the Soviet ambassador, during the election campaign went to see Giscard d'Estaing, who was the candidate of the government coalition and the minister of finance, on the pretext of urgent business within the context of the French-Soviet Commission of Cooperation—a body that had not been very active since its creation in 1966 but had the advantage of being chaired on the French side by the minister of finance. The brief talk was widely interpreted as a gesture of the Soviet government in favor of the conservative candidate over the socialist challenger. It was, in fact, a necessary precaution, because, in the probable event of Giscard's victory, good relations with the conservatives had to be safeguarded. Furthermore, the possibility that Mitterand as President and his Communist ministers could govern effectively when they did not control the National Assembly was tenuous at best, and Mitterand's election would inevitably have resulted in a government characterized by instability and uncertainty of purpose. The economic situation of France was not favorable for socialist experiments and

Communist assumption of responsibility without a total revolution. The Communists therefore settled for détente.

PEACEFUL COEXISTENCE

In its relations with Europe, the Soviet state defines the concept of peaceful coexistence as a function of its own power to coerce, to intervene, and to defend. Variations in application are matters of degree and measure rather than of principle. It is therefore a pragmatic concept of power politics that is identical with the national interests of the Soviet state. The main element of peaceful coexistence, as understood and used by Soviet foreign policymakers, is the power to deter the adversary from war, thereby neutralizing the risk of armed conflict while leaving the Soviet Union free to pursue aggressive policies and indirect intervention. If actual warfare is excluded, political competition can be made one-sided as long as the power to make war and threats of armed conflict can still be invoked. Since the end of the conquest of Russia's neighbors in Eastern Europe and the "construction of socialism" in each country by rule of force, the main achievement of Soviet foreign policy has been to impose the Soviet concept of peaceful coexistence on the nations and societies of Western Europe, while reserving to itself the capability to resort to military solutions should international crises become otherwise unmanageable.

The Soviet political edifice built in Eastern Europe, however, has remained fragile. The USSR therefore needs political as well as military fortification along its borders with the outside world. Stalin's policy of isolating the Soviet empire behind the "Iron Curtain" during the years immediately following the conquest of Eastern Europe was absolutely necessary to provide time and opportunity for the political consolidation of the new "socialist order" and the building up of Soviet military power. The Soviet Union excluded active and relaxed relations with Western Europe as well as North America, but the isolation could be maintained only by foregoing the advantages of international cooperation, trade, and assistance. Maintenance of the Iron Curtain required a military garrison and a totalitarian police state, continued political hostility, tension, and rhetorical aggression vis-à-vis the outside world—and therefore a self-denial of influence abroad other than stark deterrence through fear. Total isolation, therefore, could not be a long-term policy in the emerging era of global communications, cultural and scientific exchanges, and raw materials interdependence, and it required absolute self-sufficiency on the part of the Soviet armed forces, Soviet society, and the Soviet economy, supported only by the energies and resources of the satellized "socialist" countries. Khrushchev came to the conclusion that this state of total isolation and systematic hostility was becoming far too costly for the Soviet Union and its clients. Furthermore, extension of the Soviet realm into Western Europe appeared to be impossible, confronted as it was with American power and Western unity.

Thus, the Soviet Union, stalled in Western Europe, could not even complete the consolidation of its conquest of Eastern and Central Europe unless the conquest was acknowledged by the West. This meant in Soviet terms "recognition of the realities created after 1945" by the United States and Western Europe. Although the Soviet Union had pursued this goal from the very outset, from 1963 onwards the emphasis was to be on détente. Within this context, the Russians ultimately concentrated on a diplomatic and propaganda campaign for a European "security system" and later for "all-European cooperation and security," to be negotiated and formally established by a conference. In the 1950s, when Soviet foreign policy was primarily concerned with the internal consolidation of the Soviet bloc in Eastern Europe and the pursuit of the cold war, its influence on the domestic politics and the societies of Western Europe was at best very limited.

DOMESTIC COMMUNIST PARTIES

The Communist parties in Western Europe proved to be poor instruments for the advancement of Soviet interests, because the goals of the Soviet Union as a major power were necessarily and openly opposed to those of their own countries in the field of security and international communications, trade, exchanges, and cooperation. Although the Communist parties of Italy and France were strong and viable political entities, after the end of the immediate postwar period they were not permitted to participate in their national governments because of the emergence of the cold war and the intensity of the East-West struggle over Europe. The socialist premier of France Léon Blum—the head of the Popular Front government of 1936—said at that crucial moment in postwar Europe that, in order to become acceptable partners again, either the French Communists would have to change their allegiance to the Soviet Union or the Soviet Union would have to change its attitude toward Europe.

The national interests of the Communist parties of Western Europe had to be sacrificed by the Soviet Union in order to maintain the status quo in Europe until a political thaw could take place without, at the same time, eroding Soviet control over Eastern Europe. Furthermore, Communist parties were not well suited for the promotion of Soviet policies in the West. The Communist organizations in Western Europe served mostly as a set of drums resounding under the heavy strokes of propaganda orchestrated in Moscow to remind the peoples of Eastern Europe that the cause of Soviet communism had adherents on the other side of the Iron Curtain. They also contributed to social unrest and, with organized labor, provided opposition to American influence, the Atlantic Alliance, and the unification and defense of Western Europe. They were, however, effective only when they joined forces with socialist and other democratic parties.

Apart from such campaigns—mostly short-lived—West European Communist parties inadvertently reinforced the domestic positions of those center-right, or "national coalition," governments that were the partners of the United States and initiators of the unification process of Western Europe. By cutting off between one-third and one-half of the industrial labor vote from the electoral constituency that supported socialist policies and left-wing parties, they assured the victory of center-right majorities of government. In Italy and France, for example, they forced the socialist parties to adopt a centrist orientation and form alliances with the parties to their right. By posing as aggressive, extremist movements openly giving allegiance to a foreign power and flaunting a high degree of enforced party discipline after the Soviet example, they fed the fires of anticommunism and reinforced the policies of governments that were committed to strong defense efforts and close alliance with the West.

The Communist-directed but allegedly nonpartisan organizations of the "antifascist" and "peace" movements in Western Europe fared somewhat better, but only as long as there was confusion about their aims. Once their political identity had been established, their usefulness diminished. The same was true of the groups professing "friendship with the USSR." Thus the politics of confrontation that were designed to help consolidate Soviet hegemony over postwar Eastern Europe and to strengthen the Soviet regime internally in the USSR also brought about the Atlantic Alliance, the creation and arming of the Federal Republic of Germany on an equal footing with the other countries in Western Europe, and the beginning of West European unification. Perhaps the most important result of the policy of confrontation was the major defense and armament effort by the West, which continued for a period of twenty years. Among the effects of the cold war, the military response to confrontation in Europe had the strongest impact on Western society.

DÉTENTE

At the very time that the Soviet Union was heavily engaged in the arms competition, striving for parity with the United States in nuclear weapons, Soviet and Communist propaganda was enjoying success in another direction. As the Soviet government inaugurated in the mid–1960s its conciliatory policy of détente, it found increasing support in European countries from political groups other than the Communist parties and the left-wing supporters at the fringes of communism. Some of this support dated back to the immediate postwar period when the Soviet Union had advocated complete but uncontrolled disarmament. Some support was also engendered when the Soviets, still lacking a nuclear capability, launched a worldwide propaganda campaign against nuclear arms. With the advent of détente, however, a new perspective of prolonged and consolidated peace in Europe was opened by Soviet diplomacy, with the voluntary, if hesitant, collaboration of most Western governments and the popular support of political parties, trade unions, and the academic community. Behind this collaboration was the emergence of a pacifist and universalist spirit in the West that was a reaction against two decades of inconclusive political tension and confrontation with the Communist world. Western nations and their governments had also by this time accustomed themselves to the political status quo in Germany and the area of Soviet hegemony. The evolution of stable governments in Eastern Europe seemed to promise better relations with the West, and a general relaxation of tensions ensured that the territorial borders and the legitimacy of the Communist regimes would not be questioned.

"Détente" became a catchword throughout Europe. Its content remained to be defined, but its very imprecision had the definite advantage of allowing for latitude of interpretation. This vagueness brought on a great debate in Europe, and with it, many illusions. Détente acquired a mystical quality and became a symbol with an intrinsic value of its own—a value not to be questioned by skeptical judgment, for fear that its fragility may cause it to vanish. The pursuit of détente became an unquestioned virtue and in political statements often stood as self-explanatory. Détente, originally conceived as a relaxation of tensions that would lead to negotiation of the political disagreements in Europe, thus became for many Western political leaders an end in itself, and the ideal of détente acquired a charismatic appeal notwithstanding its elusive quality. "There is a thing mightier than all the armies of the world," Victor Hugo once wrote, "it is an idea whose time has come." So in the minds of many people in Europe and North America, the time had come for a change in the world of conflict and confrontation, armaments and alliances, power politics, and the rule of the mailed fist. Nevertheless, statesmen and high public servants, such as the two successive secretaries general of NATO during the last decade, Manlio Brosio and Joseph Luns, warned against illusions and disillusionment. Skeptics coined the term "détente euphoria" and warned that this new political state of mind was a serious threat to the security of the West. Critics of détente policies also dismissed it as a "myth."

Any discussion of détente must inevitably address itself to the question of the essential relationship between the Soviet Union and the countries of Western Europe. What is détente all about? What are the goals of Soviet foreign policy in Europe? What are the political conditions in the various countries of Western Europe and what are the expectations of their leaders vis-à-vis the Soviet Union and Eastern Europe?

It is widely assumed that the main goal of Soviet policy toward Western Europe is the consolidation of the status quo. Egon Bahr, the chief architect of former Chancellor Brandt's *Ostpolitik,* made a distinction between the "territorial" and the "political" status quo. The former relates exclusively to borders in Europe, whereas the second is concerned with the existing political order in the countries of Eastern and Western Europe. Bahr stated that the goal of *Ostpolitik* was to create the necessary conditions for a peaceful change in the "political status quo," particularly in Germany, by recognizing the "territorial status quo."

Bahr hoped that the formal recognition of East Germany as an independent and "equal" state in Germany (equal to the Federal Republic) would make it possible to promote greater internal freedom in East Germany and Eastern Europe and generate a progressive relaxation of pressure on the people, a reduction of ideological confrontations, and an opening of the borders for wider exchange between East and West. Some years earlier, Bahr had called for a similar relaxation when he suggested a "change by rapprochement" as far as the two parts of Germany were concerned. Underlying all of Bahr's proposals was the assumption that the recognition of existing international boundaries would neutralize antagonisms and reduce tensions.

Such recognition of the territorial status quo was expressed in the treaties of Moscow and Warsaw (1970) by indirect and implicit formulas in which the signatories mutually renounced the use of armed force to change the existing borders in Europe. The Soviet Union and Poland interpreted these implicit formulas as a definitive and valid recognition of borders that could be changed only by mutual consent—which both states absolutely exclude as a matter of national policy. The treaty of Warsaw contained an explicit reference to the Oder-Neisse border, which was, of course, the main subject of that treaty. However fuzzy in juridical terms, the formulas served the main purpose of Soviet policy in both Poland and West Germany: Namely, to recognize the current territorial boundaries and end the contention over the validity of the Polish annexation of former German territory. If the political issue of a change in boundary were to arise in the future, the parties to the treaties would stand on their respective positions as stated and explained at the time of the conclusion of those agreements, and any changes to be made would have to be accomplished within the context of the treaties.

The settlement of the boundary issue can be considered as final as anything ever is in history. Western Europe as a whole supports the settlement, and all European governments consider the question closed once and for all, which is in itself a considerable modification of the original declared political goals of the Atlantic Alliance, of the three allied powers, and the Federal Republic. As late as 1965 it was stated in a formal "Three-Power Declaration on Germany" that:

in the absence of a real solution of the German problem, based on the exercise in the two parts of Germany of the right of self-determination, the situation in Europe as a whole will remain unsettled and that in consequence peace will not be fully assured on that Continent. This solution is necessary not only in the interest of the German people, which asks for reunification, but in the interest of all European peoples. . . . Settlement of the cardinal issues [remains] one of the essential objectives of the Alliance.[1]

In the meantime the allies would continue to "promote and extend their contacts and exchanges with the Soviet Union and the countries of Eastern Europe" and "continue to seek an improvement in their relations with these countries."

The "peaceful settlement in Europe" was still the objective in December 1967, when a "policy of détente" was formally proclaimed as "the second function" of the Alliance "in the search for progress towards a more stable relationship in which the underlying political issues can be solved." The allied governments had in mind a policy of balance of power, and this was to remain based on "military security" and "collective defense" as "stabilizing factor[s] in world politics" and as "the necessary condition[s] for effective policies directed towards a greater relaxation of tensions." Consequently, it was stated, "the way to peace and stability in Europe rests in particular on the use of the Alliance constructively in the interest of détente. The participation of the USSR and the USA will be necessary to achieve a settlement of the political problems of Europe." Even then, however, the fifteen allies asserted that:

no final and stable settlement in Europe is possible without a solution of the German question which lies at the heart of the

[1]Text attached to the communiqué of the North Atlantic Council Ministerial Meeting, London, 12 May 1965, in *NATO Final Communiqués* (Brussels: NATO, 1974), p. 163.

present tensions in Europe. Any such settlement must end the unnatural barriers between Eastern and Western Europe, which are most clearly and cruelly manifested in the division of Germany.[2]

Under those conditions and in the context of these objectives, "realistic measures to further a détente in East-West relations" were envisaged though not specified. The allies did, however, provide a general definition of their understanding of détente: "The relaxation of tensions is not the final goal but is part of a long-term process to promote better relations and to foster a European settlement. The ultimate political purpose of the Alliance is to achieve a just and lasting peaceful order in Europe accompanied by appropriate security guarantees." Part of the envisaged "process of active and constant preparation for the time when fruitful discussions of these complex questions may be possible bilaterally or multilaterally" would be studies of disarmament and "practical arms control measures, including the possibility of balanced force reductions." They would in the view of the Western allies bring about "an effective détente." After the intervention of Soviet forces in Czechoslovakia on 21 August 1968 and the ensuing military occupation and political submission of that country, the Atlantic Council refused to recognize the validity of "agreements concluded under the pressure of occupying forces" between Czechoslovakia and the other Warsaw Pact countries, in particular the USSR.[3]

The allies also rejected as incompatible with the principles of the UN Charter and "dangerous to European security" the contention of the Soviet leadership that the Soviet Union has the right to intervene in the affairs of states that are deemed to be within the so-called "Socialist Commonwealth." A policy of détente was nevertheless pursued, and negotiations were conducted on the basis of the political situation created by the Soviet takeover in Czechoslovakia. During the period

[2]Text attached to the communiqué of the North Atlantic Council Ministerial Meeting, 14 December 1967, report to the Council by the Harmel Studies Group (voted by the Council), "The Future Tasks of the Alliance" in *NATO Final Communiqués*, p. 198.

[3]Communiqué of the North Atlantic Council Ministerial Meeting, 16 November 1968, Brussels, in *NATO Final Communiqués*, p. 212 ff.

from 1969 to 1973 the Western allies virtually recognized the state of affairs in Eastern Europe, thereby consolidating the Soviet position in the area. The primary objective of Soviet policy in Europe was finally achieved when the Atlantic Alliance recognized the de facto political and territorial status quo in Europe, as established by the aggressive action of the USSR in Eastern and Central Europe. The restrictive qualifications to this political recognition of the fait accompli, which were contained in all official statements by Western governments and even in the agreements with the USSR, could not alter the political substance. There had been no negotiation to bring about the "final and stable settlement of the political problems of Europe" that the allied governments in 1967–1969 had hoped to achieve. The only action that could be considered to have produced "a more stable relationship" had been the recognition of the GDR and the agreement between the four occupation powers in Berlin on the status of West Berlin. This latter settlement had been the most important objective of Soviet policy in Germany after it had become evident that the Soviet Union could neither force the three Western powers out of West Berlin nor completely sever the ties between that city and West Germany. The process of politically integrating West Berlin into the system of the Federal Republic had, however, been effectively halted; the political presence of West Germany in Berlin had been curtailed; and the scope and significance of ties with the West diminished. At this price, the freedom of communications and the security of the enclave of West Berlin in the territory of East Germany could be guaranteed. The relations between the city and West Germany remained, however, a critical and controversial issue between East and West.

By the end of 1972, the goals of Soviet détente diplomacy in Europe had become clear. East-West relations were to be improved, but only if the West recognized two elements of the status quo: (1) effective Soviet military and political control over most of Eastern and Central Europe (including Czechoslovakia) and (2) the division of Germany. The prerequisites for improved relations between the two parts of Europe were thus clearly spelled out. Western governments would have to respect the political order in the "socialist countries" and the ties established between them. According to the Soviet point of view, Western pressure on the countries of Eastern Europe to change their political systems or to loosen their ties to the Soviet Union would violate the spirit of détente. At the most, the Western countries could advocate "peaceful change" without, however, pressing the point. This line of argument became apparent during the negotiations at the Conference on Security and Cooperation in Europe (CSCE) held in 1973–1975 at Geneva and Helsinki. Although the Soviet Union did not attain all of its diplomatic objectives at the meetings, the underlying goal of Soviet diplomacy was achieved. The political restructuring of the countries of Eastern Europe was conceded by the Western members of the conference to be an accomplished fact, and Soviet hegemony over the area implicitly recognized—all in spite of general commitments by both East and West to defend the national sovereignty and territorial integrity of all countries. The Soviet Union chose to play the role of a "status quo power"—that is, a satisfied power with no other political objectives than the preservation of the status quo and its defense in international crises; the United States appeared to be a partner in this task. It was this pattern of external support of Soviet hegemony over one-half of Europe that Soviet diplomacy had sought to invoke ever since the period of overt crisis and confrontation in 1961 and 1962.

The question that arises from this apparent stability of relations and the distribution of power in Europe is whether or not the Soviet Union is now satisfied. In other words, is Soviet policy toward Western Europe essentially defensive, or is it potentially offensive, including options of military pressure and war? The USSR's demonstration of superior military strength, including nuclear as well as conventional power, and its position of geographical and strategic predominance both serve to impress its smaller and less powerful neighbors and produce subtle psychological effects long before any open threat is made or a military force is moved up to a border or across it. In the absence of a real balance of power, the manifest superiority of one country can influence the political imagination, the strength of will, and the national purpose of other countries.

James Schlesinger, the then U.S. secretary of defense, in 1974 put this psychological reality into an equation with strategic superiority— what he called "asymmetry of strategic options" as the basis of a political "asymmetry of pressure"—and concluded that if, in the future, the Soviet Union should achieve military, and specifically nuclear strategic, superiority over the United States, "the hypothetical leaders of the West would need more strength of will" in a power contest or confrontation with the Soviet Union than the "hypothetical leaders of the East," in order to meet the political challenge of their respective adversaries. This is the real problem underlying the "finlandization" issue in Western Europe. Weak countries tend to appease the dominant power by adapting their national interests to the demands of the greater power. In this way the war-making potential of the dominant power determines the political precondition for the stability and security of all other countries in the area. This is nothing more than the political use of military power or, to use Henry Kissinger's terms, the reality of "usable military power" in international relations in the absence of war. Always present, however, is the veiled threat to use superior power to coerce if necessary.

A promise not to use this threat is purely theoretical. The mere existence of superior power—the capability to decide a given conflict by applying force—leads unarmed or weak countries to avoid a contest of wills. Peaceful coexistence based on an asymmetrical distribution of power in a given geostrategic situation or regional system of states favors the dominant power. If the concept of peaceful coexistence leads to unilateral disarmament or restraint, the ability of the weaker countries to resist threats is diminished. This is what hegemony is all about.

Soviet policy is formulated to convince the people of the West that the USSR is the dominant military power in Europe and that Western countries should adopt a policy of unilateral restraint. This goal can succeed only if the Soviet policy finds supporters in the countries against whom the power politics are applied. Therefore the impact of Soviet diplomacy and political propaganda must necessarily be concentrated on the body politic of those countries, in this case the domestic political forces and the social fabric of West European countries. Governments can withstand external pressure by concentrating their resources in an alliance for collective defense and joint action, but if governments are exposed to domestic pressure, their power to resist can be diminished. This is particularly true of pluralistic societies based on free debate and on a constitution with checks and balances limiting the exercise of power. The multiparty system permits not only a discussion of issues but also a division of national purpose. A totalitarian power such as the USSR, however, can enforce internal conformity, suppress dissension, and monopolize information. Through a program of propaganda, it can divide public opinion in other countries, thereby reducing the freedom of choice of its adversaries. It thus makes use of public debate and domestic opposition in other countries to further its own aims. It plays on internal conflicts of interest and party rivalries as well as on civil strife and social unrest, economic crises, and international complications. The experience of the countries in Eastern Europe that have been ruled by Communist minority parties shows, however, that closed and tightly controlled nations are, in the long run, in danger of explosion due to suppressed tensions. Furthermore, these countries are less adaptable to change and less flexible in crisis. With this qualification, it can be said that the Soviet Union has so far enjoyed a certain advantage over Western Europe in the field of international power politics and in the area of the negotiation of unsettled issues. Soviet policy does—as it must—try to influence the domestic debate on East-West relations in the free and open societies of Western Europe and North America. Whenever it succeeds in finding allies or at least a benevolent neutrality in public opinion, it can bring pressure to bear on a reluctant government.

This indirect drive for political influence on the home base of foreign governments is one of the main goals of Soviet policy in Western Europe and one of the major concerns of the Western countries exposed to it. In the present era of détente, Soviet influence is promoted less by domestic Communist parties—always an object of suspicion—than by the diffuse political and ideological currents that sweep across party lines and make strong impressions on large segments of the population, such as the younger generations, for whom the hard times of World War II and the political tension of the cold war have no real meaning, and the elitist minorities of high social standing, such as the academic and literary communities—the "intelligentsia" of Russia's prerevolutionary days. Soviet propaganda and doctrinal writings have always, however, aimed beyond such minorities, and in every case the working class has remained the primary objective. Close alliances between organized labor and other "progressive social forces" for the "class struggle" inside each country and the "struggle for peace" on the international field are still regarded by Communist political strategists as the most effective vehicle for extending Soviet influence.

It was less obvious, but still apparent, that in the same year (1969) the Soviet government had serious reservations about the reliability of the "socialist-liberal" coalition government of Chancellor Brandt as a partner in the grand negotiation on the status quo in Germany. These doubts were aired unofficially and became the subject of general diplomatic discussions in the European capitals until the "Eastern treaties" finally were ratified by the Bundestag in 1972. In the eyes of the Soviet leadership, and particularly its main vassal in East Berlin, the Brandt government constituted a certain risk to the political order and cohesion of the GDR, as was shown by the destabilizing effect of Brandt's presence in Erfurt in 1970. After the return visit to West Germany of Willi Stoph, the chairman of the GDR Council of Ministers, for the meeting in Kassel shortly afterwards, no more such visits were arranged. The SED, which was the ruling party in the GDR, reduced contacts to a minimum, and its new party secretary, Erich Honecker, proclaimed for the socialist state in Germany a policy of political isolation (*Abgrenzung*) from the "capitalist and imperialist" Federal Republic. Only after the visit of Leonid Brezhnev to West Germany in the spring of 1973 did Honecker arrange for Herbert Wehner, the chairman of the SPD parliamentary group in the Bundestag, and Wolfgang Mischnick, chairman of the FDP group in Parliament, to visit East Berlin. He personally announced the talks and even advertised his meeting with the two West German politicians on television. Although this initiative has been interpreted in various ways, it is evident that Honecker wanted to put himself on the international scene and not let Brandt appear to be the only significant German spokesman on close and cordial terms with the Soviet leadership.

Since 1969, the relations between Moscow and Bonn have held the center of the European political stage. They exemplify very clearly the problems confronting both the Soviet Union and Western Europe, for it is in Germany that the Soviet policy of firming up the status quo and consolidating its Eastern conquests meets with its main challenge. Under conditions of peace and cooperation—a complex combination of competitive and cooperative relations that do not exclude political pressure and maneuvering for dominant influence in Western Europe—the use of military force for overt aggression or the support of subversion and revolution becomes virtually impossible. It is, however, under these very circumstances that political influence can best be exercised to take advantage of the opportunities presented by the expectations, hopes, or illusions that have arisen in other countries.

For the Soviet Union, the fundamental question in its relations with the various countries of Western Europe is how far these nations are willing to go in accepting Soviet domination over the Continent as a precondition of security and peace. This question has several aspects. In the case of West Germany, for example, which of its foreign policy options has priority over the others: Good relations with the Soviet Union at the expense of all other possible objectives of foreign policy? Close ties to the United States and a solid military alliance in NATO and political unity of action? As to Western Europe, what should be its posture in regard to the United States and the Soviet Union? Should it play an independent role as a "third force" in international politics with a symmetrical neutrality between the two superpowers? Or, on the contrary, should Europe maintain an organized alliance with North America and membership in the Atlantic community? Or, finally, should Western Europe make an arrangement with the Soviet Union on the basis of cooperation in an "all-European system of security" as advocated by the countries of the Warsaw Pact since the mid-1950s— that is, under conditions of an acknowledged Soviet hegemony over Europe, a situation that Brezhnev in his speech in Bonn in 1973 called "Europe, a continent of peace"?

PROSPECTS

The Soviet Union has always tried to convince the people of Europe that the presence of American strategic power on the European conti- nent will not last forever, that it is of necessity a transient phenomenon, and that, after the present brief moment in history has passed, the fundamental reality of geography will assert itself. When that day dawns, Western Europe will find itself alone face to face with all the inescapable realities of its geographical position, the most important of which is its vulnerability to the huge Russian nation that dominates Eastern Europe and occupies the Eurasian continent from the Baltic and Black seas to the Pacific coast. A close cordial relationship with this vast country and its great military power, natural resources, and im- mense tasks would constitute a source of unparalleled physical strength and offer unique opportunities for industrial and commercial activity.

Because, without the counterweight of American power, the security of the peripheral West European peninsula would have to be founded upon peaceful relations with the Soviet Union, there would be no alternative to voluntary adaptation to this distribution of power. Rapprochement with the Soviet Union would be inevitable, and cooperation could be advantageous for both sides.

Having advanced this argument piecemeal along with anti-American and "anti-imperialist" propaganda as well as threats of war, Soviet spokesmen finally adopted more reassuring language. This change was the only new feature of détente, because Soviet military power and combat readiness were not only maintained at a high level but built up further and extended to the seas, while no substantial changes were made in the internal system or in the control over Eastern Europe. Soviet diplomacy and propaganda thus succeeded beyond expectation in reconciling the appearance of forbidding military strength with the reassuring image of the Soviet Union as a "peaceful power" (Konrad Adenauer in 1966).

The aggressive foreign policy formerly pursued by the Soviet Union was not altogether useless. Although it threw the West European nations together in fear under the mantle of American power and leadership, thus helping to unify Western Europe and consolidate the Atlantic Alliance, Russia's threatening pose also inspired a yearning for peace and security in Western Europe that could not be stilled in a situation of conflict and constant danger, whether real or imaginary.

Because nothing could remove Soviet power from the heart of Europe and the approaches of the Atlantic Ocean, accommodation appeared necessary. The policy of "containment" had been successful only so far as it has denied the new dominant continental power access to Western Europe beyond the dividing line that ran across Germany, and it had contributed inadvertently to the consolidation of the new Soviet Russian empire. Thus for better or worse, Western Europe would have to come to terms with Russia.

The West Europeans are slowly coming to recognize the inevitability of this imperative, just as did the East Europeans under conditions of duress a generation earlier. Soviet policy needs only to exploit this process gradually, avoiding harsh shocks. Previous Russian experience in the exercise of power and in the treatment of other peoples does not, however, provide any useful precedents for the exploitation of this new challenge and opportunity. The Soviet regime is by its very nature repressive. The type of actions required to gain effective control over Poland, Hungary, Czechoslovakia, and East Germany and to suppress national unrest in non-Russian parts of the Soviet Union— especially in the annexed Baltic countries but also in the Ukraine—are ill suited for dealing with Western Europe. Regulation and limitation of freedom and human contact as well as control and coercion are inescapable elements of the authoritarian bureaucratic tradition of both Imperial Russia and the Soviet state.

In spite of these shortcomings, the Soviet cause is slowly but surely finding wider acceptance in West European societies—not on the merits of the Soviet economic system or political style but on the strength of the awe-inspiring power of the Soviet military presence. Educated minds in West Germany, France, and the smaller West European nations have, of course, devised rationalizations for a benevolent and reasonably accommodating attitude toward the Soviet Union. Popular concepts such as the establishment of a "stable order of peace," reconciliation and rapprochement between the nations, and cooperation between "different social systems" which are opposed to each other in principle but are obliged to work together toward the same ends if common challenges are to be met and the higher interests of humanity are to be safeguarded, may be sincere aspirations and, for the future, even realistic goals. For the moment, however, they represent courses of action that run the risk of strengthening the Soviet international position and serving the political interest of the USSR in Europe while weakening the political resolve and cohesion of the Western alliance, subtracting from Western defense efforts and encouraging the mood for surrender of vital security interests to the Soviet power. It should be noted that so far the NATO allies have withstood such temptations and, on the whole, managed their détente policies effectively in the ongoing security negotiations with the USSR and Eastern Europe.

Although the Soviet government has steadfastly advanced a configuration of plans for European security, general disarmament, and the reduction of military forces, defense budgets, and arms production, which has been totally unacceptable to the West, it has also advocated a number of altruistic proposals for international efforts to safeguard common resources and the environment. In the latter area, the Russians have found partners in Europe and in the world at large who are willing to cooperate on reasonable terms. The example of global Soviet-American cooperation across a broad field of subjects— including the limitation of strategic armaments, joint enterprises in space and scientific research, common endeavors in combating disease, mutual assistance in the development of advanced technology, rehabilitation and protection of the global environment, and, in the future, the joint stewardship of the resources of the oceans—all this cannot fail to impress the West Europeans.

It has been Soviet policy in this respect to play down issues of military security in favor of "political security" based on peaceful coexistence and organized cooperation. The countries of Western Europe, torn between nationalistic goals and the pragmatic requirements for supranational unity in Western Europe, are also at the same time confronted with the typical problems of modern industrial societies. They must find answers to issues involving the environment, access to natural resources, and political developments in the outside world. Hence the new Soviet approach falls on receptive ears. The "socially relevant forces" in Western industrial society are less concerned with military security, defense, international strategy, and contests of will in power politics than they are with civilian and humanitarian tasks and domestic conflicts and social reform. They can, therefore, be counted upon to act as valuable and altruistic allies in helping to advance Soviet influence in their countries regardless of the shadow cast over Europe by the military power of the Soviet Union.

Soviet propaganda in Western Europe plays up to the imagination and willingness to accept new ideas inherent in the modern Western elite and exploits their yearning for détente and a world free from power conflict and military confrontation. There is a clear continuity from the early "international peace movement" and the campaign against (American) nuclear armaments, through the pacifist "unilateral disarmament" school of thought and the "positive neutralism" of the late 1940s and early 1950s, to the "mass movements" that the Warsaw Pact resolution on security in Europe sought to mobilize in the 1960s in order to put pressure on the Western governments to accept proposals for a European security conference. The private, widely publicized meeting of a conference of diverse organizations and groups that was convened at Brussels in 1973 to "support" the official negotiations of the CSCE shows how domestic supporters of Soviet policy can be mobilized in the very countries whose governments are negotiating with the Soviet government on matters of security. It is clearly the aim of the Soviet Union to encourage these forces to participate in the power structure of Western Europe, so long as their influence tends to moderate any official resistance in those countries to adverse interests of the Soviet Union. The Soviet position would be quite different, of course, if serious demands were made by these groups for peaceful economic and cultural changes in Eastern Europe or for relaxation of the military control imposed on the socialist countries in Eastern Europe by the Soviet armed forces.

The question arises, however, how far the Soviet Union wishes to go in supporting sympathetic forces in the governments of Western Europe. Propaganda literature in the Soviet press and semiofficial Soviet commentaries appear to indicate that the Soviet Union is indeed interested in this type of promotion. It is not certain, however, that the Soviet Union would really want to see strong socialist governments in power in West Germany, France, or Italy, for such regimes might raise issues of European security and cooperation in the spirit of "socialist internationalism" and might seek a fundamental change in Western Europe's relationship with Eastern Europe. Thus far, the Soviet Union has shown an essentially conservative tendency, which is understand- able enough because it is now in a period in which it seeks to consoli- date the gains made after World War II.

This does not mean that in the future the Soviet Union will remain satisfied with the status quo. The prospect of changes occurring in the overall political structure of Western Europe and in the domestic governments of various countries in the western and southern nations of Europe seems obvious. The Soviet Union must and will take an active interest in such changes, whether or not they conform to the preferences of the present Soviet leadership. Although the nature of these future developments is, of course, uncertain, the Soviet govern- ment, like any other, has its own interests to protect or enhance should profound changes take place in Italy, France, Yugoslavia, Greece, Turkey, West Germany, or even Spain.

Portugal is a case in point. The active interest of the Soviet Union in the Portuguese revolution of 1974 is evident. Western intelligence sources have reported that several hundred East European Communist agents have been brought into this country since 1974. The Soviet Embassy in Lisbon is the center of coordination of Communist activities throughout Portugal. The infiltration, which is being launched from Prague, was in readiness before the revolutionary coup d'etat of the Armed Forces Movement. Arms, radio and other communications equipment, and foreign currency, as well as political instruction and indoctrination literature in the Portuguese language have been sent to Portugal in large quantities. Under the supervision of Soviet agents, a Communist party militia and a security service have been organized and armed, with the active collaboration of Marxist and left-leaning officers in the Portuguese armed forces.

The number of personnel in the Soviet Embassy in Lisbon in 1975 was greater than the entire foreign ministry staff of Portugal before the revolution. This does not include the various Soviet missions and liaison offices outside the embassy. Other East European countries are equally active and represented by numerous political staffs. The new Communist party of Portugal offers the Soviet Union an opportunity in Western Europe without precedent. For the first time since 1943–1946, a Communist party in the West is directly associated with other political forces in a popular revolutionary movement and an antifascist alliance, participating in government on a basis of independent strength. Avalho Cunhal was the first party secretary general in Western Europe since Maurice Thorez in France to have held cabinet rank in a coalition government. Here the Soviet Union had found a favorable set of circumstances including a military dictatorship of revolutionary forces and socialist inspiration. Similar conditions could be created in the future, certainly in Spain, perhaps also in Greece and even in Turkey, if the opportunities implicit in the Portuguese situation were to be exploited adroitly.

The example of the Portuguese revolution and its political evolution toward a power combination between the Communists as the "party of revolutionary order and democracy" and an authoritarian military rule with socialist goals has also had a negative effect on Soviet activities in Western Europe. The dangers of popular-front-type alliances with the Communists have become apparent once again to many a socialist or left-wing liberal in France, Italy, Greece, or Germany. This is the reason why the secretary general of the Italian Communist party, Berlinguer, has openly criticized certain aspects of the Portuguese revolution and warned against a course of confrontation with the other democratic parties and against a monopoly of power by the Communists and the military. (The secretary general of the French party, Marchais, has refused to associate himself and the French Communists with this open criticism.)

Western Europe, as a set of nations with different internal political structures and varying degrees of social integration, political stability, and wealth, has, taken as a whole, relatively little independence, power, or overall stability. The shock of war in October 1973 in the Middle East and the ensuing oil crisis revealed the weakness of the European position. The European Economic Community (EEC) proved to be even less solid and united than it had appeared to be. The conflicting national interests and contradictions dividing the partner states of the EEC and the uncoordinated actions of the community members demonstrated to the Soviet government that the political unity of Western Europe was illusory and insufficient to produce concerted actions because national interests were still far more powerful and contradictory than had been thought. The oil crisis thus exposed a serious flaw in the Western structure of unity. Domestic interests and conflicts could still be exploited as effective impediments to European integration and the formulation of a united West European policy. The Common Market, recognized by the USSR as a viable economic entity, no longer appears to be a formidable economic force, and a West European power concentration based on the EEC does not loom on the horizon of 1980, whatever the nine governments of the community may pretend. Furthermore, the emergence of popular-front governments, especially in France and Italy, could very well reduce the basis and scope of the movement toward Western unity to such a degree that it would lose most of its significance.

At this point, the Russians have two alternatives: (1) they can work closely and cordially with a Western Europe that would in return confirm the present division of Europe and thereby permit the Soviet Union to strengthen its political-economic system in Eastern Europe, or (2) they can work against Western unity as they have in the past, in order to extend, in the long run, Soviet hegemony over all of Europe. If a gradual balkanization of Western Europe were to ensue, the resulting disunited and politically weak area might seem to offer a better prospect for the kind of political security sought by the Soviet Union than a united Western Europe made up of major nations and integrated on the basis of a functioning economic community.

At a time when the West is confronted by an economic crisis characterized by the energy problem, high unemployment, and inflation, the forces of social conflict in all countries grow stronger and governments lose power. There is a potential for revolution in the current situation, including the possibility of anarchy and civil strife. The Communist parties and trade unions of France and Italy—the only ones that count in the present situation, because the future of Spain is still in balance, and West Germany, like Britain, offers an inhospitable terrain for Communist politics—have so far shown themselves prudent and cautious in the face of crisis. As noted earlier, the Russians have in the past preferred to deal with a conservative French regime. Now, however, in a time of social unrest and growing opposition to conservative governments within the industrial and urban labor class, Soviet policy must take into account the possible evolution of new left-wing political parties and the emergence of left-of-center government coalitions with Communist participation. The Soviet Union has been prepared for such eventualities for a long time, even if it has done nothing to further them. It can reasonably expect such governments to contribute to the progressive paralysis and final dissolution of the Atlantic Alliance as well as the EEC, even though they remain formally committed to a united Western Europe and the continuation of NATO. Again, Portugal is a case in point, if only a minor one, and Greece offers distinct prospects in this respect.

For the Soviet Union, the retreat of American power from Europe and the erosion of the defenses of Western Europe, centered on the disintegration of NATO, are long-term objectives. There is one condition attached to this prospect, however. Such results must come about without a shock that would, by the sheer force of its impact, rekindle the drive for unity in the West and lead to a new concentration of military power. If such a shock were avoided, Western Europe could be counted upon to disintegrate by itself, as a result of its own internal dissensions and contradictions. Soviet policy must therefore encourage nationalistic resistance to efforts to instill supranational West European discipline and Atlantic solidarity. It must emphasize alternative options to the concept of Western unity, in particular options that favor "all-European" solutions, cooperation, and security arrangements.

The idea of a "socialist Europe," as advanced by the French socialists, may not mean much to the Soviet Union; indeed, it might even have frightened the leadership in Moscow, were it not for its esoteric substance. But this concept can be used as another elusive ideal with which to capture the imagination of the Western intelligentsia and to suggest to them that there is a realistic alternative to the existing and rather imperfect EEC and the Atlantic Alliance. The immediate concern of Soviet policy in this respect is to gain influence over those who can block the European evolutionary process of integration and help reinforce Soviet influence over the existing governments. To accomplish this, the Soviet Union could invoke the higher alternative of all-European security and cooperation whenever West European governments try for a greater degree of West European unity.

The ideological solidarity between the Communist parties of Western and Eastern Europe still remains to be tested in the practical politics of governments. Furthermore, the Soviet Union has no effective mechanism for the direct control of Communist parties in the West, nor is there any evidence that these parties are likely to submit voluntarily to Soviet will as was the case in Stalin's day. If they are to survive in countries having a democratic system of government and free elections, these parties must be responsive to their electorates and minimize the political liability of appearing to be an instrument of the Soviet Union. They are, first of all, partners and competitors of their socialist and other political allies, and they are exposed to election risks as well as to risks of labor strikes, price-wage inflation, and other domestic economic factors. Domestic concerns therefore govern their politics, and they must win or lose their elections at home. The secretaries general of the Italian and French Communist parties, Berlinguer and Marchais, have stressed this preoccupation in public appearances during 1974 and 1975. Under these conditions, the main interest of the Soviet Union is, at least for the present, to preserve stable relations with Western Europe, to avoid shock reactions in individual West European countries, and to make use of the new "advances of socialism in the capitalist society" without letting too much influence from any new socialist-Communist governments in the West to penetrate the East.

Soviet-East European Relations

CHRISTOPHER CVIIC

Outward signs of Soviet imperial presence in Eastern Europe are relatively few and far between, so it would be easy for a casual visitor to miss them altogether and conclude that there was no such presence. Of course there are those large, ornate Soviet Embassies in Warsaw, East Berlin, Budapest, and other East European capitals, special Russian-language bookshops and houses of Soviet culture, and monuments to Soviet soldiers killed during the last phase of the war against Hitler in 1944 and 1945—but not much else. The slogans extolling friendship with the Soviet Union and its peoples are really loud and obtrusive only in "super-loyalist" countries, such as Bulgaria, or in countries whose loyalty to that Soviet friendship has recently been tested and found wanting, for example, Czechoslovakia.

Even the Soviet army, whose thirty-one divisions are a physical guarantee of Moscow's grip on its "socialist commonwealth" in Eastern Europe, is not all that much in evidence. These Soviet divisions are stationed in four out of Russia's six Warsaw Pact partners in Europe (the German Democratic Republic [GDR], Poland, Czechoslovakia, and Hungary); Romania does not want them, and Bulgaria does not need them. Yet it is possible to travel the length and breadth of the most heavily garrisoned of them, the GDR, without actually seeing a single Soviet soldier or officer in uniform. Obviously, Russia's East European partners think it prudent to keep those guests carefully tucked away, out of the local population's view, presumably because that population might resent their presence.

Nobody seems to resent the Soviet tourists, who are in evidence, and in ever larger numbers, too. Perhaps this is because these extremely plainly dressed men and women who shuffle so diffidently in and out of their hotels in Prague, Warsaw, Budapest, and other big East European cities do not have the words "I am a Soviet citizen" written all over them, and they lack the bearing of a proud citizenry of an imperial superpower.

Yet the visitor who simply went by the evidence of his eyes and decided that there was no such thing as Soviet rule in Eastern Europe because he could not see any outward signs of it would, of course, be wrong. Three decades of Russia's control over the area may not yet have left much of a physical, visible imprint there—certainly nothing to compare with that left behind in their former overseas dependencies by the excolonial powers whose rule after all lasted a good deal longer. Or, for that matter, the ubiquitous impact of the United States even in those parts of the world that have no direct connection with its military power and political control.

Nevertheless, Russia must be regarded as a serious imperial power with a sense of mission and an inflexible will to fulfill it that has not shown signs of weakening at any time since the Soviet army first filled the vacuum left in Eastern Europe by Hitler's retreating armies in 1944–1945. In the 1950s and early 1960s, when the process of decolonization was at its height in Africa and Asia and when the Soviet Union itself was going through a turbulent political period following Stalin's death in 1953, there was never any suggestion that Stalin's successors might be considering a parallel process for Eastern Europe, a sort of decolonization that would result in Russia's granting full external independence to the countries there. Even when the United States, in the wake of the Vietnam War, began its retreat from its overexposed imperial positions in the world, there was no sign that the Russian leaders were thinking of following suit. The question simply does not seem to arise. Today, as in the late 1940s, the Soviet Union's "socialist commonwealth" in Eastern Europe looks firm and solid, with no "liberation movements" working to undermine it, and no foreign backers to support their efforts. This is the measure of Russia's success in playing its imperial role in Eastern Europe, to which it seems to be so deeply committed.

That commitment has been put to the test three times: in East

Germany in 1953, in Hungary in 1956, and in Czechoslovakia in 1968. In each case the Soviet Union defended the threatened status quo with armed forces. Force was very nearly used in Poland in October 1956 to prevent Wladyslaw Gomulka from coming back to power. However, the prospect of a full-scale armed clash with Poland, and allegedly also the pressure from the Chinese, persuaded the Soviet leaders to settle for assurances of good behavior from Gomulka, which he honored to Moscow's complete satisfaction. Later, in December 1970, Gomulka reportedly asked for Soviet troops to help shore up his tottering regime, but was given short shrift by Moscow. After careful consideration, Moscow settled instead for another change of leadership and another set of assurances from Gomulka's successor, Edward Gierek. The gamble seems to have worked again: Just as Gomulka had "normalized" the country and silenced the intelligentsia in 1956–1957, so Gierek managed to defuse the social and economic discontent that was one of the major causes of the disturbances in Poland's northern ports and elsewhere.

Yet on the debit side, from Moscow's point of view, are the successful defections of Yugoslavia, Albania, and Romania (Romania's is still only a de facto, not a de jure defection; it remains a member of the Warsaw Pact, Comecon, and other bloc bodies, albeit a detached and critical one). It is difficult to be certain why Russia decided against intervention in the case of these three countries, while acting in East Germany, Hungary, and Czechoslovakia. It is probably true that until fairly recently Moscow had viewed southeastern Europe as a low-priority strategic area, in contrast to Central Europe, where the three interventions occurred. Today the picture is different as a result of the Soviet Union's deep involvement in the Mediterranean and the Middle East. Some of the implications of this apparent change of priorities will be discussed after a brief outline of the circumstances surrounding each of these three cases of nonintervention.

Yugoslavia probably got away without being invaded because Stalin was overconfident. In 1948 when the quarrel with Yugoslavia came out into the open he calculated that a mixture of economic boycott, military threats, and political intrigue would suffice to bring the Tito regime to heel. By the time that calculation was proved wrong (1950–1951), the United States and its allies had already extended a discreet protective umbrella over Yugoslavia. A Soviet invasion against Yugoslavia, however informally protected by the West, would have carried with it the risk of a wider conflict that Stalin was not ready for. So he concentrated instead on making the rest of Eastern Europe safe from the Titoist disease of "national communism," leaving it to his successors to try and square Yugoslavia by other means.

When Albania's leader, Enver Hoxha, quarreled with Nikita Khrushchev in September 1960, an attempt was made to unseat him and replace him by a pro-Moscow leader, but without success. There is no evidence that the use of military force was contemplated. In any case, Russia did not at that time have sufficient naval forces to launch an assault on Albania from the sea. An attack with land forces would have involved the crossing of Yugoslav territory and the certainty of a conflict with Yugoslavia, which would not have tolerated this violation of its sovereignty despite its own quarrel with Albania. Yugoslavia's connivance in the occupation of Albania could not be assumed because of the deep suspicions felt by many Yugoslavs against Moscow. Moscow eventually decided to cut its losses, even though they included that of the submarine base at Vlorë (Valona).

Romania, too, probably owed the success of its own bid for independence in 1964 to the fact that, like Albania and Yugoslavia, it was part of a low-priority strategic area. The geographical position of Romania, of course, would have made an invasion a good deal easier than in the case of Yugoslavia or Albania. With no direct access to any Western country, Romania would have presented few military problems as a target for an invasion. On the other hand, that probably made it easier for Soviet leaders to decide against an invasion in the knowledge that one could be mounted fairly easily, if and when it should become necessary to do so. Romania was fortunate in another sense too. Its quarrel with Russia had come out into the open at a time when the Soviet Politburo was deeply divided. Khrushchev, who had been criticized for the humiliating outcome of the confrontation with the United States over Cuba, for exacerbating the quarrel with China, and for the failure of his agricultural policy, was on his way out. That was clearly no time for another deeply damaging public quarrel in the communist family. But the Romanian leaders, too, helped their cause by choosing the ground for their challenge to Moscow very carefully.

Unlike Hungary in 1956, Romania did not try to leave the Warsaw Pact nor did it seek any major changes in it, as Czechoslovakia did in 1968. There was no talk of liberal reforms that could have carried a dangerous ideological infection elsewhere in the bloc. Instead, Romania, with the tacit support of several other East European countries, hammered at the perfectly respectable theme of economic equality within Comecon. In other words, the Soviet Union was being denied a chance to intervene in Romania on the pretext that "socialism" was in danger there. Romania was fortunate in another sense, too; unlike Hungary, it did not have any Soviet troops stationed on its territory, the last Soviet troops having left in 1958. An intervention, therefore, would have been less simple than in Hungary, for example. In time Romania extended its challenge to the Soviet Union to other issues. For example, it established diplomatic relations with West Germany in defiance of a strict Soviet bloc injunction not to do so until Moscow had given its approval, and it refused to go along with the Soviet bloc's pro-Arab line in the June 1967 war. But by then the time for disciplinary action had passed. Like Albania, Romania had become something of a protégé of China, a nation with which Khrushchev's successors were still vainly trying to come to terms. Forceful action against Romania on insufficient ideological grounds would have put an end to any remaining hopes of a deal with China.

Even allowing for these three cases in which Russia's imperial will was thwarted, it is nevertheless possible to argue the proposition that throughout the past three decades Russia has held on to its wartime gains and shown no slackening of its imperial will. Indeed, in the past four years the Soviet Union has been working hard not only to consolidate the inner core of its "socialist commonwealth" but also to recapture the ground that it has lost in the past two decades to the "national communists" in the Balkans.

But what is it that makes Eastern Europe so important in the eyes of Moscow that it seems prepared to pay such a high price for maintaining its presence there? What is the Soviet Union's stake there? The military attractions of a presence in the heart of Europe must be uppermost in the minds of the Soviet leaders, for such a presence above all enables Russia to exercise political and military pressure against Western Europe. Given Russia's enormous preponderance over NATO in conventional arms, such pressure could easily be exercised without an armed attack against any Western state actually taking place. Eastern Europe's role as a glacis for the expansion of Soviet influence and power in Western Europe is particularly important at a time when the Soviet Union appears to have embarked on a forward policy in Europe.

Much has been made of Eastern Europe's other, defensive role as a buffer zone to protect Russia against an invasion from the West. Whatever might have been the traumatic Russian experience of such invasions in the past, including the very recent experience of Hitler's invasion in 1941, the importance of such a zone in purely military terms has surely diminished since Russia's achievement of nuclear parity with the United States. Once the Soviet Union had become a nuclear power on a par with the United States, the idea of an attack from the West by, say, West Germany trying to get back both East Germany and its lost territories in Poland became completely unthinkable, even as a remote contingency. Even earlier the talk of a "rollback" of communist power in Eastern Europe during the Eisenhower presidential campaign in the United States in 1952 had been mere rhetoric. In reality, the West's posture vis-à-vis the Soviet Union since 1945 has been consistently pacific and defensive. The United States failed to use the brief period of its atomic monopoly to extract any concessions from Stalin. Given Stalin's pathological mistrust, it is perhaps understandable that he feared such an attempt might be made, and so went ahead to create a buffer zone among other things. But his successors have had ample proof of the West's peaceful intentions toward the Soviet Union and of the West's acquiescence in the status quo in Eastern Europe. This was demonstrated by the Western powers' passivity at the time of the East German uprising in 1953, the Hungarian revolution in 1956, and, most tellingly, the crushing of the Czechoslovak liberal Communist regime after August 1968. A Western crusade to liberate Eastern Europe from Soviet rule was, from the practical point of view, a nonstarter even in the relatively self-confident 1950s and 1960s. It is totally preposterous in the 1970s when the West is in a state of disunity and disarray. Soviet propaganda continues to talk of the "threat from the West," but if Russia has a security problem it is on its eastern border with China. On the contrary, it could be argued that, far from being a good buffer zone, Eastern Europe has been from Moscow's point of view an area of strife and conflict. Stalin's insistence that the East European regimes, with the curious exception of Finland, must be of the same political hue as the Soviet one has created more problems than it has solved. This is best borne out by the fact that the only armed interventions the Soviet Union has had to mount in Eastern Europe have been against its own national allies, not against an external "imperialist" enemy. In the light of that experience, it is indeed possible to argue that a series of friendly, even pro-Soviet, but noncommunist governments on Russia's western borders would perhaps have served the interests of its security better than a string of unstable and unreliable communist states subject to constant internal upheavals.

The economic argument for controlling Eastern Europe was very compelling following World War II, when Russia required industrial plants and equipment, raw materials, and agricultural produce for its reconstruction. Eastern Europe was relatively undamaged by the war, and so it became a big supplier of Soviet needs. Whether this happened in the form of reparations from former enemy countries (Finland, East Germany, Hungary, Romania, and Bulgaria) or from nominal friends and allies, like Poland, Czechoslovakia, and Yugoslavia, was immaterial. Even friends were paid only what the Soviet Union was prepared to pay, and so this phase of economic relations between Russia and Eastern Europe has left deep scars. "Unequal treatment" was one of the Yugoslavs' grievances against Russia in 1948, especially in the so-called "mixed enterprises" that Russia had established with Yugoslavia and a number of other East European states. Cheap coal from Poland sold to Russia at prices far below those on the world markets was a deep grievance right up to 1956 when Russia dropped the practice. Romania objected in the early 1960s to being assigned the role of a supplier of raw materials and agricultural produce for the rest of Comecon and demanded its right to industrialize like everybody else in the bloc.

Today the situation has changed in Russia's favor. It still needs its East European partners, especially the more advanced ones like the GDR, as suppliers, for example, of engineering goods and other types of specialized equipment that Soviet industry is not able to supply.

Russia's huge and still desperately undersupplied domestic consumer goods market readily absorbs vast quantities of shoes, textiles, and other consumer goods from Eastern Europe. Russia sells to Eastern Europe industrial goods and plants and equipment. But what the East Europeans want from Russia above all is oil, gas, and other fuels and raw materials, of which most East European states are desperately short. Apart from Romania, which still has considerable oil reserves, and Hungary, which satisfies about one-fifth of its oil needs from domestic production, other Comecon members in Eastern Europe (and that, of course, goes for Cuba and Mongolia too) are almost totally dependent on Russian oil supplies, not only for heating and transport purposes but also for their new chemical and petrochemical industries. But apart from oil, Eastern Europe relies on Russia for most of its natural gas, iron ore, cotton, phosphates, and other raw materials, including grain and other agricultural produce.

All Comecon countries have embarked on nuclear power station programs to help alleviate their shortages of energy. But these programs will take a long time to implement and are enormously costly. Meanwhile, Russia will have the whip hand over them. In theory, of course, it should be possible for East European countries to acquire oil and other fuels and raw materials that they need from the world market. But that would mean diverting scarce convertible currency away from purchases of advanced Western technology that East European countries need to modernize their industries. This need is felt particularly in Czechoslovakia, which in the immediate postwar period passed on its advanced technology to Russia and the rest of Eastern Europe. But while these countries have surged forward, Czechoslovakia has lagged behind, largely because of its isolation from the West. The problem is less acutely felt in the GDR, whose direct link with West Germany and thus with the Common Market led to its being termed the "seventh [now tenth] member of the EEC." But even countries with relatively new industries, such as Poland and Romania, need to keep importing modern machinery, equipment, and know-how from the West. Higher oil and commodity prices have put them all in a difficult position. In order, therefore, to alleviate their problems and indirectly help keep them loyal, Russia has had to forego some of the advantages that the enormous increases of oil prices in 1973 and 1974 have offered it as a major producer and exporter of oil. Instead of charging its Comecon partners the full world price for oil, which has quintupled since October 1973, it had increased its oil prices by only about 150 percent by the beginning of 1975—a kind of imperial subsidy well known to older imperial powers. Therefore, in general terms the boot is now on the other foot, and in the economic sense at least, Eastern Europe needs the Soviet Union more than the Soviet Union needs it, especially now that Russia is better able to pay for its own imports of technology and know-how from the West. Indeed, in the new pattern of economic relations that is emerging in the mid-1970s, an important new instrument of political control has been put into the Russians' hands.

Apart from a fairly clear-cut and well-defined military stake that the Soviet Union has in Eastern Europe as a forward base for westward expansion and, less important now, as a buffer zone to protect Russia against attack from the west, and a new rather more marginal economic stake, there is another stake that is much less easy to define, but nevertheless extremely important. It is a mixture of ideology and politics and has to do with the Soviet Union being both a Marxist and a multinational state. Above all, it has to do with the type of control that Stalin established over Eastern Europe at the end of World War II.

As has already been hinted above, Stalin had the option of establishing a series of pro-Soviet, friendly but independent, states, such as Finland is today. He rejected that option, presumably because he thought that it would not work and that those states, if left to themselves, might again become both anticommunist and unfriendly. In any case, he gave Finland an especially lenient treatment only because, as he told a Yugoslav visitor, he knew that the Americans "had a thing" about the country, and so he did not want to risk trouble with them for the sake of that "peanut."[1] The others, in contrast, got exactly the same kind of regime he had established in Russia: a Marxist dictatorship based on the use of mass terror. Stalin apparently toyed with the idea of creating several federations in Eastern Europe linked with the Soviet Union. Yugoslavia and Bulgaria would form one group, the Ukraine, Romania, and Hungary another; Poland, Czechoslovakia, and White

[1]Adam Ulam, *Stalin, the Man and His Era* (London: A. Lane, 1974), p. 594.

Russia, a third (presumably he had other ideas for Germany). But it never got beyond the stage of discussion.[2] The idea cropped up once again in a letter that the Soviet Central Committee sent to the Yugoslav Central Committee on the eve of the break between Yugoslavia and the Cominform in June 1948. In that letter, dated 4 May 1948, it was asserted that one of Tito's closest colleagues, Edvard Kardelj, had told the Soviet ambassador in Belgrade in 1945 that "Soviet-Yugoslav relations should be based on the prospect of Yugoslavia's incorporation in the Soviet Union."[3] Neither Kardelj nor the Yugoslav government has ever confirmed the truth of this Soviet allegation, but at the very least it shows that the idea of some sort of a constitutional link between the Soviet Union and Eastern Europe had continued to preoccupy Stalin.

If Stalin did indeed ever seriously entertain this idea, he probably dropped it for several good reasons. A direct incorporation of large chunks of Eastern Europe into the Soviet Union would have caused a tremendous outcry among the Western allies as well as in Eastern Europe. Local opposition would have made the first and most important task, the "sovietization" of these countries, much more difficult. Besides, there was to be considered the effect of a sudden encounter between the more prosperous and, by and large, more free-and-easy East Europeans and the Soviet citizens living under strict Stalinism. No wonder then that Stalin settled for a halfway house: Full sovereignty and other trappings of formal independence for Eastern Europe, combined with direct rule from Moscow backed by the presence of the Soviet army and supervised by Soviet officials at various levels of government. As long as Stalin was alive, this arrangement worked. But as soon as he died, and the chain of command reaching from various parts of communist Eastern Europe became confused, the problematical character of the setup began to be clear. These new East European dependencies proved to be extremely troublesome to Stalin's successors—in fact far more so than the Soviet Union itself. They saw them as a bunch of virulently nationalist, virulently anti-Russian states that resented having been put under the rule of a culturally inferior country whose political system was totally alien to them.

[2]P. Auty, *Tito* (London: Longmans, 1970), p. 250.
[3]*The Soviet-Yugoslav Dispute* (London: Royal Institute of International Affairs, 1948), p. 38.

There were of course pockets of friendly feeling for the Soviet Union in countries like Bulgaria, which tsarist Russia had liberated in 1876–1877, and Czechoslovakia, where traditional pan-Slav, pro-Russian attitudes mingled with deep bitterness against Czechoslovakia's former Western allies, Britain and France, for having left it in the lurch in 1938. There was also the more negative but nevertheless (from Moscow's point of view) helpful fact of deep anti-German feeling, especially in Poland and Yugoslavia. But the local Communist parties nearly everywhere (except in Czechoslovakia) were weak. Marxism itself had very weak indigenous roots. This of course reflected both Eastern Europe's still predominantly agrarian character and its complex national structure. In an area that was a complicated patchwork of national identities and antagonisms, national problems, however one tried to analyze their origins, not unnaturally loomed larger than the social and economic ones with which the Marxists were far more at home. In most of the countries, therefore, there was strong opposition to the new postwar arrangement on two counts: because it was communist and because it had come from Russia and been imposed by it.

Looking back on their numerous troubles with Eastern Europe since Stalin's death, some Soviet leaders may secretly wish that Stalin had in fact opted for a looser connection. That might have made the task of running Eastern Europe a good deal easier. Instead, just because the Soviet dependencies there have the same communist, or "socialist," regime as the Soviet Union itself, changes in Eastern Europe inevitably produce immediate repercussions in the Soviet Union itself. This happens if some concessions are granted. At the very least, the result is that questions are raised by orthodox party members in the Soviet Union puzzled by the apparent readiness to grant the East Europeans, who are already under "socialism," something that looks like a reversion to "bourgeois democracy."

In general, this means that their policy in Eastern Europe always exposes Soviet leaders to embarrassing and even dangerous situations because of the extremely rigid doctrinal basis of their rule. If the Soviet Union were a fairly pragmatic type of military dictatorship, based on the idea of the supremacy of the Great Russians over everybody else, non-Russians in the Soviet Union and Eastern Europe alike, the problems would in some ways be simpler. But because the Soviet Union is, on paper at least, a federation of peoples that are equal and that in theory enjoy full freedom as nationalities, what happens in Eastern Europe has a bearing on the Soviet situation in another, perhaps even more crucial, sense.

In reality, many non-Russians in the Soviet Union feel as oppressed under their own Soviet government as many East Europeans feel under their own indirect version of Soviet rule, disguised as formal independence. This is true in varying degrees of the different Soviet national groups, but it would probably be no exaggeration to say that national discontent is most acute on the fringes of the Soviet Union where most of the non-Russians brought under the rule of the tsars live. In recent years there has been a wealth of evidence of the steady growth of national discontent in the Ukraine, the Baltic republics (especially Latvia and Lithuania), the Caucasus, and Soviet Central Asia. This evidence has reached the West in numerous *samizdat* publications. For the Soviet leadership, the problem is perhaps most acute in the Ukraine, which has a population of forty million and, despite a high degree of russification in the cities, represents the most unreconciled republic. On 17 May 1974, *Pravda Ukrainy*, the main party paper in the Ukraine, carried a long report by the party secretary in the Ukraine, Vladimir Shcherbitskii, on the persistence of the problem of "Ukrainian bourgeois nationalism" in the republic.[4] Peter Shelest, his predecessor, was replaced and given another post in Moscow two years before because he had not shown results in the struggle against "Ukrainian bourgeois nationalism." Similar warnings are being issued all the time against other types of nationalism in the Soviet Union. What makes the national problem in the Soviet Union especially urgent is the fact that the national balance between the Russians and the non-Russians is changing. At the last census in 1970, the Russians had a bare majority that they soon may lose because of the enormously higher birthrate among the non-Russians in Soviet Central Asia. This prospect fills some Russians with the fear of being outnumbered by the non-Russian "Asiatics." The non-Russians, on the other hand, hope that sheer numbers may eventually lead to the end of the present Great Russian dominance in the Soviet Union. The success of the Jewish

[4]*Le Monde* (Paris), 26 May 1974.

campaign for emigration to Israel and the smaller exodus of ethnic Germans to West Germany have had a powerful effect on the other nationalities and, because unlike the Jews and the Germans there is nowhere for them to go outside the Soviet Union, have also increased their sense of frustration.

The Soviet leaders are clearly worried by the growth of this unrest among non-Russians because obviously it could become far more serious than that of the relatively less numerous Russian dissidents who are, by and large, still confined to the intelligentsia. But what worries them even more is that the national problems of the Soviet Union might be exploited by China. Soviet propaganda has complained on a number of occasions that the Chinese are using Ukrainian nationalists from Canada and other Western countries to foment unrest in the Ukraine. There is no evidence that, even if this is true, it has had any effect. One comes across publications in the West, such as the *Information Bulletin of the Ukrainian Society for the Study of the Asian Problems (USSAP)*, published in Munich, whose style and jargon suggest Chinese encouragement and probably also financial help. But in the Ukraine itself, there has not yet been any evidence of unrest fomented by the Chinese. Russian authorities must also face up to the very real possibility that the Chinese might step up similar activities among the various non-Russians in Central Asia who are not so remote from China and live on both sides of the border. Of course, this is a game that two can play, and presumably the Chinese appreciate the risks that they themselves are exposed to in the same way as the Russians. But it is almost certain that the next few years will see a stepping up of this mutual probing of weak "national" seams between China and the Soviet Union.

Eastern Europe figures in this situation because it is an obvious target for Chinese propaganda and encouragement. China has over the years supported not only Albania and Romania, as well as occasionally Yugoslavia during its periods of tense relations with the Soviet Union, but also Czechoslovakia since the 1968 invasion—this despite the evident ideological distaste that Chinese leaders must feel for the Czechoslovak "revisionists" such as Ota Šik or Jiri Pelikan. It is likely that the Chinese will go on trying to exploit the Soviet Union's difficulties in Eastern Europe by encouraging the local population to "rise and throw off the Soviet yoke." But even if future Soviet leaders felt tempted to let one or more of their East European partners go, they would still need to worry about the effect that this sort of policy might have on the disaffected non-Russians in the Soviet Union itself.

It is clear from the foregoing that having had bequeathed to them by Stalin a certain type of totalitarian control over Eastern Europe, his successors have no choice but to go on ruling Eastern Europe in a Stalinist manner. Grant the East Europeans a bit more internal liberty, and this immediately unleashes a similar demand in Russia. Grant them national independence, and tomorrow the Ukrainians and the others will be asking for it too, and the whole edifice of the Soviet Union will come down like a house of cards. This of course assumes that in the foreseeable future the Soviet Union is not going to develop rulers willing to introduce internal reforms at home that would result in greater freedoms for the citizens of the Soviet Union and both more freedom and independence for Soviet dependencies in Eastern Europe. Unfortunately, the likelihood of such leaders emerging and staying in power is remote, as the example of Khrushchev, the only leader with a modicum of historical imagination and originality thrown up by post-Stalin Russia, amply illustrated. Khrushchev, though by no means a "liberal," tinkered with relaxation at home and abroad and in the end came unstuck. In his retirement, he had to watch Russia revert to a form of neo-Stalinism.

Given these strict limits on their freedom of maneuver at home and abroad, it is easy to see why the current group of Soviet leaders have attempted to deal with the problem of the inherently dangerous and unstable situation in Eastern Europe by more indirect means. Any idea of trying to legitimize the East European regimes in the eyes of their own peoples by allowing them a degree of liberalization that would make them popular and accepted, must be ruled out. Such Dubček-style liberalization produces dangerous tensions elsewhere in Eastern Europe and the Soviet Union itself. Any attempt to allow the regime a greater degree of legitimacy by allowing it more freedom in its foreign policy also encourages the other East Europeans to do the same and thus indirectly threatens the far more important dominoes at home in the Soviet Union. What to do then?

A policy of total clampdown would have been a natural one for Stalin to follow. It is not an option that is available to his successors. Russia needs to maintain and expand its economic contacts with the West at this time in order to enable it to overcome its present economic difficulties without having to abandon its military program or having to embark on risky internal reforms that seemed the only way out of communist countries' economic troubles in the 1960s. Having decided on a policy of cooperation with the West with a view to getting this sort of economic assistance until it no longer needed it, the Soviet government could hardly shut off its East European partners from these same Western "capitalists." In any case, such an attempt could result in those countries becoming a serious economic burden on the USSR.

If these Western countries could, however, be induced to recognize the status quo in Eastern Europe and publicly renounce any intention to see it changed, this would obviously go a long way toward detaching the local populations' hopes for a better life from hopes for a change in status quo to accompany such improvements. The whole Soviet strategy since the invasion of Czechoslovakia had been aimed at demonstrating to the East Europeans the "irreversibility" of the historical process—that is, that there was no point in hoping for a democratic government or independence from Russia whereas there was a lot to be said for nonpolitical improvements. These were assured. This policy, as is well known, has worked very well from the Soviet point of view. West German treaties with Russia and Poland in 1970 and the Soviet agreement to "normalize" relations with Czechoslovakia in December 1973 have consolidated the postwar territorial situation but without introducing any of the improvements that the West has been hoping for. Instead of being a policy of *"Wandel durch Annäherung"* ("change through rapprochement"), in Brandt's phrase, it turned out to be *"Annäherung ohne Wandel"* ("rapprochement without change"). Even the agreements with the Vatican have contributed to making the local East European regimes more respectable in the eyes of noncommunists at home and abroad. The conclusion of the European Security Conference in Geneva with the adoption at a summit conference in Helsinki at the end of July 1975 of a final act was welcomed by Russia because the final act contained the formal recognition of the status quo in Europe by virtually the whole Western world.

Apart from this search for "indirect legitimacy" through approval of the status quo by the Western powers, the communist governments have sought acceptance by working hard to improve the life of the ordinary citizen, again presumably in the hope that this will make him think less about any fundamental changes in the system and indeed accept the system itself as normal. The first Soviet-bloc government that had a go at showing that socialism can be made to work was the Hungarian one after the suppression of the revolution in 1956. Under the leadership of Janos Kadar, the Hungarian government carried out a series of systematic reforms in the economy aimed at making it more efficient. As a result, Hungary has become a relatively free-and-easy country for its citizens, who prospered slowly but steadily while their modest cultural freedom expanded too. The methods applied so successfully by Kadar in Hungary were the inspiration behind the new Gierek regime in Poland after December 1970. Many people in Czechoslovakia, too, still hope that the period of Husak-style "normalization" will at some stage be followed by that of "kadarization." In terms of real improvements in the living standards and the quality of life, this has already to a certain extent happened in Czechoslovakia, though not in the cultural field. In Poland, after the 1970 political upheaval, there were hopes of at least a partial return to the relatively liberal atmosphere of the Poland of October 1956, but this has not happened. Instead, the Gierek regime has pursued an extremely cautious policy in cultural matters avoiding anything that could even remotely be considered as controversial, especially in the realm of ideas. The press censorship was lifted in the case of the party organ *Trybuna Ludu* and the weekly *Polityka* in March 1973, but the results have not been encouraging. Neither paper has become more adventurous as a result. The party congress in December 1975 ushered in a period of even greater caution on the cultural front.

As the example of Poland illustrates, the successive interventions by the Soviet government in 1953, in 1956, and above all and most painfully in Czechoslovakia in 1968 have reduced the room for maneuver for the local governments. For a while, however, it looked as if Moscow would be ready to leave it to the local leaders to judge what could and could not be done on the basis of and within the framework of a broad ideological directive. The local governments might be expected to know better in what situations they should try to defuse potentially dangerous conflicts. This can best be seen in the GDR, whose cultural policy at the moment acts as an intelligent safety valve and as compensation for the continuing policy of preventing East Germans from traveling to the West. The East German leaders have clearly accepted the idea that to allow a young student in a play staged in East Berlin to say that socialism is boring does not bring the system down, but on the contrary provides it with valuable propaganda points at home and abroad. The same probably goes for mild, carefully controlled expressions of national sentiment in Poland. The first act of the new government of Gierek was to promise to rebuild the royal castle in Warsaw, a project that has been carried out punctiliously to the great satisfaction of many patriotic Poles at home and abroad—a point in the regime's favor. Similarly, the showing of an intensely moving film about a Polish officer who fights the Germans long after Poland's defeat in 1939 was probably also seen as a legitimate safety value for pent-up Polish national feeling.

There are, however, signs that even this policy of limited small-scale experimentation in culture may be coming to an end. The new phase appears to be considerably harsher ideologically and politically. Above all, there is evidence to suggest that Soviet leaders have come to the conclusion that if further Hungarian and Czechoslovak as well as Polish uprisings are to be avoided, Eastern Europe must be yet more closely attached to the Soviet Union. Official Soviet statements suggest that the leaders are uneasy at the prospect of another military intervention that, unlike the one in 1968, might meet with resistance and spread the conflict throughout the bloc and even beyond. They are determined, therefore, to apply as much prophylaxis as is necessary to nip the disease in the bud and make another costly and unpleasant intervention unnecessary.

That fear probably lies behind the present intensive ideological drive in Eastern Europe, which is aimed at countering the dangerous by-products of "consumerism" such as "petit bourgeois mentality," "ideological indifference," or even "ultraleft radicalism," an equally unwelcome ideological deviation. What worries all orthodox Marxists is not so much those phenomena by themselves, but the everpresent danger that the ideological vacuum left by the Marxist ideology will be filled once again by nationalism. Is this really on the cards nearly twenty years after the suppression of the 1956 uprising when most of today's youngsters were not yet born? The Hungarian government seems to think so. The danger that this might once again happen in Poland, too, once the effects of the "consumer anesthetic" have worn off clearly exercises the Polish leaders. What worries Moscow is the possibility of trouble breaking out in two or more places at the same time.

The new ideological policy is based on a number of semisecret ideological cooperation pacts signed among Warsaw Pact members since 1970 (Romania is an exception). There have also been a series of high-level meetings to discuss new measures: A conference of bloc party secretaries in Moscow in December 1973 and another one in January 1974, which in turn was followed by an ideological consultation of sixty-seven parties in Prague in February of the same year. After that there was a meeting of officials of the writers' unions to coordinate policy in the field of literature and publishing, and another top-level conference of party secretaries early in 1975. Some of those meetings have also been concerned with the preparation for the world communist conference that Moscow has been pressing for since 1973 against the strong opposition of the Italian and Spanish and, in Eastern Europe, the Romanian and Yugoslav Communist Parties as well as a few others outside Europe. The main purpose of such a conference would be to strengthen the Soviet Union's position as the leading communist country and to frustrate China's attempts to question and undermine that position. But the main effort has been directed at countering the "harmful" effects of the present East-West negotiations on the populations of communist countries. Dire warnings have been sounded by a whole host of leading ideological officials against the increase in Western imperialist propaganda. What has probably worried these officials and their governments most has been the growth of unrealistic hopes and expectations all over Eastern Europe that détente might lead to more relaxation at home. Another even more serious problem has been the fact that the *Ostverträge* with West Germany had once and for all demolished the carefully built-up image of a German revanchist bogey out to reconquer Eastern Europe. Although more and more people in Eastern Europe had stopped believing in this picture, others continued to believe what they were told.

The new rapprochement with West Germany and the other Western powers—especially Brezhnev's negotiations with Richard Nixon and his successor, Gerald Ford—has made it virtually impossible once again to use the fear of German attack as an excuse for another invasion like that carried out in Czechoslovakia. This in turn has had the effect of focusing all attention once again on the Russians as the people responsible and answerable for what is happening to Eastern Europe now. The all-out campaign to ward off the danger of a new "propaganda offensive by the imperialists" aimed at the unity of the "socialist bloc" was a welcome substitute. This was especially helpful to the regimes when they needed an excuse to attack Western radio stations. The jamming of some Western broadcasts occurred at the opening of the Geneva conference in September 1973. These broadcasts were having quite an effect on the population, and the governments were even more worried by future direct television broadcasts via satellite. At several conferences the Russians have tried to legislate against all such broadcasting lacking the approval of the recipient country. So even if Moscow is not afraid of the West militarily, it is afraid of the West's political influence both in Eastern Europe and in Russia itself. The ideological campaign is still in full swing and is obviously expected to provide an answer to those fears.

But there is evidence that the Soviet leaders are not overly optimistic about the chances of an ideological campaign by itself doing the job of consolidating the situation in the bloc. Clearly, additional action is needed to meet dangerous future challenges. The answer, as far as Soviet leaders are concerned, lies in what they call the "greater unity of the socialist bloc" and the "higher degree of socialist integration." The carefully coordinated ideological campaign provides one example of this new attempt to bind the bloc together and to strengthen the weaker brethren before they actually get into trouble. An obvious area where there is already a high degree of integration is the military field. The armies of the Warsaw Pact (with the exception of the Romanian) are virtually completely integrated. A higher degree of foreign policy coordination, which would in any case have been desirable for purely practical purposes, is being promoted through the meetings of the Warsaw Pact's political consultative committee and through the more informal but probably far more important annual get-togethers of Soviet bloc leaders in the Crimea.

The instrument that the Soviet Union probably believes should ultimately prove the most effective of all—perhaps Moscow has learned this from the EEC—is that of economic integration. Although Comecon was set up in 1949, it came to be considered seriously as an instrument of political control only in the late 1950s by Khrushchev. In the wake of the Hungarian revolution of 1956 he advocated the creation of a "central planning organ" for Comecon. This plan ran into trouble with Romania as well as with some of the other smaller members, and the idea of closer integration was seriously taken up again only after the invasion of Czechoslovakia. A special Comecon summit in April 1969 resolved to take steps toward greater "socialist integration and division of labor" within the organization. After laborious negotiations lasting over two years, a "comprehensive program of socialist economic integration" was at long last agreed upon at a special Comecon summit held in July 1971. That document sets out the principles of gradual economic integration over a period of fifteen to twenty years. Although Romania has fought a rearguard action and has succeeded in detaching itself from all projects that it has not approved of, the momentum from 1971 has been slowly carried forward, with many delays and difficulties. At the end of 1973 several Comecon international associations were set up to help with the integration of the textile machinery, nuclear power stations, and electrical engineering. There are signs that Moscow intends to use its new bargaining power vis-à-vis its East European partners to push integration faster than in the past. In the November 1973 issue of the Soviet party journal *Kommunist,* Konstantin Katushev, a secretary of the Soviet Central Committee responsible for relations with communist countries and parties, specifically mentioned "joint economic planning" and "joint economic associations" as features of that higher stage of integration that he said was to be achieved within Comecon. Since then Russia has concluded joint planning agreements for the 1976–1980 period with its East European Comecon partners (though not Romania). It remains to be seen how successful this latest integration drive is going to prove. In the past, all such campaigns have tended to thin out for lack of cooperation from the smaller partners. This time, too, the Soviet Union will have to fight the trend that is hampering socialist integration: The tendency to trade more with the West. A number of East European countries, including the GDR, have actually registered a drop in the proportion of their trade with Comecon compared to that with the West—though, of course, trade with the West forms a far smaller proportion of each country's trade than does that which they have with Comecon. But the West's inflation and recession are playing into Soviet hands by forcing these smaller East European countries to limit their trade with the West anyway.

Meanwhile, will the Soviet Union decide to carry the drive for integration toward its logical conclusion and press for incorporation of some or all East European states in the Soviet Union? However improbable this prospect might seem at the moment, there is a chance that something like this might be under consideration. The statement by the Bulgarian leader, Zhivkov, at the Bulgarian party conference on 29 March 1974 that Bulgaria was going to go all out for coordination of its "cultural, political, economic, and military fields" with those of the Soviet Union in the context of its "incorporation" into the Soviet Union caused a good deal of anxiety everywhere in the Balkans. There was a suggestion that Greek leaders were worried by the possibility of Soviet divisions coming to within a few miles of the Aegean coast. Such a move would have obvious repercussions in Yugoslavia, too, where it would signal the beginning of a new "activist" phase of Soviet policy in the Balkans aimed perhaps at gaining control over Yugoslavia. It may well be that there was really nothing new in the Zhivkov speech. But on the other hand, it is possible that his statement was a trial balloon aimed at testing reactions both within the Soviet bloc and outside it.

For the moment, then, the ultimate plans of the USSR with regard to the political integration of its "socialist commonwealth" in Europe remain shrouded in mystery. But the new Soviet interest in Yugoslavia since the Tito-Brezhnev meeting in September 1971 and the wooing of Albania, which began with a series of press articles at the end of November 1973, suggest that the Soviet Union has indeed reexamined its policies in the area in the light of the new importance it clearly attaches to its position as a Mediterranean power with a strong and permanent stake in the Middle East. The looming succession crisis in Yugoslavia after Tito and the reappearance of old national conflicts in the 1960s and early 1970s offer Russia a chance of reestablishing its influence. For many years after the Tito defection, it was Russia's policy, as an absolute minimum, to deny Yugoslavia to the West. Now that President Tito's tightening up of internal controls since 1971 has achieved that goal indirectly by removing the leading liberal, pro-Western figures in all the republics, Russia is clearly pleased. On the eve of the Yugoslav party congress in May 1974, a spate of articles in the Soviet press applauded President Tito's struggle against the "enemies of socialism" in Yugoslavia. At the time of Yugoslavia's quarrel with

Italy over Trieste, when Belgrade protested against the holding of small-scale NATO maneuvers in the northern Adriatic, the Soviet army paper *Krasnaia zvezda* took Yugoslavia's side in the quarrel.

Not everything that is written about Yugoslavia in the Soviet press is completely laudatory. Russia still has some reservations about various Yugoslav liberal heresies that have not yet been extinguished. But the fact that the Yugoslav party congress was attended (for the second time only since World War II) by a high-level Russian delegation, this one being led by Kirilenko, a senior party figure and a Politburo member, suggests that Russia is taking its chances in Yugoslavia seriously.

Whereas in 1970–1971 there were suggestions that Moscow, in its efforts to regain influence in Yugoslavia, might play the nationalist card, by, for example, encouraging the Croats to hope for independence with Moscow's help, the present Soviet policy statements clearly indicate that Moscow is playing the card of centralism, dogmatism, and stricter party control. A plot by a group of "cominformist" (that is, pro-Soviet) communists was uncovered in Montenegro and Kosovo in April 1974, and sentences from one to fourteen years were handed out to thirty-two participants in the plot at two closed trials in September. The group was alleged to have been in direct touch with the Soviet Embassy in Belgrade and with anti-Tito Yugoslav émigrés in the Soviet Union. Other pro-Moscow plots were reported in the course of 1975. The uncovering of these plots led to a cooling-off between Belgrade and Moscow at the end of 1975. But Russia is actively courting the Yugoslav army, which is likely to emerge as the ultimate arbiter to Yugoslavia's future after Tito. Perhaps symbolically, on the very eve of the May 1974 party congress a high-powered army delegation, led by General Nikola Ljubicic, the defense minister and member of the Yugoslav Communist party's Presidium, visited Moscow. At the same time, General Franjo Herljevic was appointed federal minister of the interior, the first general to hold that post since World War II. Obviously Tito and his colleagues regard this policy of tightening up as part of Yugoslavia's defense against Moscow in the post-Tito era. It is more likely that this policy will ultimately help Moscow by weakening the resistance to Moscow. The situation in Yugoslavia offers Moscow its first chance to score a major success in its new activist policy in the Balkans. Altogether, after two decades of constant crises, Moscow leaders can for once feel that, largely due to the West's weakness, the balance of power in southeastern Europe is shifting toward them.

Part II
THE
MILITARY
DIMENSION

Soviet Military Capabilities and Intentions in Europe

THOMAS W. WOLFE

Under the auspices of détente—a phenomenon fed in no small measure by Moscow's readiness to explore the conciliatory openings offered by West Germany's *Ostpolitik*—the past several years have brought some relaxation of tension and improvement of relations between the two parts of Europe. By contrast with what is now widely referred to in the past tense as the cold war phase of postwar European history, there has been a succession of negotiations culminating in new East-West agreements in Europe, including the Moscow-Bonn and Warsaw-Bonn treaties and the Quadripartite Berlin Agreement.

In addition to these transactions, which can be seen in some sense as parts of a deferred settlement of the stalemated results of World War II, the SALT I accords and the rhetoric of two Soviet-American summit meetings in May 1972 and June 1973 also have contributed to the atmosphere of détente in Europe. Meanwhile, since the early months of 1973, a further series of East-West negotiations has gotten under way in Europe on European security and cooperation and on mutual force reductions. Neither set of negotiations has yet accomplished much more than to expose important differences in the conceptions of the two sides as to what arrangements would best promote European

security, but optimists would argue that even the airing of disagreement across the negotiating table is a step in the right direction.

With varied degrees of confidence, some observers today are
predicting that all of these developments point toward a basic transformation of East-West relations in Europe, including the possible
emergence at some unspecified time in the future of a new "pan-
European security system" that would embrace both halves of the
continent and render obsolete the NATO and Warsaw Pact coalitions
predicated upon defense of each half against the other. Although I do
not happen to share the view that epochal changes in the European
political landscape and in the two-bloc security system of the past
quarter century may lie just around the corner, it is undeniable that the
frozen situation of the past has been thawing in some notable respects.

At the least, even if one chooses to believe that the underlying
political and military "realities" of the East-West relationship in
Europe remain essentially resistant to change, some shift of mood and
expectation certainly seems to have taken place on both sides of the
European dividing line. How the climate engendered by détente may
influence the way each side perceives its security problems in Europe
and elects to deal with them is thus one of the many variables that any
current analysis of Soviet military capabilities and intentions must
recognize. Let us turn first to the question of appraising the capabilities
of Soviet military power in Europe today.

SOVIET AND WARSAW PACT CAPABILITIES
AGAINST NATO

Customarily, it is assumed to be somewhat easier to gauge capabilities
than intentions. Apart from the troublesome barriers interposed by the
Soviet penchant for secrecy, the task of appraising Soviet military
capabilities in Europe would seem at first glance to be no exception to
this truism. Troop deployments, weapons' characteristics, training
patterns, logistics structure, and all the other paraphernalia and practices associated with the military posture of the Soviet Union and its
Warsaw Pact partners in Eastern Europe would appear more amenable
to "objective" analysis than the slippery "subjective" business of trying
to divine the intentions that are in the minds of the Soviet leaders.

However, the history of recurrent debate in the West over the real dimensions of the Soviet military threat against Europe suggests that it may be scarcely less difficult to measure the Soviet Union's military capabilities and performance in the event of armed conflict in Europe than to come up with a confident reading of Soviet intentions. The sources of difficulty, some of which meet the eye less readily than others, are numerous.

Problems of Comparing Capabilities

There is first the problem of establishing what is called in intelligence circles the "data base"—the voluminous catalog of information about Soviet and other Warsaw Pact forces that must be compiled as the first step in estimating their capabilities. The precise state of this data base at any given time is usually a classified matter, but enough has been disclosed in the course of time to indicate that a good deal of the basic information needed for the data base has tended to be either spotty or in dispute. This can be attributed in large part, of course, to Soviet secrecy, which obstructs the "visibility" of the forces arrayed against Europe. At the same time, however, the process of acquiring a complete and reliable data base also has been affected by such factors as the tendency—at least until the past few years—to concentrate the better intelligence resources available to the West against elements of Soviet military power outside the European arena.

But, granting that considerable improvement in the data base probably has been made in recent years, the capabilities problem does not stop there. Measurement of Soviet capabilities involves much more than merely adding up the forces that can be brought to bear in Europe, even though this time-honored device is still widely in use. Essentially, the problem is that a static compilation of adversary forces yields only limited insight into what would happen under the dynamic conditions of actual engagement. To be meaningful, capabilities should be measured in terms of the opposition to be encountered and under a variety of settings and scenarios—recognizing, of course, that theoretical scenarios can never be more than synthetic facsimiles of the real world.

Over the years, many efforts have been made to deal analytically with the dynamics of interaction that would be included in a NATO-Warsaw Pact military collision. All manner of models and gaming techniques of varying degrees of sophistication have been developed for this purpose, but even the best of them still do not represent satisfactory surrogates for the complex reality of the real world. Moreover, war-gaming outcomes and "net assessment" results are notoriously sensitive to the scenarios chosen and the assumptions employed, quite apart from the intrinsic worth of a particular model as a means of simulating reality.

Several other factors contribute to the capabilities problem. One of these is the occasional tendency to employ what is called "worst-case" analysis—to posit the least favorable set of conditions for one's own side, but not to tax the adversary likewise. Justifiable perhaps as a conservative or prudential way to cushion one's own planning against unexpected adversity, the worst-case syndrome nevertheless tends toward resolving the uncertainties of a gaming situation in a direction more favorable to the adversary than either the vagaries of chance or the adversary's real-world capabilities and conduct of operations might warrant. At various times in the past, it has been alleged that the distorting effect of worst-case analysis has tended to make the Russians look taller than they actually are. To counter this defect, analysis positing a range of threats from "high" through "median" to "low" has become more common. Though perhaps preferable to analysis biased always toward the high side, such an approach is open to the objection that it dodges the issue of which threat-level best corresponds to the real dimensions of the Soviet threat.

A related phenomenon that not infrequently affects capabilities assessments is the tendency to shape the setting and other inputs of analysis in order to achieve outcomes politically or institutionally congenial to the sponsoring agency, which may be a particular national government, a regional command, an individual service, and so forth. Again, the general effect may be to stack the cards in one way or another so as to convey a picture that may either inflate or degrade actual capabilities—one's own or those of the adversary.

Even when the most scrupulously "depoliticized" and professionally competent standards of analysis are met, however, a host of problems still remains with regard to finding measures of merit and techniques for aggregating and comparing the combat capabilities of forces

as disparate as those that face each other across the dividing line in
Europe. There is no need to elaborate further at this point on the
difficulties and pitfalls that attend the assessment of capabilities,
though further examples will doubtless come into focus later in our
discussion.

Against the above background, let us look then at the picture of
current Soviet-bloc capabilities vis-à-vis NATO that emerges from
various treatments of the subject in the public domain. Perhaps the
most useful way to present this picture is to proceed from the simpler
comparisons that generally do not go much beyond adding up the
forces on each side and striking a quantitative balance (or imbalance, as
the case may be) to those more ambitious assessments that attempt to
factor in a variety of complex qualitative and dynamic elements before
coming up with a net balance between the opposing sides.

Quantitative Comparisons

By the simpler yardsticks of comparison—numbers of combat divisions, tanks, artillery, aircraft, front-line manpower, and the like—
the Soviet Union and its Warsaw Pact allies today appear to enjoy a
preponderant advantage in conventional-theater forces in Europe, as
has been the case throughout the postwar period. With the notable
exception of NATO's larger arsenal of tactical nuclear weapons and its
edge in a few other categories such as total military manpower and
numbers of antitank weapons, one finds NATO coming out on the short
side of most of the purely quantitative comparisons in circulation
today.

Most of these comparisons begin with a tally of the general-
purpose theater forces in place on each side. There are some variations
in the figures cited from one published source to another, depending
on whether the "flanks" as well as the "center" of the European theater
are included, and on other factors such as whether the counting includes combat troops only or total military manpower, tanks in operational service only or stored replacements also, tactical aircraft based in
the immediate theater only or also those that can be quickly deployed
forward. On the whole, however, the gross figures tend to fall in the
same general ball park.

TABLE 1
NATO-WARSAW PACT COMPARISON FOR THE OVERALL
EUROPEAN THEATER

	Warsaw Pact	NATO
Troops (combat and direct support)[a]	1,150,000 (485,000 Soviet)	1,113,000 (190,000 U.S.)
Divisions (including division equivalents)	78 (31 Soviet)	59 (4⅓ U.S.)
Main battle tanks (in operational service)[b]	17,600 (7,000 Soviet)	8,600 (1,350 U.S.)
Tactical aircraft	3,600 (1,500 Soviet)	2,800 (300 U.S.)[c]
Tactical nuclear weapons	3,500	7,000

[a]Ground force figures only. Air personnel number about 50,000 for the United States and slightly more for the Soviet Union in Europe.
[b]In addition to figures shown for battle tanks, the Soviet force in Europe reportedly has about 1,000 stockpiled tanks, while NATO has about 4,000 in reserve stockpile, of which about 1,300 are American.
[c]There is a total of about 500 U.S. tactical aircraft in Europe, but those based in Britain and with the Sixteenth Air Force in Spain are not shown.

Sources: The Military Balance 1973–1974, IISS, London, September 1973, pp. 87–95; Trevor Cliffe, Military Technology and the European Balance, Adelphi Paper no. 89, IISS, London, 1972, pp. 26–29; and Colonel Delbert M. Fowler, "How Many Divisions? A NATO-Warsaw Pact Assessment," Military Review, November 1972, pp. 80–87.

The compilation in Table 1 is a representative one derived from several published breakdowns.[1] For the Warsaw Pact, it gives in-place figures covering both the so-called northern and southern tiers of the Pact, but not including Soviet forces in contiguous areas of the USSR itself. For NATO, the compilation covers the three main regional commands—Northern, Central, and Southern Europe—but in the ambiguous case of France includes only the French forces stationed in Germany.

[1]By far the most helpful source of information is The Military Balance series published by the International Institute for Strategic Studies (IISS), London. Indeed, without the basic data furnished by the IISS, informed public discussion of the NATO-Warsaw Pact military relationship would be difficult to sustain.

By the arithmetic in Table 1, the Soviet Union and its Warsaw Pact allies have a substantial margin of 25 percent more divisions and tactical aircraft in place in Europe, together with a 2:1 advantage in tanks. Troop strength is about even, while NATO is ahead by 2:1 in the number of tactical nuclear weapons at its disposal. Had forces on the southern flank been omitted from the comparison, there would be a larger advantage for the Warsaw Pact in divisions and troop strength, since the NATO total in these categories is swelled considerably by the inclusion of Italy, Greece, and Turkey. In tanks and tactical aircraft, the Warsaw Pact edge would also be greater if Soviet forces in the immediately adjacent border areas of the USSR were included. Absent altogether from the comparison are naval forces, which—while accorded a significant role in maintaining or denying maritime access to the European theater, especially in the event of a lengthy conflict—are marked by so many asymmetrics that it is difficult to set them off against each other in a meaningful way in gross numerical comparisons of the theater balance. In general, NATO enjoys a substantial advantage in such categories as carriers, antisubmarine weapons (ASW) and amphibious landing forces, whereas the Soviet Union has a greater number of attack submarines and a growing force of guided-missile cruisers and destroyers that represent a serious threat to surface ships.

Leaving aside for the moment all the qualitative and interactive factors that bear on relative capabilities, the theater force equation in Europe is also affected in a gross sense by the presently available military resources that can be brought to bear in Europe from the outside. In this regard, the Soviet Union can be said to enjoy impressive but by no means undiluted advantages. On the one hand, it is greatly favored by geographic proximity and by the maintenance of a theater force establishment much larger than that of the Western allies combined. The Soviet ground forces altogether come to slightly more than 2,000,000 men and some 160 divisions today, with supporting tactical air strength of about 4,500 aircraft.[2]

On the other hand, however, this abundant array of theater forces is not a wholly unconstrained asset. The Soviet Union has several thousand miles of borders to secure against other potential threats, not

[2]*Military Balance 1973–1974*, pp. 6–7.

the least of which is posed by China. Roughly speaking, the Soviet Union today has deployed about one-fourth of its divisions and its tactical aircraft in areas facing China, while somewhat more than half of its forces and aircraft remain oriented toward Europe.[3] The remaining theater force elements presumably constitute a central reserve. The essential question with which gross estimates of the military balance in Europe must cope is how much of its European-oriented theater force strength would the Soviet Union wish to withhold or redeploy for other contingencies in a situation of major crisis or outbreak of war. No answer can be given, but most estimates seem to assume that the Soviet command would keep large forces committed to European operations. At present, about sixty divisions with supporting tactical air armies are deployed in the several western military districts of the USSR, presumably as direct backup for the European theater.

For its part, NATO has much smaller standing forces to draw upon. Under the best of circumstances, it might increase its ground forces strength in Europe by perhaps six to eight divisions within a few weeks, including modest ground force contributions, together with somewhat more rapid augmentation of air forces, from the United States. Given sufficient time and unimpeded mobilization, NATO doubtless has the potential to raise forces as large or even larger than those the Warsaw Pact could field, but in the context of forces immediately available for conventional theater operations in Europe, NATO appears to be at a decided disadvantage.

Many comparisons of the NATO-Warsaw Pact balance tend to focus on the central front, the area extending from the Baltic to Czechoslovakia, where the bulk of the forces drawn up against each other in Europe are to be found on the territory of the two Germanies. This is the traditional invasion route between East and West, as well as the focal point of the most troubled political issues in a divided Europe. It also corresponds closely to the NATO Guidelines Area (NGA) proposed for the initial effort to negotiate mutual force reductions at the Vienna arms conference. It is not surprising, therefore, that the lineup of forces in this central region generally receives a greater share of attention than the opposing forces on the northern and southern flanks.

[3]Admiral Thomas H. Moorer, Chairman, Joint Chiefs of Staff, *United States Military Posture for FY 1974*, 26 March 1973, p. 52.

Similarly, most of the gaming exercises and analytical models used as analogues for an actual clash of forces in the European theater are usually applied to the central region on the assumption that this would be the decisive sector of live operations.

The Warsaw Pact emerges from gross comparisons of theater forces in the central region with a somewhat more impressive edge over NATO than when the European theater as a whole is considered. Some of the relevant indices are given in Table 2.

As can be seen from Table 2, which takes in Soviet and other Warsaw Pact forces currently deployed in the northern tier area of

TABLE 2
NATO-WARSAW PACT COMPARISON IN THE CENTRAL REGION

	Warsaw Pact	NATO
Troops (combat and direct support)	800,000 (430,000 Soviet)	600,000 (190,000 U.S.)
Divisions (including division equivalents)		
Armored	26 (14 Soviet)	8 (2⅓ U.S.)
Mechanized	30 (13 Soviet)	11 (2 U.S.)
Other	2	2
Total	58 (27 Soviet)	21 (4⅓ U.S.)
Main battle tanks (in operational service)	13,800 (6,850 Soviet)	6,000 (1,350 U.S.)
Artillery pieces	("more than double" number held by NATO)[a]	
Antitank weapons		(numbers favor NATO)[b]
Tactical aircraft	2,700 (1,250 Soviet)	1,720 (230 U.S.)
Tactical nuclear weapons	3,500	7,000

[a]The precise number of Pact artillery pieces is not given in published sources, although it is said by Western defense officials to be "more than double" NATO's number (see Moorer, *United States Military Posture for FY 1974*, p. 56). An educated guess, arrived at by using figures in *Military Balance 1973-1974*, p. 80, for divisional artillery and allowing for artillery formations at other levels, might put the Pact number at about 4,000-6,000.

[b]Numbers are not available, but are said to be growing in NATO's favor. See Moorer, *United States Military Posture for FY 1974*, and *Military Balance 1973-1974*, p. 90.

Eastern Europe (that is, the GDR, Poland, and Czechoslovakia),[4] the Pact outnumbers NATO almost 3:1 in divisions and nearly 2:1 in tactical aircraft, while having an advantage of more than twice as many artillery pieces and main battle tanks. Some compilations, incidentally, credit the Warsaw Pact with about 15,000 operational tanks to 6,000 for NATO. The tank margin is at least partly offset, however, by NATO's growing but unspecified number of antitank weapons. As before, the ratio of tactical nuclear weapons is 2:1 in NATO's favor in the central region.

Geographic Imbalances

In addition to such quantitative data, several other built-in imbalances in the geographic disposition of theater forces in Europe tend to tip gross comparisons of conventional forces in favor of the Warsaw Pact. One is the geographic fragmentation of the NATO area, which is split by the neutral wedge of Austria and Switzerland as well as by France, so that NATO's ability to shift forces from one sector to another is compromised. By contrast, the Warsaw Pact side, with the exception of a possible noncooperative Romanian "wedge," can move its forces more freely along what amounts to a continuous coherent front.

A second imbalance is NATO's relatively shallow rear and lack of elbowroom for deployment in depth, as contrasted with the deep rear afforded the Warsaw Pact by European Russia. NATO's logistics back-up, with lines of communication that stretch overseas to the United States, also compares unfavorably in geographic terms with the situation of the Warsaw Pact, which draws its support from a continental Soviet Union operating closer to the European theater on interior lines. Both this logistics handicap and the restricted room for operational maneuver in NATO's case are accentuated by a certain maldeployment of American forces—a legacy of the postwar occupation zones—that finds the U.S. Seventh Army in southern Germany with its lines of communication from the north exposed to penetration across the north German plain. By contrast, the Soviet forces poised in

---

[4]On the NATO side, Table 2 takes in forces deployed in Central Europe by the United States, Canada, and Britain, as well as those of West Germany, the Netherlands, and Belgium. It also includes the French forces stationed in West Germany, though these have not actually been committed to NATO.

Germany suffer no geographic discontinuity with their supporting rear. Another imbalance growing in part out of NATO's geographic disabilities is that it has at its disposal fewer and hence more crowded and less well dispersed airfields than does the Warsaw Pact.

But now, having briefly surveyed some of the factors that give Soviet bloc forces a marked quantitative edge in most categories of conventional military power in Europe, we come to the much more complex matter of factoring in qualitative differences and interactive conditions, which gross force comparisons, by their very nature, tend to slur over. Certainly, if a case can be made that Soviet capabilities are actually somewhat less formidable than first meets the eye, it must rest upon close inspection of qualitative factors that are inherently more difficult to get a handle on than mere counting of relative numbers.

Qualitative Appraisals of Ground Forces

A customary starting point for qualitative appraisals is the different size and makeup of Soviet and other similar Warsaw Pact divisions, compared to those on the NATO side. Soviet divisions are smaller—9,000 to 11,000 troops, compared to about 16,000 for U.S. and most West European divisions. Soviet divisions also have a smaller "divisional slice"—that is, the combat division itself, plus other combat and logistics personnel directly supporting divisional activity. The estimated figure generally ascribed to the Soviet divisional slice is 15,000 to 20,000, compared to about 60,000 for the United States. These disparate manpower numbers, together with a somewhat richer mix of weapons and equipment in U.S. and some NATO divisions, logically suggest that individual divisions of the opposing sides should not be rated on a par with each other.

Although it is generally accepted that on paper the attributes of comparable types of divisions give those of the United States and NATO greater firepower and more sustained combat ability, the problem that arises is how to measure with any degree of precision the relative effectiveness of NATO divisions against their Soviet counterparts. And further, how to do this so as to approximate the variety of conditions that would obtain on a real battlefield, where not only objective attributes of the contenders, but such subjective factors as combat morale, motivation, and leadership would also count.

Many scoring systems have been tried, but even when they are confined to measuring such "objective" indices as firepower, mobility, weapons effectiveness, and survivability, the scoring methods yield far from uniform results. By varying the weighting given, for example, to firepower versus mobility, quite different scores may be registered. It is essentially the old problem of apples and oranges writ large. Some of the past attempts at trying to translate the differing attributes of divisions into meaningful comparative terms came up with the rough answer that one U.S. division could be considered the equivalent of one-and-a-half to two Soviet divisions.[5] Perhaps this is about as close as paper exercises in comparison can be expected to come, though not all would agree that the ratio today is quite so favorable.

A second qualitative issue relating to divisions turns on the question of their peacetime manning levels and combat readiness. Soviet divisions are kept in three categories of readiness,[6] those of the other Warsaw Pact countries in two.[7] Only the category 1 Soviet divisions are close to full strength with complete equipment. Approximately seventy-five Soviet divisions fall in this category, with forty-six in category 2, and fifty-three in category 3. Although many NATO formations are also below their full manning levels, the fact that a large number of Soviet divisions would have to be filled out by calling up personnel and drawing equipment from depots is often cited to make the point that the Soviet theater force establishment as a whole is on the leaner peacetime footing than gross numerical comparisons usually indicate.

On the other hand, however, all of the thirty-one Soviet divisions deployed in Eastern Europe and perhaps twenty or so of those in adjacent military districts of the USSR are considered to be at the category 1 level. So far as the in-place forces confronting NATO are

[5]For a discussion of this question, see Thomas W. Wolfe, *Soviet Power and Europe: 1945–1970* (Baltimore: Johns Hopkins Press, 1970), p. 172.

[6]Category 1, three-fourths to full strength, with all equipment; category 2, one-half to three fourths strength, with combat but not full support equipment; category 3, one-third strength, equipment status uncertain. See *Military Balance 1973–1974*, p. 6.

[7]The East European divisions have uneven peacetime manning levels. Category 1 divisions are up to three-fourths strength; category 2, at about one-fourth strength. See *Military Balance 1973–1974*, p. 11.

concerned, therefore, the manning situation offers no particular comfort. The principal issues arise around how reinforcement of the European theater would be affected by the requirement to bring Soviet category 2 and 3 divisions to higher states of readiness, and how long this would take.[8]

One issue centers essentially on a prehostilities situation: How much time would NATO have to carry out its own mobilization before a Soviet buildup could be completed? This in turn involves estimates of how early NATO would become aware of Soviet buildup activities (that is, the amount of "strategic warning time" available), as well as estimates of what readiness levels the Soviets would wish to attain before risking active operations. Needless to say, the range of uncertainty involved here is great, so that appraisals of the relative readiness of the two sides if and when a day of squaring off should arrive are necessarily sensitive to the assumptions made with respect to warning time and readiness levels.

Another reinforcement issue picks up in effect where the prehostilities one leaves off. It centers on the question of how rapidly and massively the Soviet Union could pour reinforcements into Europe if for some reason hostilities should begin without a prior buildup having taken place. Here appraisals are especially sensitive to whether or not the standard yardstick of "uninterrupted mobilization" is employed. By this yardstick, the Soviets generally are credited with the potential to increase their theater forces on the central front in Europe to seventy or more divisions in thirty days,[9] compared with a Western potential of reinforcing to a maximum of perhaps forty divisions in the same region. Critics of this reinforcement picture, however, may question both the assumption that movement of Soviet forces into the theater would proceed on an "uninterrupted" basis and the likelihood that sufficient numbers of understrength Soviet divisions could be

[8]No hard estimates of the time needed to ready category 2 and 3 divisions are available in the public domain, and this subject has long been a contentious one. Past published statements of U.S. defense officials have placed the time required to bring all divisions in these categories to full readiness at from three to six months. An educated guess might put the time required in the case of at least category 2 divisions somewhat lower, perhaps no more than two months. See Wolfe, *Soviet Power and Europe: 1945–1970*, p. 171.

[9]*Military Balance 1973–1974*, p. 89.

brought to combat readiness rapidly enough to make such a substantial reinforcement schedule feasible. (The same objection, of course, also applies to NATO's chances of realizing an unimpeded buildup to its full potential.)

A further imponderable but salient consideration also intrudes upon calculations of realizable reinforcement rates. This is the question whether any major conflict in Europe would remain on a conventional basis, or would have escalated to the nuclear level in the time frame posited. Were the latter the case, all bets would be off, so to speak, and any advantage the Soviet Union might otherwise have for rapid reinforcement of its conventional theater forces would have lost much of its meaning.

Technology and Materiel Factors

Qualitative comparison of the arms and equipment to be found in the NATO and Warsaw Pact armies is obviously one of the ingredients that must go into assessing their relative capabilities. Given the technological and other disparities in the way the two sides are equipped, however, comparison presents a good many problems. Moreover, determining the point at which a superior technology on one side may represent an adequate offset to greater numbers on the other is at the best a shaky art.

In comparisons of equipment, the Warsaw Pact is usually credited with the advantages of standardization and interchangeability that come from being almost completely equipped with Soviet-designed materiel, whereas NATO, while having higher qualitative standards in many equipment categories, has not standardized to the same degree and hence encounters supply incompatabilities and problems of interchange.[10]

The question of how much advantage the Soviet bloc derives from its large margin in tank divisions and total number of tanks is particularly sensitive to qualitative weighting. The current main battle tanks in NATO are the U.S. M-60, the British Chieftain, and the German Leopard. Though introduced earlier than the Soviet T-62 medium

---

[10]*Military Balance 1973–1974*, pp. 87–90.

tank,[11] about 1,000 of which have been deployed in East Germany over the last few years, the NATO tanks are judged to have more accurate firepower and greater operational efficiency than the T-62, and they clearly outclass the older T-54 and T-55 medium tanks that still account for the bulk of Soviet and other Warsaw Pact armor.[12] However, even though NATO tanks may be considered generally superior to those of the Warsaw Pact, their qualitative edge seems hardly enough to re-dress the numerical advantage of the other side. This leaves it up to antitank weapons, a category in which both new technology and num-bers of ground and air-delivered munitions seem to favor NATO. At this juncture, it remains a moot question whether the antitank weapons coming into service in NATO are as yet numerous and efficient enough to offset the Warsaw Pact's tank and to shift the balance of advantage in tank warfare to the defense, or whether a standoff is the more likely prospect.

In conventional artillery, with which both the Soviets and the United States began to strengthen their field formations in the 1960s after an earlier period of thinning out,[13] the greater qualitative im-provements have probably been on the U.S. side, particularly in am-munition and electronic surveying and fire-direction devices.

The present situation finds the Warsaw Pact with a numerical advantage of about 2:1, but this is partly offset by the greater destruc-tiveness and perhaps more accurate fire of NATO's artillery, as well as the ability to sustain higher rates of fire conferred by a larger logistics "tail." The greater number of mortars and higher proportion of self-propelled weapons in NATO's inventory also help to narrow the gap in conventional tube artillery, but on the other hand the Warsaw Pact

[11]Both the T-62 and the NATO tanks reflect incremental changes in tank design, rather than radical advances. The U.S. main battle tank XM803 would have incorpo-rated some major changes, but the program was canceled. A new version of the German Leopard with a larger gun than the T-62 (120 mm versus 115 mm) is being built, but it is still of a less advanced generation than the aborted XM803.

[12]*Military Balance 1973–1974*, p. 90; see also Michael Getler, "Soviets Add 1,000 New Tanks to East European Arsenals," *Washington Post*, 12 February 1972.

[13]U.S. artillery decreased with the adoption of the small Pentomic division in 1957, until the army went back to a larger division size in 1963. In the Soviet case, the thinning out of conventional artillery began in the late 1950s in connection with Khrushchev's military reforms, and the trend was reversed after the mid-1960s.

forces have large numbers of multifire artillery rockets, giving them a marked advantage in this type of saturation system, which NATO has been slow to adopt.[14]

Logistics factors represent another significant ingredient in assessments of relative capabilities. Here the picture is mixed. As noted earlier, both geographic and man-made conditions favor the Warsaw Pact in a number of ways—interior lines of communication, depth and coherence of the rear area, standardization of equipment, and so on. On the other hand, NATO fields formations with a richer combat and logistics support tail that makes for greater staying power, and its air resupply lift still tops that of the Soviet Union, although the latter is developing a strong air resupply capability also.

With regard to the effect of logistics on the staying power of divisions, incidentally, some analyses suggest that comparisons using a larger divisional slice for U.S. and NATO units tend to give a misleading impression of relative Soviet logistical support capability. The argument is that while the Russians have a smaller support slice for their smaller divisions, they also have more divisions, so that total numbers of personnel assigned to combat support functions do not differ markedly on the two sides.[15] However, policies for replacement of combat attrition, which also affect staying power, are different on the opposing sides. The Pact replaces whole units after attrition, whereas NATO's policy is to bring units already in the field back to strength by individual replacements. The effect here is said to be to give NATO units longer combat life on the line than Pact divisions. Which policy is best depends critically on whether a very short or a lengthy campaign is assumed.

Perhaps the most murky aspect of the logistics issue as it pertains to Soviet capabilities is the question of what rates of expenditure of critical stocks of such items as ammunition and fuel would apply in a European conflict, and the closely related question of whether sufficient amounts of such stocks are stored in forward areas to sustain intensive Soviet operations under conditions in which supply lines from the USSR were to be subjected to interdiction. Again, a sensitive

[14]See Cliffe, *Military Technology and the European Balance*, pp. 10–11.
[15]See Fowler, "How Many Divisions? A NATO-Warsaw Pact Assessment," p. 82.

variable is how long intensive fighting might last, for in a very brief campaign limited forward stocks might see an attacking force through. The results of analysis directed at these questions are generally not revealed in the public discourse, but the findings one way or another certainly can be expected to shape significantly the perceived magnitude of the Soviet military threat against Europe.

Quality of Opposing Air Forces

Up to this point, our discussion of qualitative considerations to be taken into account in appraising Soviet capabilities has dealt mainly with ground forces. However, the relative quality of the opposing air forces, and the interplay between air and ground operations, also must be factored into the theater forces equation. No less than in the case of ground forces, qualitative factors and air reinforcement potential have a significant bearing on how relative air capabilities are perceived, especially in the central region, where in-place numerical comparisons customarily show the Warsaw Pact ahead of NATO in tactical aircraft on the order of about 2,800 to 1,700, with Soviet-manned aircraft out-numbering those in U.S. units by more than 5:1.

With regard to air reinforcement, NATO's situation is generally considered to be fairly good, with the important proviso that sufficient habitable airfields are available to accommodate the additional American aircraft that could be redeployed to the central region from other areas, including the continental United States. Aircraft in the United States include ten dual-based tactical squadrons in the Readiness Command, which are assigned to NATO. Carrier-borne aircraft also represent potential reinforcement, although their use would be largely limited to the flanks rather than the central region. The Soviet Union, of course, also has the option of moving in tactical air reinforcements, along with the advantage of having far more airfields with aircraft shelters in the theater of operations than does NATO. However, the limiting factor for the USSR is that with a total inventory of about 4,500 tactical aircraft, and with perhaps one-third or more of them tied down elsewhere, the numbers that could be committed to European operations would no more than match, and might fall slightly below, NATO's buildup level, other things being equal.

On a qualitative basis, the opposing tactical air forces are both equipped with advanced types of front-line combat aircraft and are in the process of further modernization. The principal front-line aircraft of the Soviet tactical air forces is the FISHBED-J and other versions of this MiG-21 fighter, together with the SU-7 FITTER ground attack and YAK-28 light bomber aircraft. Newer-generation aircraft now coming into service with tactical units include the high-performance MiG-25 FOXBAT air-superiority fighter, the MiG-23 FLOGGER, a variable-wing ground-attack aircraft, and the SU-20, an improved version of FITTER. The FENCER A, another variable-wing fighter-bomber, is expected to follow these aircraft into service. Non-Soviet Warsaw Pact air forces are equipped mainly with older versions of the MiG-17 and 19, and some MiG-21s. On the opposite side, the mainstay of the U.S. tactical air units is the F-4 PHANTOM in its various versions for fighter-bomber and interceptor roles, together with A-7 attack aircraft and the variable-wing F-111 fighter-bomber (based in Britain). Of the later-generation U.S. aircraft—the F-15 EAGLE air-superiority tactical fighter, the A-10 attack aircraft, and the F-14 TOMCAT air-superiority fighter—only the TOMCAT has yet become operational, and because it is carrier-borne, is not likely to appear in the lineup on the central front in Europe. Most of the aircraft in the non-U.S. NATO forces, except Britain, are various F-100 series aircraft of roughly comparable vintage to aircraft in non-Soviet Warsaw Pact units.[16]

Though there have been occasional combat "tests" now and then outside Europe between such Soviet aircraft as the FISHBED-J and the American-built PHANTOM,[17] qualitative comparisons of the opposing air forces in Europe are difficult for a number of reasons, including the rather different priorities on each side in aircraft design

[16]For sources drawn on for this paragraph, see: *Military Balance 1973–1974*, pp. 7, 11–13, 70; Cliffe, *Military Technology and the European Balance*, pp. 15–16; *Statement by Admiral Thomas H. Moorer Before the Senate Armed Services Committee*, 5 February 1974, pp. 15, 17; Moorer, *United States Military Posture for FY 1974*, pp. 35–36; John Erickson, "Soviet Strategic Policy," *Strategic Review*, Spring 1973, pp. 62–66.

[17]A case in point was the reported shooting down in July 1970 of four or five MiG-21 FISHBED-Js, presumably Soviet-piloted, by F-4E PHANTOMS of the Israeli Air Force. See Erickson, "Soviet Strategic Policy," p. 63.

and mission. The Soviet and other Warsaw Pact forces are primarily structured for air defense and close battlefield support of the ground forces, and their aircraft reflect this by having less range and payload than NATO tactical aircraft. On the other hand, NATO has put more emphasis on offensive penetration capability for such missions as airfield destruction and interdiction, and its aircraft can deliver more ordnance deeper into enemy territory than can Pact aircraft. In general, the Pact air forces have more aircraft optimized for interceptor and air-superiority roles, whereas NATO has a higher proportion of multipurpose aircraft that can perform well in attack roles as well as in air-to-air combat. In the field of very advanced air-delivered weapons, such as laser-guided bombs and other precision-guided munitions, the U.S. air elements in NATO would appear to have an appreciable edge over their Soviet counterparts.[18]

But whatever balance of qualitative pros and cons may be struck, the fact remains that net assessment of relative capabilities of tactical air forces in Europe and of their influence on the outcome of any theater campaign that might occur is still subject to great uncertainty. Potential outcomes vary over a wide range favoring now one side, then the other, depending on such variables as the circumstances under which hostilities break out, the degree of surprise, availability of airfields and aircraft shelters, pace of mobilization and reinforcement, mobility, tactics, integrity of command and control systems, and the like.

One further factor that deserves particular mention is the extent to which a high-density environment of antiaircraft defenses on the ground may blunt the effectiveness of air operations, a question that has acquired a new edge since the latest Middle East war of October 1973. Though both sides in Europe have defenses incorporating a variety of weapons from surface-to-air missile batteries to shoulder-fired missiles, the denser protective system is that provided by Warsaw Pact field forces and fixed installations. The question of whether such defenses or the technology and tactics of defense suppression could be expected to score most heavily in a European theater conflict was not answered conclusively by the proxy test in the Middle East of Soviet-

[18]*Military Balance 1973–1974*, p. 91.

style ground defenses against tactical aircraft. At the least, however, that experience has added another element of uncertainty to the calculation of air-ground theater outcomes in Europe.

East European Contributions to the Warsaw Pact

Among the many qualitative issues relevant to appraisal of the theater force balance in Europe, another that merits mention concerns the effectiveness and reliability of the forces belonging to the East European members of the Warsaw Pact. These forces account for more than 60 percent of Pact divisions and tactical aircraft in the European theater as a whole, and for upward of 50 percent of the in-place Pact divisions and tactical aircraft in the central region. Their quality therefore has considerable bearing on the overall capabilities of the Pact in the event of military operations in Europe.

Expert opinion has long been divided as to how the non-Soviet Pact forces might acquit themselves in an East-West conflict. Both from the standpoint of military effectiveness and with regard to their responsiveness to Soviet direction, these forces have varied considerably from one country to another. Over the past decade, however, a large effort has been invested in joint training exercises and equipment modernization, together with organizational reforms of the Pact structure intended to integrate the East European forces more closely into Soviet planning.[19] The 1968 invasion of Czechoslovakia, in which small forces from other Pact countries cooperated with the Soviet intervention forces,[20] did not shed much light on the military effectiveness of the East European contingents, because no armed resistance was encountered. However, this episode at least suggested that from a political standpoint the participating East European armies could be regarded as an asset to the Soviet Union rather than a liability.

Today, with Czechoslovakia's forces restored to their pre-1968 status as part of the northern tier group of the Warsaw Pact, and with the presence of five Soviet divisions in Czechoslovakia to help ensure that the rehabilitated Pact partner does not backslide, the consensus among most Western observers is that the non-Soviet Pact forces

[19]For a more detailed discussion, see Wolfe, *Soviet Power and Europe: 1945–1970*, pp. 471–485.

[20]The participating non-Soviet forces were from the GDR, Hungary, and Bulgaria.

opposing NATO in the central region can be expected to meet standards of combat capability and readiness not greatly below those that characterize the Soviet Union's own theater forces in the European arena. The military value of the southern tier members of the Pact, on the other hand, is generally considered to be a good deal less than that of the northern tier group.

Whatever the military effectiveness of the non-Soviet Pact forces may be, one of the prime military benefits of the Warsaw Pact to the Soviet Union doubtless continues to lie in the right of access to East European territory that it gives the Soviet Union's own theater forces.[21] The military security system erected by the Soviet Union in Eastern Europe has always rested primarily on a sizable forward deployment of Soviet forces in the area, directly reinforceable from the USSR, and only secondarily on the collective defense contributions of the other Warsaw Pact members.

Although the various military advantages of a forward position can be said to accrue to the Soviet Union mainly from its own deployed forces and not those of its Warsaw Pact allies, it would appear nevertheless that the Pact's collective contributions to the Soviet military security system have tended to grow with the passage of time. Besides access to real estate, the Soviet Union derives valuable military benefits in the form of joint exercises, standardization of equipment, development of a common infrastructure, and the working out and periodic testing of arrangements for command and control of the Pact forces. In short, if the Warsaw Pact were to be completely dismantled on short notice, the effect would probably be to degrade at least temporarily the capabilities of the forces presently opposing NATO.

Soviet Theater Doctrine and Its Bearing on Threat Analysis

Along with numerical and qualitative comparisons of theater forces and their equipment, another consideration that is customarily factored into assessments of the Soviet military threat against Europe is Soviet

---

[21]Right of access also is important to the Soviet Union, of course, in terms of the "disciplinary" actions it has found it necessary to take from time to time against errant East European countries. Politically and ideologically, it has proved convenient to Moscow to enforce the Soviet writ in Eastern Europe behind the facade of "collective" Warsaw Pact approval.

theater-warfare doctrine—or, perhaps more accurately, Western perception of Soviet doctrine and strategy for theater warfare in Europe. Although enunciated doctrine is by no means an infallible guide to actual practice, it does give some indication of how Soviet and other Warsaw Pact forces might be used in European operations and thus tends to become an important input to threat analysis. One might add, incidentally, that doctrine also may serve in some sense as a clue to intentions, although care must be taken not to lose sight of the line of demarcation between the two—lest doctrine be interpreted as an unequivocal manifestation of intentions.

The evolution of Soviet theater-warfare doctrine, especially as it applies to Europe, has been examined at length elsewhere;[22] for the purposes of this discussion, a brief recapitulation of its main features will suffice. In both a defensive and an offensive context, Soviet military doctrine has consistently placed a high value on the forward positioning of Soviet theater forces in Europe. Defensively, doctrine has prescribed the forward deployment of Soviet forces to buffer the Soviet Union itself against any military threat that might arise across the historical invasion routes from the West; a similar doctrinal basis applies with respect to the forward extension of integrated air defense coverage throughout the belt of East European countries, which has served to enhance the buffer role of the region. In an offensive context, in which East European territory is seen as a forward staging area and springboard for combined theater forces, Soviet military doctrine has unflaggingly stressed the need for waging a swift offensive campaign across Europe, should war occur—partly perhaps on the assumption that the Soviet Union had best get a theater campaign in Europe over with quickly before larger Western resources could be mobilized and brought to bear in the area.

The doctrine of a swift and decisive offensive in a European campaign seems to have remained equally applicable under nuclear and nonnuclear conditions in Soviet planning. In the Khrushchev era,

[22]See, for example, John Erickson, *Soviet Military Power* (London: Royal United Services Institute for Defence Studies, 1971), especially pp. 65–73; and Wolfe, *Soviet Power and Europe: 1945–1970*, especially pp. 197–216, and 451–458. An excellent concise summary of Soviet theater doctrine also may be found in Cliffe, *Military Technology and the European Balance*, pp. 29–35.

Soviet forces facing Western Europe were reequipped and trained for rapid exploitation and follow-up of nuclear strikes, at some expense to support and conventional staying power. Today, while greater attention is given in Soviet theory and practice to the possibility of substantial nonnuclear operations in Europe, Soviet doctrine continues to emphasize prompt seizure of the initiative and rapid penetration throughout the depth of the theater, with tank and airborne forces being allotted an even more important role than previously.

Several points stressed in Soviet theater-warfare doctrine that have had a distinct influence upon the way the Soviet military threat against Europe has been perceived in the West are worth noting. For example, in keeping with the idea that the initial attack is of prime importance, Soviet doctrine has underscored the value of surprise and deception as a means of seizing the initiative for one's own forces and of disorganizing those of the adversary. Parenthetically, one might note that Egyptian forces seem to have taken this page from their Soviet tutor's doctrinal book in the October 1973 war. At the same time, however, another tenet of Soviet doctrine stresses the importance of ensuring that an initial attack is launched with preponderant forces and with ample reserves in place. These doctrinal prescriptions are to some extent at cross purposes, for the assembling of preponderant forces could give the adversary at least strategic warning that something was in the wind and thus sacrifice the advantage of surprise. Pondering these contradictory points of doctrine, Western analysts may come to quite different conclusions. Some analysts assert that NATO faces a deceptive foe who may try to launch a sudden surprise attack without warning, whereas others feel that a sudden attack without detectable advance buildup is unlikely. Needless to say the latter interpretation may be slightly more comforting, but on strictly doctrinal grounds alone, it is no more plausible than the former.

Perhaps the chief source of doctrinally engendered uncertainty as to where the borderline lies between plausible and implausible Soviet threats is the persistent Soviet tenet that no matter how hostilities might begin, any conflict in the "heart of Europe" between the opposing blocs would pose great danger of escalation to general nuclear warfare. Though this view has been somewhat tempered in recent years by the admission of Soviet theorists that conventional operations on a considerable scale or even limited use of tactical nuclear weapons in Europe ought not to be "excluded" from the realm of possibility, there has been no basic revision of the idea that a military conflict, once it has arisen in the center of Europe, is likely to assume cataclysmic dimensions. One notable effect of this image of Armageddon has been to make it seem highly implausible that the Soviet Union would take the risk of trying to overrun Western Europe in the manner prescribed by its theater doctrine, even if the theater balance were to be indisputably tilted in Soviet favor.

In a sense, Soviet adherence to the doctrinal caveat that a major European conflict may bring disastrous escalation seems to testify that deterrence is working and that the "dynamic equilibrium" between the opposing coalitions remains intact. What this dominant perception of the implausibility of a Soviet military thrust in the center of Europe also does, however, is to obscure the possibility that Soviet military action might occur elsewhere, as on the northern or southern flanks of Europe under circumstances in which no frontal challenge to central NATO interests were laid down. At the least, the risks to the Soviet Union, and hence the degree to which such military threats are plausible, would seem to be of a different order from that which applies in the case of the central region.

Summing Up of the Capabilities Question

The task of appraising the Soviet military threat against Europe obviously involves more than net assessment of the theater balance in Europe between the opposing sides. External strategic forces, for example, though deployed for the most part well beyond the geographic confines of Europe,[23] are nevertheless coupled to it by a nexus of political and deterrent factors. Indeed, the contingent recourse to strategic nuclear power, although just offstage so to speak, has probably been the dominant "reality" bearing on European security throughout most of the postwar era. Ultimately, should a major clash of

---

[23]An exception on the Soviet side is the force of some 600 medium and intermediate range ballistic missiles (MRBM/IRBM) emplaced in European Russia and targeted specifically against Europe. This MRBM/IRBM force is organizationally a part of the Soviet Strategic Rocket Forces, but is constrained by range to employment against targets in Europe and around the European periphery.

arms actually take place in Europe, at least a portion of the strategic nuclear arsenals of the superpowers would probably come into play. However, for the purposes of this discussion, we shall simply let the matter of external strategic forces rest there for the time being and turn now to a brief summing up of factors relevant to Soviet theater force capabilities against Europe.

The only conclusive proof of Soviet military capabilities against Europe would come if there were a direct collision between the opposing military systems that have been at a standoff in Europe throughout the postwar period. The nearest approach to a live demonstration of Soviet capabilities lies almost six years in the past, when Soviet theater forces almost as large as those now in place in the central region, together with a few other Warsaw Pact divisions, invaded Czechoslovakia.[24] Although this was a coordinated operation on a scale far broader than ordinary field exercises of the Warsaw Pact, it lacked the one essential ingredient of a realistic test of theater forces in action: organized armed opposition. The insight it provided into Soviet capabilities, therefore, while illuminating with regard to air-ground mobility, logistics support, communications, ability to achieve tactical surprise, and many other aspects of Soviet performance,[25] fell short of revealing how well the Soviet theater forces might do under actual combat conditions against a strong adversary.

In the absence of such direct testimony, the measurement of Soviet capabilities has perforce been left to analytical techniques of varying degrees of sophistication—from gross numerical comparisons that generally credit the Soviet theater forces with a decisive edge in most categories of conventional military power to more subtle methodologies that at least tend to modify the picture of incontestable Soviet superiority in theater forces. Even the most refined methods of analysis, however, appear incapable of resolving satisfactorily the wide

[24]The forces introduced into Czechoslovakia included about 22 Soviet divisions, plus a contribution by non-Soviet forces amounting to the equivalent of 4 or 5 divisions, backed by up to 700 tactical combat aircraft and 250 transport aircraft. See Wolfe, *Soviet Power and Europe: 1945–1970*, p. 469.

[25]In general, the Soviet performance was given good marks by Western military authorities, including General Lyman L. Lemnitzer, then the NATO commander, although some shortcomings, especially in ground logistics, were also noted. See Wolfe, *Soviet Power and Europe: 1945–1970*, p. 474.

range of uncertainties to which comparative assessment of the opposing forces in Europe is subject.

This is not to say that no judgments, however tentative, can be made. If, for example, Soviet threat at the "low" end of the threat spectrum is premised (that is, an attack without substantial reinforcement of forward forces, but one that at the same time does not come without warning), then NATO can perhaps be expected to hold its own in the event of a clash of arms in Europe. On the other hand, against a threat at the "high" end of the spectrum, and if recourse to nuclear weapons is excluded, NATO could find itself in grave difficulty. Needless to say, it does not necessarily follow—as some unfinished scenarios of a conventional war in Europe seem to imply—that resort to nuclear weapons would in fact, as a kind of *deus ex machina,* automatically salvage the situation. "Out of the frying pan into the fire" might more aptly describe this "solution" of the conventional war problem.

To the extent that Soviet conventional-theater capabilities might be successfully countered by a NATO strategy of flexible response pegged somewhere in between containing a small probe and being obliged to consider a nuclear exchange, time would appear to be an especially critical factor. Fundamentally, if sufficient warning time were available to permit NATO to mobilize its forces, it might be able to mount a credible forward defense in accordance with its strategy of meeting an aggression at the level of force the adversary chooses to employ—which in essence is what flexible response means.[26] But if time were short and events should move swiftly, NATO might not find it possible to carry out a conventional direct defense successfully. It would then have to make up its collective mind whether to use tactical nuclear weapons,[27] and to face whatever might lie beyond that fateful

[26]Flexible response also implies, of course, that if a conventional defense fails to halt an attack, the next step to be considered would be use of tactical nuclear weapons to persuade the aggressor to stop by posing the risk of escalation. (See footnote 27.)

[27]According to a Senate Foreign Relations Committee staff report on NATO's nuclear strategy made public in December 1973, and said to give the first public description of the options agreed upon by the allies for using nuclear weapons, two categories of nuclear warfare are specified—"selective" use and "general response." The first of these categories presumably would be the first to be considered. The report states that "NATO strategy 'specifies that selective employment would be used on a controlled or limited scale either for demonstrative or tactical purposes' to confront the

step. The first "selective" use of tactical nuclear weapons or a broader "general nuclear response" would require both NATO consultation as well as the approval of the President of the United States.[28]

What these considerations suggest is that the NATO allies have never quite managed to gear themselves to deal on even terms with the upper levels of the military threat posed by Soviet conventional power in Europe. Another way of putting it is that NATO has not optimized its posture to meet the conventional threat on conventional terms, but rather has maintained a posture that depends essentially on trading space for time—when, unfortunately, NATO is short on space to trade,[29] from both a military and political standpoint. The implied prospect of escalation to tactical nuclear warfare and the contingent coupling of external strategic forces to the defense of Europe have served to "check" the Soviet conventional threat, but the ultimate credibility of the nuclear options has long been somewhat questionable, and is probably becoming more so in the present "parity" environment.

Patently, a profound dilemma inheres in the proposition that the NATO posture in Europe has never really "corresponded" to the Soviet conventional threat in a way to permit dealing with it successfully without subjecting the countries to be defended to enormous and perhaps irremediable collateral damage. But it is also true that however poorly NATO's posture may have "fit" the Soviet conventional threat, that threat has never been exercised.

Rather, through conditions of cold war and détente alike, and despite an imbalance of conventional power in Soviet favor, the opposing military forces in Europe have remained in a state of rough equilibrium. Many factors other than those to be viewed in terms of a functional military logic alone help to account, of course, for the

---

aggressor with the risk of escalation so that he would halt the attack." See John W. Finney, "A NATO Nuclear Strategy," *New York Times*, 2 December 1973.

[28]Finney, "A NATO Nuclear Strategy."

[29]One might also argue that the Russians have "optimized" their conventional posture to exploit NATO's lack of geographic depth and to deny NATO the time it requires to mobilize its greater war potential. But even so, the military dilemma remaining for the Soviet side has been how to carry this off without risk of nuclear escalation.

maintenance of this equilibrium. But here we are interested primarily in how stable the balance may be in a military sense, and especially in the question of whether military trends at work today promise to strengthen the stability of the theater balance or to upset it.

The military factors making for a stable military balance in Europe as well as those that threaten to upset it can be viewed on two planes: Those external to the European theater and those internal to it. Obviously, the two planes intersect at many points. Though our focus thus far has been on the intratheater picture, a few words about extratheater factors are in order here.

It is a widely held view, seemingly confirmed by the history of the past quarter century, that military stability in Europe has been largely the product of the external strategic power relationship between the United States and the Soviet Union. In essence, so long as the strategic balance favored the United States, and the U.S. strategic deterrent remained clearly coupled to the defense of Europe, a conventional-theater imbalance did not appear to matter too much, and stability seemed assured at least from the Western viewpoint. Conversely, with the onset of strategic "parity" and the further possibility of a large shift of strategic force advantage to the Soviet Union, both implying some decoupling of the external U.S. deterrent, it has seemed to follow that the theater balance in Europe can be expected to grow increasingly precarious.

Whether this will prove to be the case remains to be seen. But in any event the external strategic relationship is probably still to be regarded as the main agency upon which military stability in Europe depends. This does not mean, however, that intratheater military factors are of no consequence.

Generally speaking, the theater standoff in Europe has not been a static affair. The "dynamic equilibrium" often referred to is another way of describing a more or less continuous qualitative competition between the two sides. The European theater has been the arena in which qualitative advances in conventional arms usually have been first introduced, as well as the focal point for tactical nuclear systems. In the Soviet case, with few exceptions, top priority has regularly gone to the GSFG (Group of Soviet Forces, Germany) for improvements in battlefield mobility and firepower, construction of aircraft shelters,

POL pipelines for better logistical support, and a variety of other measures to upgrade theater force capabilities. In the U.S. case, the Vietnam War had the effect of diverting some attention from Europe, but many of the qualitative advances it spurred in such fields as helicopter gunships, sensors, artillery, and air-delivered munitions have also been adapted to the European theater.

The qualitative competition in Europe, though uneven in tempo at times, seems to have speeded up in the last few years. In particular, there have been qualitative leaps forward in antitank weapons and precision-guided air-delivered weapons of various kinds, as well as a tougher ground antiaircraft environment. It is not easy to sort out what these qualitative changes may do to the balance of theater force, or which side they may tend to favor. At first glance, the new weapons trends might seem to go a considerable way toward reducing the conventional offensive advantages of the tank-heavy Warsaw Pact forces, although some of them may cut the other way, especially the dense antiaircraft threat against NATO tactical aircraft.

If, however, it turns out that qualitative improvements in conventional weapons technology—along with, perhaps, some restructuring of NATO forces—do promise to redress some of the imbalance between NATO's posture and the Soviet conventional threat, then the stability of the theater balance may begin to look less vulnerable to changes in the external strategic equation than might otherwise be the case.

The upshot of the foregoing discussion of Soviet military capabilities against Europe can be said to amount to this: The most reasonable measurement of Soviet capabilities today appears to lie somewhere between the older prudential view that Soviet theater forces possess overwhelming superiority that would permit them to overrun Europe in a matter of days and what might be called the newer revisionist view that an actual test of Soviet arms against NATO would probably show that Soviet capabilities have been greatly overrated. In making one's own choice between these two schools of analysis, it is well to bear in mind that the first school has tended to assume worst cases for NATO and to posit conditions favoring the Soviet side, whereas the second is prone to stack the conditions so as to maximize NATO's capabilities and degrade those of the Soviet Union. Let it be added, however, that even this caveat is perhaps a bit overdrawn for the sake of making a point. Few members of the first school would any longer maintain that "all the Russians need to reach the Channel is shoes," whereas no one of the second persuasion is likely to hold that NATO can afford to grow complacent about Soviet capabilities against Europe.

SOVIET MILITARY INTENTIONS IN EUROPE

Whatever the capabilities of the Soviet theater forces arrayed against Europe may be, the most interesting question to be asked undoubtedly is this: To what uses may the Soviet leadership intend to put these forces? Because the Soviet leaders themselves probably do not know the complete answer to this question, intentions being contingent upon many circumstances that no leadership can fully foresee, it is not surprising that the estimates of others as to what purposes Soviet arms may be meant to serve are at bottom little more than speculation. Certainly, no systematic methodologies for divining Soviet military intentions have been invented. Nevertheless, some of the intended uses of the Soviet military power deployed in Eastern Europe can be determined with somewhat more confidence than can others.

One of the more obvious purposes the Soviet theater forces are intended to serve is the defense of Warsaw Pact territory, including of course that of the Soviet Union itself, against attack. Because an unprovoked attack by the NATO allies or any other Western country seems out of the question, this function of the Soviet forces would appear to merit no further discussion in terms of Soviet intentions. However, the matter is not quite that simple. In the event of a major crisis, for example, the question of what kind of military action should be taken in the interest of defense could well be put before the Soviet leadership, raising such issues as whether or not the situation called for preemptive or forestalling moves. What the military plans and intentions of the Soviet Union might be in this regard is far from clear, although Soviet crisis behavior in the past would tend to suggest that a cautious rather than trigger-happy approach might be the rule.

Enforcement of Soviet Hegemony in Eastern Europe

Another rather obvious function of the Soviet theater forces in Eastern Europe is to help bind the Warsaw Pact together and bring any errant members back into line. On the past record, there seems little doubt that Soviet forces are still intended to enforce the Soviet writ in Eastern Europe if it should be seriously challenged by an ally. Again, however, it is less clear what Soviet military intentions might be toward any outside party seeking to intervene or otherwise restrain a Soviet "policing" action within the Warsaw bloc. In the case of Czechoslovakia in 1968, there were some intimations that the Soviet Union was prepared to take military action against any outside meddling in what it chose to describe as a "family affair" within the socialist common-wealth.[30] But on neither this nor previous occasions of Soviet discipli-nary action (East Germany in 1953, Hungary in 1956) were Soviet intentions with regard to outside interference put to test, because the West stayed out. Certainly, there is no greater inclination today on the part of the Western powers to oppose any use of military force the Soviet Union may see fit to apply within its own sphere of influence.

A somewhat more borderline question as to how far Soviet hegemonial prerogatives extend might arise, however, in a case like Yugoslavia, if, for example, there should be a turbulent post-Tito succession crisis in which the Soviet Union were to decide that its interests required active intervention on the side of a pro-Soviet fac-tion. How the West might react, whether it would warn the Soviets to keep hands off, and whether in such a case the intentions of the Soviet Union would be to go ahead anyway with military action to seal off Yugoslavia at the risk of tangling with the Western powers—all of these questions are too "iffy" to permit prediction. But at least one point might be ventured: If the Russians should intend to bring military pressures into play in Yugoslavia, the chances are that they would try to wrap their approach in the mantle of "collective" Warsaw Pact defense of "proletarian internationalism."[31]

An even more nebulous state of affairs involving the role of mili-

[30]For a discussion of this question, see Wolfe, *Soviet Power and Europe: 1945–1970*, p. 392.

[31]The Soviet Union has been engaged since 1968 in erecting an elaborate theoret-ical edifice on the foundation of "proletarian internationalism" to justify its hegemonial rights of intervention in Eastern Europe and to reconcile them with individual "socialist sovereignty." Yugoslavia lies on the borderline, but is still in the shadow cast by this construct, which has sometimes been rather loosely described in the West as the "Brezhnev Doctrine." See Thomas W. Wolfe, *Role of the Warsaw Pact in Soviet Policy, P-4973*, The Rand Corporation, Santa Monica, Calif., March 1973, pp. 3–4.

tary force as an instrument of Soviet hegemonial policy can be imagined if at some future time the Warsaw Pact were to be dissolved in connection with some new all-European collective security arrangement. Under such circumstances the Soviet Union might fall back on its bilateral defense treaties with the East European countries to justify any "protective" military measures deemed necessary to ensure the allegiance of its socialist camp partners, provided of course, that these treaties were to remain in force and that other impediments to Soviet intervention were not created by an European-wide collective security system. Again, this is such a hazy area that it seems futile at this point to try to spell out how the Russians would seek to preserve their military leverage upon the East European countries, or what specific military actions they would find it expedient to take to protect their interests.

The Issue—or Nonissue?—of a Premeditated Attack on the West

Although the postwar period has seen Soviet theater forces in Europe employed only against countries within the Soviet bloc, the paramount issue of Soviet military intentions is whether these forces are ever likely to be launched across the political dividing line in a premeditated attack on Western Europe. For many people, perhaps most, this may seem to be a nonissue, or if it ever was one, then a relic of the past no longer germane under nuclear-age conditions that seem to make incredible the prospect that either Soviet bloc forces or those of NATO would initiate major hostilities against each other in the heart of Europe. Détente has probably deepened this general conviction, although it also has stirred in some quarters incipient concern that greater relaxation of vigilance may take place on NATO's side of the dividing line than on the other, thus putting temptation in the way of the Soviet leadership to start thinking seriously about the hitherto unthinkable.

Whether such concern is justified, only those privy to what is actually going on in the minds of the Soviet leaders can be sure. But so far as mere guesswork may take one, it would seem that if the Soviet leaders want to assimilate Western Europe's resources and bend its political processes to their will—the two fundamental objectives of conquest usually attributed to them—they might think of better ways than a direct military assault that could end up not only pulverizing most of the resources they were after, but also putting the Soviet Union itself in jeopardy.

Precisely what alternatives to military conquest the Soviet leaders may have in mind is a large question in itself, which opens up avenues of discussion well beyond the compass of a paper on military capabilities and intentions. But as a general proposition it can be said that the preferred alternative from the Soviet viewpoint would probably be to see Western Europe eventually succumb to Soviet influence under a combination of enticements and pressures, helped in this direction by a growing sense of impotence in the face of preponderant Soviet military power.

Assuming, however, that for some reason or other the Soviet Union should attempt an outright invasion of Western Europe, the way the Russians would intend to use their forces is perhaps best indicated by their theater doctrine—both as expressed in Soviet military literature and as applied in joint Warsaw Pact exercises of varying size. Pact exercises usually are based on scenarios that begin with an attack by the West, but if in an actual war outbreak situation the initiative had been taken by the Soviet side, then the customary doctrinal prescription presumably would prevail—a swift offensive attempt to break through NATO's forward defense and penetrate the north German plain, along with possible attacks on the flanks. The objectives of flank operations might be as follows: In the north, to secure a foothold in Norway, which would give access to the North Atlantic and push out the perimeter for protection of important Soviet military and naval assets in the Kola Peninsula area; in the south, to seal off the Eastern Mediterranean in order to deny adversary access to the southwestern regions of the USSR and perhaps to split the southern flank countries of NATO off from the rest of the alliance.

But even Soviet doctrine, as noted earlier, does not necessarily furnish an infallible guide to practice, so that actual operations might well depart from a doctrinally derived blueprint. In particular, Soviet doctrine furnishes ambiguous clues at best as to Soviet intentions with regard to the critical question of making the transition from conventional to nuclear warfare. In any event, an attempt here to trace Soviet military intentions through all the permutations of a major campaign against Europe would involve a full-fledged war-gaming exercise well beyond the scope of this paper.

Military Intentions Around the Rim of Europe

Short of an outright Soviet military thrust through the central region, the proposition is sometimes advanced that the Soviet Union might try to bite off small chunks, perhaps on the northern or southern flanks. As noted earlier, the risks to the Soviet Union—if it could politically and militarily isolate an operation on one of the flanks from a frontal challenge to the West—might seem sufficiently diminished to make such a flank threat more plausible than a major attack.[32] To the extent that military intentions may be a linear function of opposing capabilities and the risk they pose, a case can probably be made that the Russians at least have studied the possibilities afforded by Europe's exposed flanks, and perhaps even filed away a few operational plans for pushing out their military perimeter around the edges of Europe.

But a serious intention to realize such plans would seem to be conditioned by many other factors. Such moves almost certainly would mean sacrificing further détente, which the Russians still seem to want, albeit not on terms the West would prefer. Not least, the possibility that a flank adventure could not be kept isolated, but rather might draw the Soviet Union into direct confrontation with the United States and NATO, would seem to be a major constraint upon the Soviet Union—unless disarray in the Western Alliance had assumed rather extreme proportions.

Another scenario short of a premeditated frontal attack on Europe that is sometimes projected—indeed, it probably dominates today's scenario field—is that of a series of Soviet military moves taken in connection with some third-party conflict. Areas like the Middle East and Persian Gulf provide the usual *mise-en-scène*. Though it might not be the original intention of the Soviet Union to engage its forces, events might take charge, as the scenario runs, and draw the Soviet leadership ever deeper into commitments from which it would be averse to withdraw, such as that implied by Brezhnev's message to the White House on 24 October 1973 advising that the Soviet Union

[32]See page 161.

might "consider acting alone" unless its suggestion that both powers "send forces to enforce the cease-fire" was accepted.[33]

Although there is still contention as to what the military intentions of the Soviet Union in the October Middle East war might have been had not Kissinger's quick trip to Moscow resolved the cease-fire enforcement issue, there was no direct intervention by Soviet forces. Rather, the Soviet Union seemed relieved, in the words of at least some of its spokesmen, that a "dangerous confrontation" between the two great powers had been averted.[34] Whether this precedent will prevail when and if a new crisis arises, or whether on the next occasion greater Soviet military involvement may ensue, is anybody's guess.

MBFR and Its Bearing on Soviet Military Intentions

Finally, to step back from such possible eventualities as Soviet military operations in or around the rim of Europe, one may ask where such a current actuality as the Vienna negotiations on mutual force reductions fits into the picture of Soviet military intentions in Europe. The Soviet Union, it may be recalled, was in no hurry to get these negotiations underway,[35] acceding only after the Western states insisted that the CSCE (Conference on Security and Cooperation Europe) must be accompanied by parallel talks on MBFR (Mutual Balanced Force Reductions). Once the latter negotiations were joined, however, and after preliminary Soviet maneuvers had succeeded in getting the word "balanced" deleted from the title of the talks,[36] the Soviet Union began

[33]David Binder, "An Implied Soviet Threat Spurred U.S. Forces' Alert," *New York Times*, 21 November 1973.

[34]Hedrick Smith, "Soviet Concedes Accords Averted Clash with U.S. in Mideast," *New York Times*, 16 November 1973.

[35]For background on Soviet MBFR attitudes, see Thomas W. Wolfe, *Soviet Attitudes Toward MBFR and the USSR's Military Presence in Europe*, P-4819, The Rand Corporation, Santa Monica, Calif., April 1972, pp. 10–12. For treatment of MBFR issues from the Western viewpoint, see Christoph Bertram, *Mutual Force Reductions in Europe: The Political Aspects*, Adelphi Paper no. 84, IISS, London, 1972; John Yochelson, "The Search for an American Approach," *Survival*, November–December 1973.

[36]The disputed word "balanced" originally reflected NATO's concept that the Soviet side should take proportionately larger cuts to balance disparities in force levels, compensate for the larger distance of U.S. withdrawal, and so forth. Obviously attentive to how semantic details might influence the negotiations, the Russians insisted on dropping the term and got their way. The title officially agreed upon is "Mutual

to lay some of its cards on the table, including a three-stage reduction proposal tabled in early November 1973.

All of the details of this proposal have not been made public, but enough has been disclosed—partly by Soviet leaks to the *The Times* (London) and other media—to give a fairly good idea of what the Russians have in mind.[37] Their proposed plan would begin with a small "symbolic" reduction of men and equipment by the end of 1975, to be followed during the next two years by successive reductions totaling 15 percent of forces on each side. The cuts proposed would affect both indigenous "national" forces and "foreign" forces in Europe and would be spread across all types of units, including nuclear delivery forces and weapons in the treaty area. At the end of the reduction process, the effect would be to leave the Warsaw Pact with a continued margin over NATO in the categories in which it had an advantage at the start of the process. The precise terminal margin would depend on what base figures the "equal percentage" reductions were to be taken from—figures that apparently were not furnished with the Soviet proposal.[38]

By contrast with the Soviet scheme, the proposal offered by the NATO side later in November 1973 was built around a "common ceiling" concept of drawing down forces on both sides in the NATO Guidelines Area (NGA)[39] to a common manpower level of about 700,000. This ceiling, to be reached over a period of several years, would be confined mainly to Soviet and U.S. ground forces elements. The proposal, which omitted aircraft and nuclear units, would have the effect of cutting down Soviet armored preponderance. Justification of the nonsymmetrical character of the NATO proposal was said to rest on geography, which would permit the Soviet Union to keep its with-

---

Reduction of Forces and Armaments and Associated Measures in Central Europe"—which yields the acronymic mouthful: MURFAAMCE. This paper will use simply MFR.

[37]See Richard Homan, "Soviets Leak Troop-Cut Plan," *Washington Post*, 18 November 1973.

[38]It may be noted that the Soviet "equal percentage" formula for reductions was a less drastic approach than a one-for-one reduction principle previously broached. The latter, given larger Soviet forces at the start of the process, would have pared U.S. forces in particular to a much lower level than their Soviet counterparts.

[39]NATO Guidelines Area: the GDR, Poland, and Czechoslovakia on the Warsaw Pact side; West Germany, the Netherlands, Belgium, and Luxembourg on the NATO side.

drawn forces nearby in European Russia, while American units would be pulled back across the Atlantic.[40]

Not surprisingly, the Soviet Union has made known its distaste for the NATO proposal, charging that it is an evident "maneuver" to bring about unequal troop reductions "at the expense of the socialist states" and that it deals only with conventional land forces, and not critical nuclear units and aircraft.[41] The NATO plan's application "only to Soviet and American troops stationed in central Europe," leaving unaffected "the well-trained West German Bundeswehr, the British Army of the Rhine and other armed forces of the NATO allies," is said to contradict "the principle of avoiding infringement on the security of any country whatsoever."[42] By way of undercutting the NATO rationale that mutual force reductions should contribute to stability in Europe by "correcting" present disparities in the theater balance that favor the Soviet side, Soviet spokesmen have advanced the view that the current force relationship already provides a stable "balance," and hence any reduction agreements should not disturb this "historically evolved balance of forces in the center of Europe."[43]

Soviet complaints that the NATO proposal tries to play down the effectiveness of West German forces, which it would leave largely intact, as well as the provision in the Soviets' own plan to make early cuts in these forces, suggest that the aim of curbing West German military capabilities stands high on the Soviet priority list. Likewise, Soviet criticism of the NATO plan for failing to include forward-based American air units and tactical nuclear weapons suggests that the

---

[40]The NATO proposal also has not been officially unveiled in public, in keeping with the confidentiality agreement previously reached. However, many of its features have been disclosed, both by leaks that preceded its tabling and by subsequent criticisms of it by Soviet and East European commentators. See Drew Middleton, "Troop Cut Offer by NATO Reported," *New York Times*, 16 September 1973; "West Called 'Not Helpful' in Talks on Troop Cuts," *New York Times*, 14 December 1973; Christopher S. Wren, "Soviet Says NATO Blocks Gains in Troop-Cut Parley," *New York Times*, 18 December 1973.

[41]I. Melnikov, "A Responsible Task," *Pravda*, 17 December 1973; Vladimir Komlev dispatch, "West Seeks Unfair Advantages at Vienna Talks," Radio Moscow, 15 December 1973; Aleksandr Urban, "Vienna Measures of Military Relaxation," *Literaturnaia Gazeta*, no. 51, 19 December 1973.

[42]Melnikov, "A Responsible Task."

[43]Urban, "Vienna Measures of Military Relaxation."

Soviet Union intends to press hard in the MFR negotiations, as it has in the parallel SALT forum, for cutbacks in these forces (part of the so-called forward-base-system package), which it regards as a strategic threat to Soviet territory. One rather unexpected feature of the Soviet position, however, is the rather restrained way in which overall reduction of the U.S. military presence in Europe is treated in the Soviet MFR proposal. This might be interpreted to mean that the Soviet Union has some concern that a too abrupt American withdrawal could stimulate EDC-type developments and especially the emergence of an autonomous "third" nuclear force in Western Europe involving France and England, with perhaps tacit West German cooperation.

Whatever the immediate negotiatory aims of the Soviet Union may be in the Vienna MFR talks, the larger question bearing on Soviet military intentions in Europe is how far the Soviets are prepared to go in a détente environment toward reducing the massive military presence upon which they have habitually counted for more than a quarter-century to back up their policies toward the West and to enforce their hegemony in the East. The Soviet MFR proposal itself reflects no disposition to embark upon a hasty dismantling of the military security system the Soviet Union has built in Eastern Europe. Although displaying a willingness to accept some lowering of the level at which the military balance in Europe is now maintained, the Soviet Union appears to feel that the balance could be disturbed by efforts to improve NATO's posture. To prevent that from happening, it apparently hopes to structure an MFR agreement that will give it control over force balance and changes in composition during the process of reduction.

Such an approach to reduction of forces in Europe does not appear to involve a basic reordering of Soviet security priorities, and therefore is probably one that the political leadership in the Kremlin can "sell" without great difficulty to the Soviet military command, whose generally conservative instincts might be expected to call into question the wisdom of any more radical reduction scheme. This is not to imply, however, that a marked dichotomy exists between the political and military leadership,[44] with the former eager to liquidate the Soviet

[44]Whether the relationship between Soviet political and military leaders reflects a unity of outlook or a distinct cleavage of views as to what best serves Soviet security is a

military lodgement in Europe except for the stubborn counsel of the latter.

Rather, both would appear to share an interest, perhaps from a somewhat different perspective, in not going too far down a new and untried military security road in Europe. In the case of the military command, a professional military calculus alone would account for reluctance to give up a firm military foothold in Eastern Europe. In the case of the political leadership, the purely military implications of wholesale withdrawal from Europe, especially if it were on a nonunilateral basis, would probably be of less moment than its potential political consequences.

Should Soviet withdrawal be construed on both sides of the European dividing line as having actually defused the Soviet military threat against Europe, the terms of East-West competition would have undergone a basic change. In the new environment, the paramount factor in future competition would tend to shift from the military status of the competing parties to the political-economic vitality of their respective systems. Though compatible with détente, this situation might seem to place the Soviet Union in a poorer competitive position than if its policies were backed by the continuing threat of employable force in the European arena.

---

perennial question addressed by "Kremlinology," but one that has acquired a new edge at a time when the Soviet Union is engaged in negotiations along a wide front involving readjustment of the East-West power balance. For expressions of the view that an internal defense debate is underway between leadership constituencies headed by Brezhnev on the one side and men like Marshal Grechko and Admiral Gorshkov on the other, see Stephen S. Rosenfeld, "Kremlin Defense Debate," *Washington Post*, 8 February 1974, and Victor Zorza, "Soviet Naval Debate," *Washington Post*, 5 February 1974, a strong argument for the case that there is no essential disagreement.

Soviet Military Posture and Policy in Europe

JOHN ERICKSON

Military obligations dictate, you say? But in fact we have only one-tenth of the military obligations that we pretend to have, or rather that we intensively and assiduously create for ourselves. . . . For peacetime we armed to excess several times over. . . we maintain this army solely out of military and diplomatic vanity.—
Alexander Solzhenitsyn (Letter to the Soviet Leaders)

The above statement comes from Alexander Solzhenitsyn and such a comment on the psychology of Soviet military power cannot be lightly brushed aside as either irrelevant or irresponsible, much less uninformed. For all the continuous scrutiny of "hardware" or the daily inspection of order of battle, Solzhenitsyn seems to have gone directly to the heart of the question, even if literary comment is not normally admitted into military analysis—more is the pity, perhaps. There is a certain irony in all the efforts to understand particular aspects of Soviet military policy when we fail in general to grasp or to identify the essentials of the system, and here Russian literature (and Soviet literature, for that matter) can be most informative and illuminating. Much of the present Soviet concern over *effektivnost'* in the field and in command—"performance," in short—can be examined through those insights into behavior afforded by literature and literary comment. The social profile and predicament of the officer, for example, is displayed

169

throughout the nineteenth-century Russian novel, and there is much to suggest that the present position has not altered substantially.

To put it another way, and to use this time the formulation of a military analyst, the perception and implementation of "military requirements" (Imperial Russian and Soviet Russian alike) have consistently outpaced social and economic developments. Military exigencies set the Russians on their forced march through modern history and it is not unreasonable, therefore, for Solzhenitsyn to ask when this might stop, because there is more to it than mere *folie de grandeur*—with modern military technology behind it, there is more to the posturing than sheer vainglory or mere strutting. The substance of Soviet military power is all too real and can no longer be explained away by that oft-repeated maxim about the "defensive bias" of Soviet military policy—and yet at the same time it is not entirely satisfactory to argue the primacy of some indeterminate concept of "superiority" in view of the operational and technological complexities of the modern military scene. Lack of military substance has also in its time been reflected in Soviet political stances. "Socialism in one country" was itself a formulation closely related to Soviet strategic inferiority, embodying a truce with a hostile, encircling world, whereas "peaceful coexistence" in Khrushchev's time represented the same kind of standoff. The problem at the moment is to find the same kind of perceived relationship between Soviet military capability and political objectives, not least in the miltary aspects of "détente."

To embark upon an examination of the specific topic of Soviet military policy in Europe with such imponderables might at first sight seem strange, even misplaced, but the basic issue (of which the European emplacement is only a part) is Soviet reliance on military capability at large, the relationship between diplomatic political and military processes, and, finally, Soviet objectives in general. Referring to "military influence" on Soviet policy provides no effective guide whatsoever, if only because we are substantially ignorant of the institutional processes that go to make up this "influence"; even to speak of "the military" tends to beg the question, or a large part of it. The extent and pervasiveness of "military influence" is a familiar topic of debate, even if it is bereft of substantial insights into actual processes of policymaking and policy formulation. There is, additionally, the problem of the mechanistic operation of the weapons acquisition system, which demonstrates a momentum of its own (and not only in the Soviet Union). Innovation, testing, procurement, and production cycles all play their part in establishing the Soviet "military picture" and can be applied to both strategic weapons and equipment (or reequipment) for the theater forces. What precisely does "modernization" entail and through what phases does this pass? The problem is complicated by the fact that the Soviet command never throws anything away (to use a rather colloquial formulation), and "modernization" is accompanied by miserly retention of all items of equipment, due no doubt to a great deal of military bookkeeping, costing, and sheer bureaucratic inertia. Thus, whereas there are undoubtedly dramatic aspects to the weapons buildup, there is also the inertia of routine processes and the sheer weight of military bureaucratism.

All this simply serves as a series of caveats—against a simple assumption of a quest for "superiority," against an equally simplified notion of "military influence" at work in the system, against a failure to appreciate some of the characteristics of the Soviet weapons acquisition process with its attendant bureaucracy, and, finally, against any notion of a possibly irrational factor in this addiction to, or reliance on, the crude effectiveness of military "muscle." Nevertheless, the language of the Soviet military professionals does nothing to reassure. General Milshtein is at pains to point out that political détente is neither "durable nor irreversible" if the present arms race continues, and the introduction of that notion of "durability" (or the lack of it) is perhaps the most sombre undertone here.

Thus we come back to all the psychological factors adduced by Solzhenitsyn, to the persistent magnification of "military obligation," to vanity in the sense of asserting a newly won status, and to the addiction to military power as the nostrum for internal and international "order." It is perhaps relevant to point out here that members of the American academic-strategic community bear some considerable responsibility in this matter, for there has been a consistent effort on their part to translate the terms of the Soviet military effort into "equivalencies" that make comforting sense in the context of American doctrine (though not without mocking a deplorable Soviet lack of theoretical sophistication) and yet take no account of a fundamentally different political and psychological climate relating to military force. There is, for example, absolutely no comparison between the interpenetration in Soviet life between military and civilian agencies (ranging from civil defense to the educational system) and that general situation which pertains in the United States in which the disarray and disillusionment following Vietnam have severely affected the military both as an establishment and as a profession.

It is this sense of Soviet cogency that informs this present paper, the aim of which is to examine Soviet capabilities in Europe as they developed during the period 1968–1974. There are a number of specific reasons for this choice, not the least of which is the fact that the general historical background to Soviet power in Europe over two decades at least has been covered by Thomas W. Wolfe[1] in a study that can be taken as definitive for the point of view of the emplacement and objectives of Soviet power in Europe under both the Stalinist and Khrushchev regimes. The object of this examination is, therefore, to look at the situation in the following terms:

1. The momentum of the military buildup since 1968, comprising both manpower levels and equipment (including also the non-Soviet elements of the Warsaw Pact). Is this really a "buildup" in the recognizable sense of the term, or can it be explained away in the light of replacement-modernization programs, and what degree of deliberate "superiority" does this embody, assuming that it is a planned and programmed increase?

2. In what form does this force structure and the capability at large correspond to military requirement, as an expressed requirement and as a reflection of Soviet perceptions of NATO performance, as well as the evolution of Soviet military doctrine in relation to theater forces—or even an "autonomous" doctrine relating to the European theater as a special case in Soviet military-political planning?

3. The relationship between military force and political processes, including constraints on Soviet force levels in Europe. How much is "enough" and to what degree are the Soviet requirements of internal policing, defense, and preemption effectively satisfied, leaving an

[1]Thomas W. Wolfe, *Soviet Power and Europe: 1945–1970* (Baltimore: Johns Hopkins Press, 1970).

appreciable margin of force that presents the disparity between a professed interest in "relaxation of international tensions" and the high visibility of military power?

The bulk of this discussion is based on Soviet, GDR (German Democratic Republic), Polish, and Czechoslovak materials (see Selected References, pp. 207–209), though the proviso of caution in handling such sources must be paraded at once. Information on Warsaw Pact organization, equipment, and training does, of necessity, overlap between Soviet and non-Soviet sources and all is virtually grist to the mill—a good example is provided by a recent Polish publication, *Technika wojskowa LWP XXX lat rozwoju 1943–1973* (Warsaw: MON, 1973), or the military journals of the non-Soviet members of the Pact. Yet another example is furnished by the question of the logistics of Soviet and Warsaw Pact forces in the European theater, where information is necessarily derived from a wide variety of sources, or yet again the organization, disposition, and training of airborne forces and special service units.

Much more difficult is the problem of handling data—quantitative and qualitative—bearing on the "military balance" and the force reduction problem in Europe. Estimates are subject to a number of drastic revisions, in both directions—upward and downward—so that it is difficult at times to discern the criteria upon which they are based, though specific political convenience in assessing "the threat" seems to intrude in rather obvious fashion. (The same phenomenon on the Soviet side can be observed in the public discussions of NATO and the "threat" it poses—a recent example of that was provided by A. Antonov's article "NATO in Conditions of Détente" in *International Affairs*, February 1974.) Soviet tank strength is an everpresent puzzle, for numerical estimates and presentations are subject to so many interpretations. The augmentation of tank strength in the European theater is obvious, but the line between modernization of existing forces and actual reinforcement is difficult to draw. Let us, therefore, call these "gross statistics." The buildup in Soviet armor between the Elbe and western Russia has been gradual but nonetheless imposing, bringing the force level up to some 40,000 AFVs (armored fighting vehicles) of which 15,000 would be covered by the proposed force reduction negotiations, while at the same time the buildup in artillery has produced a strength of some 18,000 tubes (over 100 mm) and over 1,000 FROG and SCUD missiles—representing at least a 15 percent increase in tube artillery and a 25 percent increase in battlefield missile strength.[2] Increase nevertheless does pose a problem in relation to the opposing NATO and Warsaw Pact concepts of force reduction. The mutuality and balance of the NATO proposal would mean a common ceiling, whereas the Warsaw Pact's insistence on equality of reduction must inevitably fail to affect the degree of preponderance that is apparent even from these "gross statistics." This is an aspect that must be discussed somewhat later in this paper.

As for doctrine, the military journal *Voennyi Vestnik* provides a general commentary on the general shifts in emphasis, though for obvious reasons it does not specify the operational details; nevertheless, it is possible to discern that major shift in the past year or so to what might best be called an "independent conventional option"—that is, the possibility and even the desirability of conducting a prolonged phase of conventional operations in the European theater, as opposed to the "switch on/switch off" nuclear-conventional relationship that has so far predominated. As for military exercises, these have been included but with a certain note of caution, for the exercise—by its very nature—is artificial and demonstrably so in terms of its time scale. That nuclear weapons are "introduced" on the third day, say, is no guarantee that this is the working operational code, for it may simply conform to the exercise time available. Finally, there is the naval and air component to be considered, for the former in particular represents a singular element in the Soviet Union's "European presence"—both in inshore, coastal waters, and sea-lane terms. The flanks of the European theater also represent a somewhat different quantity for the Soviet Union in the context of access, egress, emplacement, and reinforcement, not to mention the linkage with the Middle East on the

[2]See *Aviation Week & Space Technology* (hereafter cited as *AWST*), 11 March 1974, p. 43: this is the suggested total for Soviet armor in the land mass between the river Elbe and a north-south line running through Smolensk. The percentage increases in artillery pieces and battlefield missile strength are also derived from this account (also p. 43). See also *White Paper 1973/1974*, The Security of the Federal Republic of Germany and the Development of the Federal Armed Forces, Press and Information of the Government of the FRG, 1974, p. 13 (table).

southern flank. On the northern flank the visible extension of the line marking the Soviet Union's maritime frontier has long been an accomplished fact, embracing as it does the extent of the northern theater and reaching out to the more distant line of the "UK-Iceland" gap.

The choice of the period for investigation and study—1968–1974—is by no means an arbitrary selection. It avoids both some extended and indeterminate time frame and a snap inspection of a very limited period that might prove to be merely an exception. The Soviet invasion of Czechoslovakia in 1968 signaled something of a climacteric in Soviet policy and at the same time visibly altered Soviet military disposition in Central Europe, not least with the addition of a whole new army group to the prevailing order of battle. By the same token it is possible to argue that the Warsaw Pact organization as such experienced a trauma all its own. If General Sejna is to be believed, the Soviet command in 1968 simultaneously entertained plans for action against northern Yugoslavia, which could have involved operations by Hungarian units against western Austria—a recent disclosure that seems to have come as no great surprise to the Austrian General Staff.[3] Nor does the matter end there. Though SHIELD 72 was officially proclaimed to be a practice defense against "revanchist aggression," its main purpose has been demonstrated as a staff exercise designed to study the invasion of Yugoslavia mounted from Czechoslovakia via Austria—with the river-crossing demonstration at Melnik being nothing more than a public diversion. This "exercise pressure" is also exerted against Romania, usually with the purpose of testing reactions and to what degree the Romanian Army does (or does not) comply with orders in the face of what might well be a local invasion.

Thus the Czechoslovak operation might serve as a model for a number of contingencies internal to the Warsaw Pact area (and extending even into what some choose to call the "gray areas" of the European periphery). It also serves as a baseline for measuring Soviet and Warsaw Pact strengths in terms of manpower levels, equipment, and overall combat capability, while in 1972–1973 Czechoslovakia was "restored" to the military comity of the Warsaw Pact, first

[3]See analysis of Warsaw Pact exercises, including SHIELD 72, in *Frankfurter Allgemeine Zeitung* and *Die Welt*, 16 and 18 March 1974.

in the demonstrative multinational exercise of SHIELD 72 and later in the spate of military activity, all in the guise of "exercises." The suggested time frame seems to justify itself as a unit of study and as one in which it might be possible to make comparisons of levels of capability. It is that element—capability—which forms the focus of the first discussion in this paper. What does the Soviet command have at its disposal (and what has it recently acquired by way of reinforcement)? In what fashion is this force deployed and for what purposes might it be suited?

FORCE LEVELS AND MILITARY CAPABILITIES

The present balance, insofar as it can be called that, dates back essentially to 1968, when the Soviet incursion into Czechoslovakia resulted in the addition of five or six divisions (or their equivalent) to the Soviet order of battle in Central Europe. This addition to Soviet military strength in Europe also coincided with the increased momentum of the general buildup of strategic weapons. The point here is not the missile buildup, but the place of the ground forces in this scheme of things. In general, whereas the proportion of the military budget devoted to the ground forces has fallen since the 1950s to well below 50 percent, actual expenditure has increased, as might be expected in view of the increased commitments of the ground forces to east and west alike. By the same token the level of Soviet investment in, and commitment to, the Warsaw Pact organization has remained high, with Soviet forces providing some 60 percent of the total capability of the Pact. In round numbers, more than 50 percent of ground forces strength is committed to the European theater, and in spite of the buildup on the eastern frontiers facing China there is no sign of any diminution in this scale of commitment.[4] Though rising cost was at one time anticipated as a major constraint on the Soviet military presence in Europe, this does not seem so far to have acted as a real brake on

[4]See *Bonner Rundschau*, 21 August 1974, for a summary from the Federal German Ministry of Defense publication "Information for the Troops," emphasizing the buildup in armor and tactical aircraft. Soviet deployment on the eastern frontiers facing China involves only one-quarter of Soviet potential, and the modernization of the weapons and equipment of these units in the east has not reached the standard of Soviet forces in the European theater.

force levels as such, which were first increased (1968–1969) and then made more effective (1971–1972).

Though there are inevitable discrepancies in the figures for Soviet and overall Warsaw Pact manpower (depending upon which main sector is or is not included for the purposes of reckoning), there is general agreement that manpower levels as such seem lately to have flattened out. One very approximate estimate is that on the crucial central sector—running from the Baltic to Czechoslovakia—some 825,000 men of the Warsaw Pact face 750,000 NATO troops, but such a statement has very little real meaning. In his annual report for 1974, Defense Secretary Schlesinger referred to "the deployed threat," comprising those Warsaw Pact forces which could be launched "with very little warning" against "the Center (that is, the Federal Republic of Germany)," amounting to twenty-seven Soviet divisions in GDR, Poland, and Czechoslovakia, and thirty-one indigenous (non-Soviet) GDR, Polish, and Czechoslovak divisions and 2,800 tactical aircraft— in sum, fifty-eight divisions representing a "very immediate and palpable threat" to the central region.[5] The 8,000 and more tanks available to the Soviet forces also underline the offensive potential in this region. To this order of battle it is also necessary to reckon with, though not necessarily count in, the Soviet southern group in Hungary with four divisions, which brings the total order of battle up to thirty-one Soviet divisions, though again these must not be counted purely as "divisions" but also in terms of "division force equivalents," an estimate of which is given in Table 1. Schlesinger's report gives a total of 925,000 men for the deployed manpower in these Pact forces, which takes account of the fact that Warsaw Pact divisions maintain a lower logistics structure in peacetime than do NATO divisions.

After the "deployed threat" comes the "mobilized threat," which could amount to eighty to ninety divisions deployed in the central region, and, with the reinforcement coming from the military districts of the USSR itself, a figure that could be reached within a "relatively short period of mobilization." The 1974 "Pentagon study" also cited an

[5]For the latest figures, see Secretary of Defense James R. Schlesinger, Annual Defense Department Reports FY 1976 and FY 197T (Report to the Congress, 5 February 1975) under I-19: deployed manpower is "over 930,000 men," with about 2,900 tactical aircraft and more than 16,000 tanks.

TABLE 1
WARSAW PACT GROUND FORCES IN CZECHO-SLOVAKIA, THE GERMAN DEMOCRATIC REPUBLIC, AND POLAND

Country	Divisions	Division equivalents (effective)	Manpower (in divisions)	Division-force equivalents	Total manpower
Indigenous Forces					
Czechoslovakia	4 Tank	3 Tank	25,200	108,000	145,000
	8 Motor-rifle	5 Motor-rifle	52,500		
GDR	2 Tank	2 Tank	16,800	81,000	90,000
	4 Motor-rifle	4 Motor-rifle	42,000		
Poland	5 Tank	4 Tank	33,600	135,000	190,000
	8 Motor-rifle	6 Motor-rifle	63,000		
	1 Airborne				
	1 Amphibious				
Total Indigenous	11 Tank	9 Tank	233,100	324,000	425,000
	22 Motor-rifle	15 Motor-rifle			

Soviet Forces[a]				
In Czechoslovakia	2 Tank	16,800	67,500	70,000
	3 Motor-rifle	31,500		
In the GDR	10 Tank	110,000	250,000	370,000
	10 Motor-rifle	140,000		
In Poland	2 Tank	16,800	27,000	30,000
Total Soviet	14 Tank	315,100	344,500	470,000
	13 Motor-rifle			
Total Warsaw	23 Tank	548,200	668,500	895,000
Pact Ground Forces	28 Motor-rifle			
	25 Tank			
	35 Motor-rifle			

[a]The divisional deployment of Soviet forces in Hungary: 2 tank and 2 motor-rifle divisions (manpower, 39,000; division force equivalent, 60,000); Soviet air force strength in Czechoslovakia, GDR, and Poland is about 60,000 men.

Sources: A variety of press reports, for example, *Die Welt,* 1 February 1974; *Die Welt,* 16 February 1974; *Soldat und Technik,* no. 3 (1974), p. 116 (on Hungarian deployment, strength, GSFS); *White Paper 1973/1974,* Bundesministerium der Verteidigung (Planungsstab); and *Die Welt,* 16 August 1974, on Soviet front-line air strength (Sixteenth Air Army), deployment of combat helicopter regiments, reconnaissance (MiG-23) units at Brieg. See also the important study by Steven Canby, *The Alliance and Europe: Part IV Military Doctrine and Technology,* Adelphi Paper no. 109, The International Institute for Strategic Studies, London, Winter 1974/1975, pp. 3–4, on the terms "division slice," "division-force equivalent"; also pp. 9–11 on the structure of Soviet units, including logistics arrangements.

"augmented threat" of 126 to 128 divisions, but the report of February 1975 does nonetheless assert that the force assembled under the "mobilized threat" would have "a significant probability of breaking through NATO's forward defense." There is, additionally, one major asymmetry that must be introduced at this point—namely, Soviet medium-range attack capabilities, the IRBM/MRBM force, which at an earlier stage may have been designed to implement a "hostage concept" vis-à-vis Europe as a major Soviet response to the intercontinental threat posed by the United States. Those days are long past, however, and yet this type of capability has been maintained and expanded beyond any comparable European capability and even beyond the range of potential and predictable targets. (It might be possible to argue, albeit in very hypothetical terms, that the "hostage concept" has been given a fresh lease of life in inhibiting and containing any U.S. or European response in the event of major hostilities on the Soviet Union's eastern frontiers—not to mention the Soviet proclivity never to throw anything away.)

Such assessments of strength on the ground bring a great element of military metaphysics into play, such as matching actual combatant units, weapons performance, and available air support. Although there must be inevitably a Soviet attempt to match NATO capability, the real question seems to be the degree of superiority (if any) that the Soviet command intends to assure and to retain. Manpower levels themselves do not provide a very reliable guide here, because recent Soviet techniques have involved adding more new equipment without increasing the nominal order of battle. Augmented weapons stocks in Soviet divisions in the GDR are sufficient to equip an additional company, while additional aircraft are assigned to existing regiments (again, without increasing the order of battle as such). Here the cycles of Soviet reequipment and modernization are important and seem (very approximately) to follow four- or five-year periods, with the curve presently flattening out, followed by a period of absorption, and succeeded in turn by yet another bout of modernization.[6] There are

[6]See General George S. Brown (USAF), Chairman, Joint Chiefs of Staff, *United States Military Posture for FY 1976*, pp. 60–61. The USSR seems to improve its ground forces in three cycles, developing a powerful tank force, deploying armored troop-carrying fighting vehicles, and then introducing self-propelled artillery, thus enabling

also other odd aspects to general manpower levels, some of which may fall under the heading of rationalization, but which at the same time cannot be excluded from an awareness of removing categories of forces from any proposed force reduction. For example, in the GDR, the special border forces have now been removed from Warsaw Pact authority and thus cannot be considered to be part of the "military establishment" as such, though there are also commonsense reasons for this adjustment to present arrangements. The whole question of paramilitary forces—of some strength in Central and Eastern Europe—and of possible "substitutions" (national forces taking over second-line duties normally assigned to Soviet divisions) obviously assumes some considerable significance.

Let us examine, therefore, some of the characteristics of the Soviet buildup in terms of increased combat capability, mobility, and firepower, if only to amplify some of the basic military statistics of the European theater. The most obvious increase has been in armored strength, which now stands at a ratio of some 18,000 to 19,000 Warsaw Pact tanks against NATO's 6,700 AFVs, with Soviet divisions in the central sector disposing of more than 8,000 tanks (which represents an increase in the order of 30 percent since 1968). In general terms, Soviet tank production over the period 1968–1974 stands as follows: 24,300 T-55s and 20,400 T-62s; and so that it is not surprising that there has been this increment of strength in the European theater, with a new model yet to make its appearance in strength and an air-droppable tank also coming into service.[7] In addition to the actual increase in the number of AFVs, a form of dual-basing permits armor to be kept in home bases and also in field storage, thereby facilitating training, higher combat readiness, and a reduction in unnecessary movement (though I would also refer to the Soviet unwillingness to withdraw equipment, even if it ages). Nor is it possible to exclude the increase in

---

the artillery to "keep pace with highly mobile tank and motorized rifle units." (The new self-propelled artillery includes the 122-mm D-74 ordnance and the 152-mm mounted on SA-4 GANEF transporters.)

[7]On Soviet tank strength, see *The Guardian* (London), 10 February 1973; also, *Frankfurter Allgemeine Zeitung*, 21 April 1973, mentioning a total Soviet tank force facing NATO as 20,000. See also *Force Reductions in Europe*, an SIPRI Monograph (Stockholm-New York-London, 1974), p. 84, which gives Soviet tank strength as 20,000 for the northern and central regions.

armed personnel carriers, which has averaged around 1,000 additional carriers per year since 1969, or some 4,000 gross over the past four or five years. Tank reinforcement has already been mentioned, with modern T-62s for Soviet forces in the GDR increasing their first-echelon strength from 5,040 to 6,500 and additional reinforcement throughout the central sector bringing the total of first-line strength to 8,700 tanks for fifteen tank divisions—an increase of over 30 percent over the past two years.[8] In line with this steady modernization—or reinforcement—increasing numbers of T-62s have been reaching the indigenous forces of the Warsaw Pact and there will be presumably yet another stage of reequipping when the new medium tank is pressed into full service, again with the likelihood that the older machines (which are not after all so old) will not be withdrawn.

Yet another singular departure of late has been both the missile buildup and the increase in Soviet nuclear munition stocks, with the latter—according to general reports—now attaining the U.S./NATO level of some 7,000 (as opposed to the previously cited disparity of 2:1 in NATO's favor), though here again the difficulty of accurate counting obtrudes at once.[9] What is certainly observable is the frequency of the practice of transferring and loading nuclear munitions in the GDR, and it is reasonable to suppose that if conventional munition holdings have been increased (as they have), then there will have been a corresponding increase in nuclear firepower. A new long-range missile now furnishes additional nuclear fire support, in addition to the FROGs and SCUDs (which have increased by some 25 percent) while conventional artillery (along with conventional ammunition stocks) has been steadily increased, to some 18,000 barrels of tube artillery (which represents a 15 percent increase in artillery strength, for weapons over 100-mm diameter). Soviet divisions now hold double their previous complement of conventional artillery, which was already in excess of the artillery component of NATO divisions (and superior in range to U.S. equivalents, though this will be corrected by improved ordnance).

Less dramatic but very relevant to the effectiveness of Soviet military performance in this theater has been the considerable im-

[8]*The Guardian* (London), 10 February 1973.

[9]See *The Times* (London), 5 February 1974: "it is thought that the Russians have also brought in a total of 7,000 tactical nuclear warheads. . . ."

provement in logistics and support, particularly for armored and missile units. The introduction of the new seven-ton truck more or less doubles Soviet capacity, as well as providing the facility to move heavy weapons quickly to required sectors. And, in line with that constant emphasis in Soviet military writing, the capacity for high-speed assault river crossings has been visibly improved (no doubt with some of the lessons of the recent Middle East war in mind). Stocks of heavy folding bridges (PMP) have been built up with respect to both numbers and capacity (supplying, for example, each of the six pontoon bridge regiments in the Group of Soviet Forces, Germany [GSFG] with an additional 120 meters of bridging), permitting each of the regiments attached to Soviet armies to erect a 600-meter bridge, while at the same time the six river-assault battalions in GSFG have each been supplied with thirty or more heavy amphibious trucks, twenty of the very heavy PTS-M amphibians (carrying a ten-ton load), and additional ferries. Soviet and GDR exercises in assault crossings obviously concentrate on dealing with the characteristics to be found on the river banks of West Germany, which are frequently built up and thus impede submersible or wading tanks.

The importance of airborne troops was highlighted during the recent Middle East war, when the mobilization of seven Soviet airborne divisions at bases in the GDR, Poland, and Hungary reportedly produced a major crisis in Soviet-American relations. For some considerable period now, airborne forces have figured much more prominently in the planning and preparations of the Warsaw Pact command. The eight Guards airborne divisions within the Soviet forces form the major striking force, committed to large-scale strategic landings in the enemy rear, but there has also been a recent growth in purely tactical airborne and helicopter-borne forces with GSFG. Two Soviet helicopter regiments stationed at Parchim and Stendal are available to lift a number of motor-rifle battalions well ahead of the main assault force, with the object of seizing and holding crucial river-crossing points. In addition to this "tactical air landing assault force," there are also the *reidoviki*, the helicopter-borne commandos who now form No. 1 Company in each rifle regiment and are used in a forward assault role. The *reidoviki*, an elite force, played out their role in the night occupation of Prague in 1968 in operational conditions.

Together with Soviet units, Warsaw Pact forces also provide elements for these paracommando missions—the Fifth Parachute Battalion of the GDR Army is one such infiltration/sabotage group, as is the Sixth Polish Airborne Division, whose men are trained in German and in Danish. The present order of battle of these paracommandos seems to consist of two GDR regiments, one Czechoslovak Special Air Service regiment, the Polish Sixth Division (which is only half the strength of a full airborne division), and a reserve Soviet regiment at Neuruppin. (It is worth a little speculation whether in wartime such units, particularly Soviet, would come under military or special intelligence command for a wide range of diversionary activities in NATO's rear.)[10]

Even on this very brief inspection (in which the choice of illustration was not intended to be arbitrary), it would appear that a number of trends can be established. Allowing for that earlier insertion in 1968 of the equivalent of five or six extra divisions into the order of battle available in Central Europe, manpower strengths do seem to have leveled off, with the exception of the addition of specialist support and special service units. With five Army HQs in the GDR (and twenty or twenty-one divisions), immediate reinforcement from European Russia and the support provided by the northern and central groups would amount to some eight armies with thirty-two to thirty-six divisions (to which earmarked forces from the non-Soviet forces of the Warsaw Pact would have to be added to derive a true mobilized total). These are forces which I have elsewhere described as encompassing "instant capability"—that is, they are at a high state of readiness in terms of manpower and equipment—but an operational requirement seems to have induced some modification in military service conditions, with a tacit extension of the period of compulsory military service which could contribute to increasing the number of age-groups (three, in fact) simultaneously under arms and thus would tend to increase gross numbers. On the other hand, such an increase hardly seems to be the object, and it may well be aimed at maintaining existing force levels in view of the extended period of training time now demanded for the Soviet serviceman and at the same time retaining much-needed

[10]For background, see "Soviet Airborne Forces" (A Staff Study), *Aerospace International*, March–April 1973, pp. 10–13; also *Die Welt*, 6 February 1974, on special paratroop formations.

specialist personnel. It has been obvious for some time that the Soviet system since 1967 has suffered from the disadvantages of the double annual intake (January and June of each year) and also the reduced period of service, yet with a more demanding training schedule, allowing even for "on-the-job" training. This aspect of Soviet organization, together with "transferring out" units or formations from under formal Warsaw Pact command—not to mention the existence of substantial paramilitary bodies—must in turn compound the problem of equitable force comparison and force reduction.

This augmentation of Soviet force levels has taken place without any visible increase in the nominal order of battle, even though armored strength has increased by one-third, artillery has been doubled, tactical nuclear warhead strength doubled, and in some respects (taking rough measurements) logistics capacity has also doubled. In the GDR, GSFG seems to be going through a number of changes, one of which seems to be a significant development in the direction of creating "battle groups" capable of operating on their own, much smaller than the "army group" concept but nonetheless quite powerful—and here crude yardsticks of "how many men" scarcely seem to apply.

To digress for a moment, the "battle group" concept has also a counterpart in the manifest concern of the Soviet command over how its forces will actually perform. The quantitative increase in combat capability also has its corresponding effort in the attempt to improve the tactical performance of forward-deployed Soviet forces, of which an important part was the reorganization of the NCO/warrant officer group beginning in 1972. This meant a short period of withdrawal of such personnel for training and further education (which showed up as a visible "sag" of GSFG units), followed by the infusion of the new *praporshchiki* and presumably concentration on the performance of the subunit. The rotation/replacement program connected with the call-up schedule also means that about one-third of the Soviet troops are replaced each year in GSFG (using *Aeroflot* transport in most instances, rather than the slower rail links), which may be useful for morale purposes but must also produce some undesirable side effects on troop training and small-unit cohesion. It is also worth noting that "détente" is very appreciably underplayed in the military-political press (both Soviet and GDR), with an unyielding emphasis on the "aggressive designs" of the NATO bloc. There is, of course, the obvious motive for not wishing to undermine or to deflect the combat motivation of the Soviet troops abroad (who will in any case take the "official line" with something of a pinch of salt), but this military leitmotif is in marked contrast with other expressions of peaceful intent and international cooperation. If anything, the disparity is particularly marked in the GDR military press.

TACTICAL AVIATION

As in the case of ground forces, tactical aircraft have been increased in number, but at the same time there has been a significant improvement in qualitative combat capability. Again, as in the case of the ground forces, existing units have been supplied with additional aircraft, though three whole new wings of tactical aircraft have been shifted to GSFG, Poland, and Czechoslovakia—normal in the sense that these were genuine replacements, but less reassuring in that they were also advanced aircraft. If anything, the basic emphasis has been on improving both all-weather performance and ordnance delivery. The new all-weather aircraft can undertake several roles, with the improved MiG-21 acting both as an air-defense aircraft and also as a ground-attack aircraft; recently the VG MiG-23 has begun to replace the MiG-21 by virtue of its improved ordnance-carrying capability (though only in limited squadron strength at the moment). The transformation of Soviet tactical airpower in the European theater seems to hinge on a slow but steady shift away from preoccupation with air defense and air superiority into providing effective close air support for ground formations (a theme that is currently being hammered home in the Soviet military press). This does not mean, however, that air defense is being neglected, for both passive and active measures are being taken in this area. A major aircraft-shelter program has been carried through, whereas mobile air defense is embodied in the replacement of the older SAMs (SA-2s and SA-4s) with the SA-6 and SA-7 systems, which were employed to some effect in the recent Middle East war. Finally, there are the implications of rapid switches in role, or versatility, to be considered. Soviet tactical air units in the GDR, which might hitherto have been considered almost exclusively a defensive force, can now be converted to an offensive role by utilizing their new fighter-bombers, capable of carrying and delivering tactical nuclear weapons. The stocks of nuclear weapons maintained at the bases of these fighter-bomber groups have been increased of late, and it is to be expected that the tactical strike capabilities of these forces have expanded in corresponding fashion.[11]

The Soviet concept of air operations and the air battle in the European theater is a topic that must shortly be discussed in somewhat greater detail, but the expansion and diversification of Soviet tactical airpower must be reckoned an accomplished fact, not merely in terms of numbers—giving the Soviet forces something more than a 2:1 advantage in numbers (4,300 to 1,890)—but also in capabilities. Nor would it be wise to ignore the growing transport/airlift capacity for the European theater and a helicopter force which, again in addition to numerical increases, has seen the deployment of "gunship" MiL Mi-24 assault-transport helicopters with GSFG.[12] The aircraft of the Soviet Military Air Transport command demonstrated their capability in the Czechoslovak operation and again during the recent Middle East war, though under somewhat different circumstances. Soviet interest in vertical envelopment operations is by no means new, and this growing capability for medium-range lift as well as tactical flexibility affords additional advantage. (It has been suggested, for example, that the Soviet command may be working its way to the "tri-cap" pattern developed by U.S. forces, and there are certainly some signs of such an evolution.) Finally, the considerable force of tactical aircraft—over 5,000 with full mobilization—is augmented by a formidable strike force of bombers that have the necessary range and performance to deliver both conventional and nuclear weapons throughout the theater.

NAVAL FORCES

If the object of Soviet air operations in Europe would be to gain control of the air in the theater, so in general terms and by the same token the mission of Soviet naval forces (though more difficult to discern) would

[11]The SU-19 FENCER A now coming into squadron service is the first Soviet fighter since wartime days designed specifically to engage ground targets; the VG MiG-23 FLOGGER has also a considerable close air support capability, whereas the SU-20 FITTER B is a further addition to this close-support/ground-attack capability even as a relatively simple adaptation of a type in previous continuous production, providing pivoting outer-wing panels and a more powerful engine (the AL-21F-3 turbojet).

[12]*AWST*, 4 March 1974, pp. 14–16, under "Soviets Deploy MiL Mi-24 Gunship."

involve an attempted domination of European coastal waters, by no means so circumscribed a task as the term "coastal" might suggest at first sight. A very general scenario (but one supported by the pattern of Soviet naval maneuvers and exercises) suggests that in the event of general war the Soviet Navy would pull back its surface units to protect key installations, while the large submarine force would form the forward "fighting line," intercepting U.S. supplies to Europe and also operating with surface units to hunt enemy submarine forces. Here the Soviet Navy enjoys an advantage in its capability for assembling multiple-strike task forces combining surface, air, and submarine elements to execute these specific and specialized missions.

The Soviet naval power base in the north is great and growing, with the most powerful of all four Soviet fleets—the Northern—lodged in the Kola Peninsula and possessing a singular strength both in submarines and naval strike/reconnaissance aviation. Its general strength is in the order of 100,000 men, 500 surface vessels, and a formidable submarine force. The obvious feature is, of course, the presence of a major element of the Soviet seaborne strategic deterrent with the Northern Fleet, whose submarines have been hitherto obliged to use the Norwegian Sea as a transit zone in order to reach their stations to cover North American targets. At the same time, the Northern Fleet has pushed out its forward deployment well into the North Atlantic. With some 170 submarines at its disposal, the Northern Fleet must play a vital part in this forward "fighting line." In combination with the Baltic Fleet, the Soviet Northern Fleet could probably deploy five or six surface/air task forces in the Norwegian Sea (all the while assuming uninhibited access from the Baltic and the Barents), with the Baltic Fleet covering the southern flank of its northern neighbor. This is simply to say that in a war situation the Soviet naval command would try—with a form of preemption, possibly—to obtain complete control of the peripheral sea areas covering the Baltic approaches and would build up its protective screen in the sea areas facing these vital egress points—that is, into the North Sea and well into the northern Atlantic. Thus, as with other Soviet forces, the Soviet Navy is being deployed well forward and in an increasingly offensive posture.

On the Kola Peninsula itself the Soviet command maintains a

naval infantry brigade, plus two motorized rifle divisions, with another five in the Leningrad Military District to draw upon.[13] The Kola forces are trained in amphibious warfare and can call on airborne forces as well as considerable air support (300 aircraft) and a well-developed infrastructure of airfields. The Baltic Fleet, while maintaining substantial support, base, and repair facilities, consists of a cruiser and destroyer force, a medium-sized submarine force (fifty to seventy submarines), FPBs (fast patrol boats), and a substantial amphibious capability (embodying two Soviet brigades, a Polish amphibious assault division, and two East German marine battalions). Between them the Northern and Baltic Fleets account for half of the available Soviet strength in cruisers, more than half of the oceangoing escorts and ASW forces, and 70 percent of the present submarine strength. Amphibious capability is well to the fore (and well practiced).[14] Between them, and assuming ease of access, the Northern and Baltic Fleets can probably deploy these five or six surface task forces and will no doubt seek to push forward deployment well into the North Sea and into the Atlantic. Although this action would take place only under full wartime conditions, it is worth remembering that this deployment is taking shape even now and actually places northern areas of the European theater behind the Soviet "defense line"—a psychological point with no mean political impact.

On the southern flank the Soviet Black Sea Fleet provides the Mediterranean *eskadra* (squadron), which is deployed in the eastern sea area. In addition to this naval element there is also an air component, tactical airpower that can be moved (as has been done in exercises) into the Mediterranean area, though lack of bases proves to be a distinct handicap. A certain degree of surveillance of the northern Adriatic area is carried out by the MiG-21s stationed in Hungary, though this is very limited, and it is here that the position of Yugoslavia assumes such singular significance for the Soviet Union. Yugoslavia has

---

[13]See the review of General Synnergren (commander-in-chief, Swedish armed forces), "Military Policy and Armed Forces, Situation and Tendencies in 1975," *Frankfurter Allgemeine Zeitung*, 31 January 1975, on Soviet strength and disposition in the Kola Peninsula.

[14]On increased Soviet activity in the western Baltic, see Drew Middleton, "Denmark Reports Soviet Navy Move," *New York Times*, 16 February 1975.

already played a considerable role in Soviet policies in the Middle East (the sealift via Rijeka and the airlift that brought Soviet squadrons onto Yugoslav airbases), so that naval base facilities, sealift, and overflying facilities all form part of the Soviet "package." The connection between the Middle East and the Soviet Union's southern European theater emplacement is both interesting and possibly unique. Soviet airborne divisions stood by on airfields in Hungary during the recent Middle East war, while the sealift moved equipment drawn from the Soviet interior and from the Warsaw Pact area.

One of the indicators of the investment in the Middle East was the unprecedentedly heavy rail traffic on the East European rail networks. This Middle East/southern flank connection becomes increasingly interesting, for it covers a very wide area indeed. Soviet interest in (if not actual pressure on) Yugoslavia becomes critically important, so that one can see at once why Hungary has been deleted from any area of "force reduction"—for here is the pressure point on Romania, Yugoslavia, and even Austria (and the recent Italo-Yugoslav contretemps over Trieste has been the occasion to affirm public attitudes over foreign intervention and the integrity of sovereign states, not without some flurries in both Italy and Austria). In other words, the integrity of the southern flank can by no means be taken for granted, with Soviet pressure growing slowly but steadily, and with the possibility of Soviet forces passing to the west of the Strait of Otranto.

The recent advent of the DELTA-class submarines, with their new 4,000-mile-range submarine-launched missiles (SLBMs) adds something of a new dimension to Soviet coverage of the NATO land mass. They supply the Soviet command with the capability of targeting the entire NATO land mass without exiting from well-protected home water, assuming, that is, an intention to use these SLBMs in this role. All this is to say simply that to the nuclear-capable land forces must be added a substantial naval component—committed most probably to the domination of European coastal waters—that includes submarine and surface units armed with cruise missiles, medium-range bombers from Soviet naval aviation, and a major missile capability supplied by the latest class of missile-launching submarines.

This bare military catalog—essentially simplified, unidimensional, and consisting of brute figures—furnishes a picture that nonetheless cannot be disputed in its essentials. The bulk of Soviet ground forces and tactical airpower that might be committed against NATO is located in the central region (the GDR, Poland, and Czechoslovakia), with the southern flank absorbing the remainder and the northern flank forces comprising a somewhat lighter ground and air force component, balanced in turn by the heavy concentration of naval power between the Northern and Baltic Fleets. The configuration of these European theater forces inevitably raises the point about the duplication of Soviet capability—those genuinely tailored to the European environment and those that are part of an augmentation of Soviet effort against the United States (a theme that Thomas W. Wolfe has explored in some detail in his monograph on Soviet power in Europe).[15] It is a reasonable assumption (explored in multiple exchanges with Soviet specialists) that no clear delineation has ever been a part of Soviet military-political thinking, much as it is virtually impossible to discern a hard and fast line between force provisions for "internal security" and basic military operational tasks. The burden of this argument is, therefore, that two elements intrude on Soviet military provision for the European theater: (1) a traditionalized investment in the commitment to an "effort" against the United States (even as American commitment in Europe shrinks) and (2) the emergence of an indigenous "theater commitment" that has localized but significant political implications (witness the invasion of Czechoslovakia, where modernized military power took on an almost unexpected utility).

The following discussion concerns the Soviet "theater commitment" and is an attempt to look at the theory and practice of Soviet military investment in Europe, to examine what military provisions or contingencies are being catered for, and, finally, to look at changes in the function of the Warsaw Pact alliance system, if indeed changes have taken place.

PERCEPTION AND FORMULATION OF MILITARY OPERATIONAL REQUIREMENTS

This is almost certainly the heart of the matter—the rationale behind the present (and previous) force structures, deployments, and oper-

[15]Wolfe, *Soviet Power and Europe: 1945–1970.*

ational practice. The burden of this paper is, in general, that military priorities precede all else (and must be included not so much under the rubric of "military influence" but rather within the theory and practice of *holding power*,[16] which is the *raison d'être* of the Soviet regime). This does not mean, however, that such military priorities can be easily defined, as this accounts for much of the complexity of Soviet military politics. The Soviet posture in Europe is demonstrably a product of what has involved a seemingly traditionalized duplication of the main effort directed against the United States—the military encirclement that Khrushchev tried to break once and for all—and also the role of the ground forces as an autonomous element within the Soviet military establishment. The issue of ground forces has given the pronouncements over "doctrine" a certain ambivalence, not to say spuriousness, for this has been special pleading—witness, for example, the debate over the place of substantial general purpose forces in terms of the "long war-short war" controversy. Whichever way that argument came out (in favor of long or of short wars), the argument still presupposed a large ground force. What is interesting of late has been the admission that a future major war situation involving theaters such as Europe could and should mean a "short war"; yet this is not adduced as an argument for reducing the number of ground forces. To this can be added arguments that also affirm the general political utility of the ground forces, an assertion supported by the events of 1968 and also by military demonstrations in the Soviet Far East. Thus the expensive ground forces are the phoenix risen from the Khrushchevian ashes.

Subsuming the second argument, the Soviet position in the European theater has passed through three stages in the past decade: (1) the sole all-nuclear option (the "one-variant war" rejected immediately on the political demise of Khrushchev), (2) an extended phase of nuclear emphasis, yet with an admission of a possible conventional phase in the initial stage of operations, and (3) a definite separation in nuclear and conventional options. To judge even superficially from recent Soviet military theory and actual preparations in the

---

[16]For a fundamental observation on Russian military power and territorial expansion, see Richard Pipes, *Russia Under the Old Regime* (New York: Scribner's, 1975), pp. 118–119.

European theater, the conventional option, extended over a significant period of time, is now admitted as realistic—and here the difficulty is to find out why. Is this a reappraisal of the changed strategic balance, a reevaluation of NATO's dilemma, or some new consideration of the utility of nonnuclear force for the attainment of prescribed, if limited, political objectives? To what degree is this a realization that "flexible response" is not as flexible as it should be and that an acceptable strategy would be to place the "nuclear onus" on NATO itself? This is to say that in several instances we are forced to discuss NATO's shortcomings rather than any predatory instinct and overwhelming advantage harbored by, and nurtured within, the Soviet forces in Europe.

It is a truism that the significance of tactical force in Europe (and elsewhere) has increased in both absolute and relative terms, for strategic forces have begun to checkmate themselves, whereas tactical force, with its strong conventional component, has taken on added significance—usable military force, if you wish. At the same time, it is impossible to dismiss the argument that NATO's failure to furnish Europe with a credible conventional counterforce capability may have provided the Soviet Union with an unprecedented opportunity, though I understand all the precautions that must hedge the argument that the Soviet command may be presently entertaining a "conventional option" in its own right. Nonetheless, what cannot be denied—statistically, geographically, or politically—is that the Soviet command uses military force in demonstrative fashion along the length and breadth of the European periphery (as will shortly be seen in looking at the pattern of Soviet military exercises). Here there is continued movement, substantial augmentation of exercise patterns, and mysterious, even unnerving, comings and goings of large bodies of men and materiel.

Since the mid-1950s the profile of the Soviet theater forces has altered very little, save for improvement and expansion. It was at this time also that Soviet doctrine espoused an unequivocal offensive emphasis. (There is no great case, therefore, for arguing that the recently promoted younger commanders in the Soviet armed forces have a greater predilection for the "offensive." Rather, what these newer commanders are engaged upon is adapting new tactical forms and more modern weapons to a preferred and prescribed offensive frame.)[17] The ground forces have for long concentrated on building up highly mobile forces, with the armored fighting vehicle as its core—the tank, in which the Soviet command continues to place such faith— supported by motor-rifle elements and nuclear (or conventional artillery) fire supply as well as increased provision for chemical warfare. The recent display of Soviet fighting vehicles in the Middle East provided much evidence of extensive preparation for chemical warfare (filters, environmental protection, and so on) and other forms of warfare. Conventional artillery strength has always been an article of faith (including self-propelled guns, howitzers, rocket launchers, field pieces, and heavy mortars), while air defense systems have long been organic in regiment strength at front and army levels. Antitank defense is provided down to battalion level, while engineering capacity (notably improved of late) is designed to provide for high-speed advance and also an extended range of operations. Soviet military writing on the European theater in terms of operational commitment very pertinently suggests that in every 5 to 10 kilometers of advance there will be a small river to be encountered, a medium-width river every 30 or so kilometers, and a major river obstacle every 100 kilometers.

Soviet forces are deployed forward "on a massive scale" (the description is that of Admiral Thomas H. Moorer, Chairman, Joint Chiefs of Staff) and are offensively designed. Now as before, formal doctrine emphasizes the primacy of offensive action. The Soviet conduct of operations in the European theater would assume an offensive cast from the outset, if not actually envisaging preemption. A mass nuclear strike delivered by missiles and aircraft would reach out to targets in great depth, with high-speed armored strike forces moving by day and by night to penetrate with the greatest rapidity into the

[17]Recent reappraisals of the Soviet theater "threat" emphasize the concentration of armor (including the new T-70 battle tank), strong units of self-propelled artillery, mobile surface-to-air missiles, and modern armored infantry combat vehicles such as the BMP with a "tank killing" capability (see *Daily Telegraph*, London, 8 March 1974). General John W. Vogt (USAF), commander of the USAF in Europe, has also emphasized the threat deriving from the improved quality and performance of Soviet tactical aircraft, accompanied by significant advances in radar technology and electronics (see *AWST*, 3 March 1975, pp. 12–13).

enemy rear and deep rear, while air-dropped, airborne, and helicopter-borne forces would also exploit the initial strike and by their special operations (seizing road and river passages) expedite the movement of the assault forces. There would be no initial mass concentration, with offensive action taking place "off the march" and with the "meeting engagement" (or a series of them) assuming great importance, intensity, and complexity—in no sense a preplanned battle, but rather one to be conducted with a series of standard operating procedures designed to hold formations and units together. Here one has to point to the Soviet dilemma of the relationship between the use of initiative, or "creative tactical instinct"—my best translation for that elusive term *tvorchestvo*—and tight discipline rigorously enforced and all under centralized control.

Colonel Sidorenko has fully prescribed these conditions for the modern land battle in his book on offensive operations.[18] The study emphasizes mobility, fire preparation and support, maneuver, logistics, and engineering support. Throughout this book, which is presumably one of the standard texts at the Frunze Military Academy, the emphasis is on nuclear operations, though Colonel Sidorenko does assert that troops will have to undertake a variety of combat actions without the use of nuclear weapons. What is striking at the moment is the manner in which the Soviet command is attending to logistics and engineering to support the panoply of operational requirements stipulated by Colonel Sidorenko. While the U.S. Army cuts its "tail," the Soviet ground forces are increasing theirs, with greater investment in motor-transport forces, not to mention bridging, field pipeline, and military-engineering equipment. A Soviet all-arms army now has a motor-transport brigade (as opposed to a regiment) available to it, whereas each regiment has a battalion (rather than a company) attached for lift and logistics. On the whole, Soviet logistics officers see a rising requirement for POL, which will steadily rise in the percentage of combat supplies required, thus increasing the 430 tons of fuel required to keep a Soviet tank division on the move for twenty-four hours. (In addition, it is worth noting the increase in preparations for chemical

---

[18]A. A. Sidorenko, *Nastuplenie* (Moscow: Voenizdat, 1970).

warfare in Soviet units. As the Middle East war showed, Soviet vehicles are well fitted out with antiradiation and filtering devices, while each regiment has now attached to it a chemical company of 200 men.)

But what, really, does this amount to? That question has been posed by a number of Soviet military specialists, one of the most contentious of whom has been Colonel Savkin. What *is* "maneuver"? This formed the subject of a short sharp exchange in the recent past, when Colonel Savkin argued that "movement" did not constitute "maneuver." Here he took issue with some of his colleagues who had compiled a study entitled *Manevr v obshchevoiskovom boiu.* Colonel Savkin has also returned to the time-honored precept of "art of operations," which few modern Soviet soldiers understand, whatever lip-service they may pay to it. Even more recently, Colonel Savkin listed the main features of the modern land battle, subsuming his arguments under the following headings:

1. The decisiveness of military operations (due to the political aims of any war and the use of weapons of mass destruction during the course of it).

2. A high degree of maneuverability.

3. Rapid and critical changes in the situation.

4. Diversity in the means of conducting military operations (nuclear and nonnuclear weapons, depending on the nature of the tactical situation).

5. Operations conducted on a broad front with the use of airborne forces.

6. The conduct of operations along divergent axes.

7. Disparity in developments at the front and in the rear.

8. An increase in morale—psychological and physical stress under battlefield conditions, thus augmenting the human factor in modern combat.

9. The instant readiness of all subunits, even when operating in conditions of conventional warfare, to switch over to nuclear operations.[19]

[19]Colonel V. E. Savkin, "Cherty sovremennogo boia," *Voennyi Vestnik*, no. 3, (1974), pp. 24–28.

Soviet interest in nonnuclear operations is, of course, a matter of some considerable importance and relevance in the present situation. Some of the clearest evidence in this direction is supplied by the modifications in Soviet airpower in the European theater—the improvement in tactical airpower in the theater certainly concerns ground attack capability particularly for nonnuclear operations. FENCER A is indeed the first Soviet fighter to be developed as a fighter-bomber in the ground attack role, though the MiG-23 has a significant ground-attack capability. The improved SU-20 FITTER B also has improved ground-attack capability. As for Soviet tactical air forces at large, it might be assumed that under conditions of general war Soviet aircraft would be directed against NATO nuclear weapons, HAWK surface-to-air missile sites, tactical airbases, and nuclear installations or depots, and only after these missions had been accomplished would Soviet airpower be turned against NATO ground forces.

The most acceptable assumption is that the Soviet air forces would go for general air superiority in Western Europe,[20] though the intrusion of the missile (SAMs) must nonetheless complicate this picture and induce the possibility of the "switch on/switch off" air battle, in both its offensive and defensive phases. Just how the Soviet command would handle the air battle is far beyond the competence and confines of this paper, but both the SAM and the investment in ECM (electronic countermeasures) must influence the traditional Soviet view of the requirements of air operations—and it is undoubtedly true that the Soviet command is making a much greater investment in all-weather ground-attack capability.

How real is the Soviet interest in what might be called an autonomous conventional option for the European theater? In the mid-1960s the Soviet ground forces departed to a very small degree from the concept of an exclusive nuclear engagement and experimented with a phase of conventional operations, though in neither equipment nor training were Soviet forces fitted for any protracted phase of conventional operations. Up to 1970–1971 the attention of the Soviet

[20]To improve NATO's performance and effectiveness, a newly formed unit—Allied Air Forces Central Europe (AAFCE)—now combines the Second Allied Tactical Air Force (2ATAF) with the Fourth Allied Tactical Air Force (4ATAF). See *AWST*, 3 March 1975, p. 12.

command remained fixed on this gruesome escalation to major nuclear operations, with the conventional phase being very much subordinate, and nuclear operations assuming an inevitable pride of place. To a considerable degree, that still holds, and ironically enough Soviet adherence to "nuclear exclusiveness" is partially due to NATO's failure to implement the force levels for an effective conventional defense, thus falling back on early recourse to nuclear weapons. That first Soviet flight into a conventional option took place when the strategic balance was demonstrably and massively in favor of the United States. Some of these earlier steps to improve performance in conventional operations included strengthening conventional artillery, placing a motor-rifle division within a tank army, increasing mobility for air-defense systems, and expanding logistics arrangements. While retaining all their existing capability for full-scale nuclear operations—and even expanding on it—the Soviet forces in the European theater seem now to have embarked also on a clear-cut "conventional option" that might be conducted for some extended period during the initial phase of hostilities.

This is not to say that the previous emphasis on nuclear operations has been in any way diminished, or the highly mobile armored strike forces displaced. On the contrary, even in this conventional mode, the same norms of high-speed advance have been retained (though the actual rate of advance reduced to some sixty-five to eighty kilometers for a twenty-four-hour period) and the primacy of offensive action remains equally intact, though after some initial defensive posturing. Much of this has been the burden of the observations of Colonel-General Nikitin (Chief of Staff/Ground Forces) on the possible operational commitments of his command. Rather than seek for the precarious dividing line between the nuclear and conventional mode, it may be that the emphasis is increasingly on identifying them as autonomous (though always with the grim reminder of the nuclear weapon in the background). Colonel Savkin is at pains to emphasize that. The process of disentangling these modes is, to say the least, difficult, but two factors seem to have combined to produce some reappraisal: an appreciation of the change in the overall strategic balance and the need to decide on what is "usable" military force (which is demonstrably force well below the strategic-nuclear level). This is a continuing

debate within the Soviet command, but the "conventional option"—
for which serious preparations seem to be currently underway—
supplies an additive to the Soviet military repertoire in Central
Europe. It proved its utility in rather limited circumstances in 1968 in
Czechoslovakia and might well have a useful future life in the affairs
of Yugoslavia, or on the northern flank or even in some carefully
staged but impressive "demonstration" at the very center of Europe's
affairs.

This gives the Soviet command three general capabilities in the
European theater:

1. A deterrence-defense capacity, which is connected with
counterbalancing NATO and is also related to the general war tasks of
the Soviet ground forces.

2. An intermediate nuclear-conventional capability, which is
more nearly a genuine theater commitment.

3. Growing conventional capability, which has implications both
for the states of the Warsaw Pact and also for those of Western
Europe—an intervention force, in short, capable of being employed
for limited political objectives.

What is common to all these three conditions is high minimum force
levels: For deterrence-defense there must always be that measure of
added strength, for "theater tactical operations" the same margin, and
yet again for a conventional backdrop the same clear edge. Equally,
Soviet tactical doctrine reinforces the supplement of strength. As for
NATO, the Soviet military press—while making a series of noises
about NATO's "aggressive designs"—nonetheless presents a careful
technical analysis of its capabilities.[21] (I am speaking here of works
intended for use in military academies and important sectors of the
military administrations.) At the same time, there is a constant drilling
on the nerve of tactical nuclear weapons, in which NATO is presented

---

[21]The latest general textbook on NATO, *Armii stran NATO; Voenno-politicheskii
ocherk*, ed. Lieutenant-General A. M. Shevchenko (Moscow: Voenizdat, 1974),
continues this practice of presenting accurate military data in terms of organization and
"hardware," but this version is distinguished by a strident propaganda tone about the
"aggressive nature" of NATO and the brutalized nature of its troops.

very much in its nuclear guise, with West Germany at its back. Ironically enough, much as the Soviet Union would be glad to see the
withdrawal of American troops and their weapons, this is much less
preferable to the implementation of any European defense community
that might bring West Germany at once into the nuclear armory; that
notion, no doubt, will serve to keep Soviet force levels high on both
military and political pleading. Equally, this vexing question of force
levels is complicated by the fact that no one on the military side (and
even on the political side) seems to have made realistic calculations
about troop levels needed for military tasks as opposed to internal
policing (including Eastern Europe). For example, a cut of some
three-fifths in Soviet strength in GSFG (lopping off about eight divisions) would still leave a force that would meet the military requirement in terms of tactical needs and "confronting" NATO, particularly in view of the strengthening of first-echelon armored
forces—but this assumes that the "policing role" can be and will be
separated out. Quite the opposite process seems to have taken place;
the steady reinforcement since the events of 1968 (and 1970 in Poland)
can furnish additional manpower related to security duties.

     To sum up in the briefest fashion, a substantial edge, or
superiority, in forward deployed and high-readiness combat power on
the ground during the entire initial phase of operations *is* the "requirement." This preponderance thrusts the nuclear onus on NATO in
unpalatable fashion. While the Soviet command is fully prepared for
tactical nuclear warfare, the general distinction between "nuclear" and
"conventional" modes is, in fact, small—conventional operations still
demand the same fit of forces, though the rate of advance has been
slimmed down and the logistics demands have been recognized as
somewhat different. Both forms presuppose a high momentum of
advance, the use of mobile strike forces, operations on divergent axes,
and a "short-war" concept (that is, not necessarily chronologically
defined but set out in terms of winning at the smallest possible cost and
with the assumption that "winning" could comprise the attainment of
specific and limited political objectives). Conventional preponderance
is now assuming a qualitative as well as quantitative cast, in view of
what has been discerned of Soviet equipment deployed and employed
in the Middle East.

This conventional preponderance as such—and superiority at large—does of itself complicate the comparison of force levels for purposes of potential reduction, a point that will be discussed in somewhat greater detail at the end of this paper. Tactical nuclear arsenals are brandished, in a sense, and the implications of the present conventional balance—or imbalance—in Europe are such that Warsaw Pact forces can mass and level armored pressure along the length of NATO's defense line, where NATO's own conventional capability is far from strong. The obvious "deterrence," therefore, is to apply limited nuclear firepower to the armored head of any thrust—this is a midway point between conventional warfare as such and all-out general nuclear collision. It has been estimated that only 300 tactical nuclear weapons (out of the thousands held in the European theater) would be needed for this bludgeoning task against an assault on the central sector, with advanced technology no doubt providing substantial improvements in response time, flexibility of use in the field, and a major reduction in collateral damage. But limited nuclear firepower is, after all, still nuclear, and it is upon this contingency that Soviet eyes remain firmly fixed. Neither side has an interest in lowering the nuclear threshold, but the Soviet response might well be conceived along the lines of thinking that the lower this threshold, the faster one ought to get under or through it, all of which constitutes a circular argument. This is to say that the Soviet military requirement in the NATO area is high for purely technical reasons and that—ironically enough—the European "inferiority complex" (the phrase is that of the then U. S. Defense Secretary Schlesinger) in relation to its own capability is not shared by the Soviet command. It would be a mistake to dismiss such Soviet preoccupation with NATO's capability as mere propaganda or crude political rhetoric and to refuse to transform this into the terms of military requirements as such. After all, that is what Soviet soldiers are for.

MILITARY INVESTMENT IN THE WARSAW PACT

During the period from 1968 to 1974, the capabilities of the non-Soviet elements of the Warsaw Pact have also grown steadily, though these same non-Soviet formations, in general at least, do not quite compare with their Soviet counterparts either in levels of training or equipment. Probably the most reliable and the most efficient of the indigenous forces are the GDR and Polish formations, with the Czechoslovaks, Hungarians, and Romanians coming appreciably lower down the list (though in any event they occupy a much less important part in the general Warsaw Pact order of battle). The modernization of the East European military establishments has nonetheless made steady progress, and general Soviet confidence in them has been displayed by the uninterrupted flow of highly modern war material. For practical purposes and for the foreseeable future, this must be accounted a continuing trend, which obviously contributes to a buildup of the military strength of the Pact as a whole. The net result has been to equip select non-Soviet formations so as to enable them to take their place beside first-line Soviet units and to utilize a portion of the military potential of the East European nations in other than purely defensive tasks. This change in the function of the Pact has clearly not been managed without some considerable dissent, notably on the part of Romania, which has opposed both the centralization, the supra-nationalism inherent in some of the suggested military arrangements, and the move toward a mobile intervention force that might be used within the Pact area or outside it. "Integration" now seems to center on setting up special combat groupings of formations that can be used in conjunction with first-line Soviet divisions. It is an unlikely contingency that all Warsaw Pact forces would be immediately mobilized, but the "predetermined forces" are available for use in large-scale operations. Recent Warsaw Pact exercises have demonstrated this "division-of-labor" concept of mixed Soviet-indigenous Warsaw Pact forces with respect to prescribed combat groupings, mobility, logistics, and specialist units. (One interesting sidelight on these composite groupings is just what the language of command and control might be—German, Russian?)

Taking a more expansive view of total Warsaw Pact capabilities (one which seems neither exaggerated nor unrealistic), this would give a lineup of some 1,035,000 troops with 23,000 tanks (3,000 of which are in Hungary) and a full air strength of 7,400 aircraft (though, again, in the all-important category of fighter-bombers there is still more or less parity between NATO and the Pact). All these forces are structured on the Soviet pattern (with only minor and somewhat idiosyncratic differences), with uniform equipment and training. It appears that the "predetermined forces" are kept well up to war strength and, to judge by comments such as those of General Sejna, are prepared to move in a very short period of time, being able to activate an alert status very speedily. Furthermore, deployment movements would not require any great distance to be covered.

The computations of comparative strength can be made in a variety of ways, all of which will produce differing results. For example, straight comparisons of NATO and Warsaw Pact divisions reveal discrepancies in manpower that apparently favor NATO, yet in the Warsaw Pact division the logistics and support elements are separated out, thus raising the proportion of combat personnel for a Warsaw Pact division and thereby investing it with greater firepower in relation to manpower strength. Nevertheless, the general conclusion must be that the volume of force being committed to the Warsaw Pact is being substantially increased, with an obvious emphasis on high mobility and augmented by firepower (with the former contrasting sharply with the static disposition of NATO forces deployed on West Germany's eastern frontiers).

Here exercises and maneuvers assume a significance somewhat greater than that normally accorded them in Western circles and by Western public opinion. "Deployment by exercise/maneuver" was again demonstrated recently in the Middle East war, when Israeli intelligence failed to discern the operational (and offensive) intention behind "exercises." There are, of course, the conventional types of exercises within the Warsaw Pact area—the military backdrop demonstrates a consistent pattern of practicing "attack off the march" without prior concentration, the assault river crossing, and the provision of close air support under all weather conditions. These are purely tactical in scope and are designed to test and practice procedures and tactical principles. But this hardly disposes of the whole question. The larger-scale "maneuvers" (let us light on that distinction) involve extensive troop movements and heavy military traffic, frequently impinging on politically sensitive areas. During the spring of 1974 the buildup for maneuvers was patently obvious, with heavy military traffic through Czechoslovakia into Hungary and with the exercise area bordering on both Austria and Yugoslavia; in addition, preparations for this exercise included closing *Wehrkreis No. III* (comprising the southern area on a line running from Magdeburg to Frankfurt-on-Oder and therefore enclosing three divisions of the GDR Army). Not unnaturally these movements caused some misgivings in Belgrade, though it is understood that these are, after all, strictly "maneuvers" which had their first stage in Hungary in February 1974. The conversations between Marshal Tito and Hungarian Defense Minister Szilege on 14 March 1974 no doubt touched on the scope and implications of the maneuvers, which appeared to be growing in scale. This interrupted Minister Szilege's planned holiday in Macedonia, but more important matters were afoot.

Naturally the training schedule has to be followed. In February 1974, staffs and signals staffs of Warsaw Pact forces exercised in Romania for two weeks; thereafter the winter exercises in Hungary began, with fairly small-scale troop exercises beginning in Czechoslovakia on 4 March; there was the usual heavy rail traffic and intensified air activity, which also involved the Trans-Carpathian (Soviet) Military District and the air force units stationed in the GDR, which flew south from the Cottbus-Dresden area. Meanwhile Polish and Soviet troops moved out into their training areas, with GDR troops embarking in regimental exercises. Opinions and assessments of the "exercise/maneuver pattern" must inevitably vary; for example, though SHIELD 72 was a formal military exercise, it has been suggested that it was in reality a staff exercise designed to study the possibility of an invasion of Yugoslavia—via Austria—from Czechoslovak bases. The less publicized GDR maneuvers, such as UDAR 72 and 73, may well have involved a basic operational intention of practicing a limited invasion of the *Bundesrepublik*, designed to win specific political concessions; at the same time, even small-scale "exercises" may be used to test the reaction time of potential opponents—bumping up against Romanian defenses, penetrating Austrian airspace, or "inadvertently" blundering into Yugoslav territory. It has to be assumed, therefore, that one object of these military undertakings is to reduce NATO's warning time and at the same time to accustom NATO's military system to "coexisting" with such substantial maneuvers. In any event, it appears less than realistic to suppose that NATO strategy can continue to rely on adequate and substantial warning time (twenty-three days and perhaps more), a period that would be characterized by a developing pattern of rapid movement from the interior to the borders of NATO countries (and other countries as well), the intensification of air activity, greatly increased radio and signals traffic and sudden wireless silence before "the assault," and the switch from training ammunition to the real thing. Also deserving note is the growing number of these exercises and maneuvers. In 1972, there were sixteen exercises in the GDR involving several divisions; in 1973 that number jumped to twenty-four, and it is more than possible that the number of exercises will increase.

All this demonstrates a significant increase in the conventional capabilities of Warsaw Pact forces, the bulk of them kept at a high state of readiness and trained for high-speed, deep-penetration operations. In sum, this is to argue that since the invasion of Czechoslovakia (and also by absorption of the lessons of the 1973 Middle East war), the whole tactical outlook of the Warsaw Pact has been given a face-lift, not to mention the whole steady shift in the basic function of the Pact, which can no longer be regarded simply as a defensive military mechanism. Though it is still open to debate whether non-Soviet forces would be allowed to conduct independent operations on any scale, they are evidently now fully admitted to the offensive operational designs contemplated by the Soviet command.

In sum, whichever way the military statistics are argued, the "military threat" has grown substantially, and, while it is perhaps an exaggeration to describe it in terms of "a vast and offensively orientated superiority," the growing power behind the conventional option, with its backdrop of surprise movement, is a latent but potent threat in every sense of that word—military, political, and psychological.

POLITICAL IMPLICATIONS
OF SOVIET FORCE LEVELS

There is that time-honored military formulation about "intentions and capabilities," which seems more often than not to confuse the issue. In a sense, this has been a brief survey of the "capabilities" aspect, but with overtones of "intentions" ascribed more to political and psychological disposition than to any narrow operational context. It has to be admitted from the outset that high minimum force levels have been and will presumably continue to be a basic feature of the Soviet military position in Europe. At the same time—and here consensus seems to prevail between the military and political leadership—Soviet security is best underpinned by military weight and that military force is not only a necessary instrument of policy but also an effective one.

The buildup in Europe is now an accomplished fact, and, though it might have peaked some time ago, the momentum is only slowly slackening; and there promises also to be another spurt of modernization up to 1976. The conventional reinforcement points almost exclusively to deliberate attempts to pile increased combat power on increased combat power, all in the face of a stabilized, if not actually diminished, NATO "threat." The Soviet attitude during the force reduction talks also underlines a basic intention to retain "equal security" in terms of maintaining this pronounced margin of superiority— that is, an attack posture. Nor does that oft-proclaimed factor, the situation on the Far Eastern frontiers, seem to have acted as a constraint on the Soviet buildup in Europe. The bulk of available Soviet forces in theater terms is still concentrated against Europe, and, though it might be argued that the Soviet posture in the Far East is essentially defensive, that in the European theater is demonstrably not so.

Even allowing for overinsurance, for the inevitable professional inflation of NATO's capabilities, for the need to maintain a high military investment in Eastern Europe—indeed, allowing for almost any conceivable rationale—the expansion of Soviet military capability in Europe seems to defy the strictly rational. As for a means of applying political pressure in general, this case seems to have been overtaken by the fact that the Soviet Union has made considerable progress in its major political program for Europe at the Conference on Security and Cooperation. The need for further coercion thus seems to have passed. The first "threat," then, in this present Soviet position is not so much in their using this military force as in simply *having it*—an overweening military presence, the high visibility of military force, and the persuasion of Eastern Europe that conformity is the only permissible stance. The second "threat" is related to this changed and changing capability of the Warsaw Pact forces, their demonstrable capacity for a rapid turnover to high-speed military operations to attain limited political objectives, with force levels now well past purely defensive requirements. Although Soviet capability does complicate the situation, the NATO strategy of relying on available warning time—23 days of political and military warning—seems now to be gravely at risk, rendered more serious by the cumbersome machinery of the Atlantic Alliance for reacting to crisis situations.

This all comes back to Solzhenitsyn's point that the Soviet leadership may place an undue and obsessive reliance on military force, on its form and function, but then Western Europe has increasingly chosen to ignore the military factor. Between them these two postures have contributed to what can only be counted a growing imbalance. In the final outcome, Europe may well become that "low-risk option" that will suit the Soviet command perfectly.

APPENDIX—SELECTED REFERENCES

General

Antonov, A. "NATO in Conditions of Detente," *International Affairs*, no. 2 (Moscow, 1974), pp. 34–41.

Canby, Steven. *The Alliance and Europe: Part IV Military Doctrine and Technology*, Adelphi Paper no. 109, The International Institute for Strategic Studies, London, Winter 1974–1975.

Erickson, John. "Soviet Military Manpower Policies," *Armed Forces and Society*, vol. 1, no. 1 (November 1974), pp. 29–47.

Force Reductions in Europe. An SIPRI monograph (Stockholm-New York-London, 1974).

Mackintosh, Malcolm. "The Soviet View of East-West Relations," *Journal of the RUSI*, vol. 118 (December 1973), pp. 9–17. "Soviet Foreign Policy Objectives in the Era of Negotiation," U.S. Army Institute for Advanced Russian and East European Studies (Eighth Annual Soviet Affairs Symposium 1973–1974), pp. 24–41.

"Neue sowjetische Panzertypen." *Soldat und Technik*, no. 1 (1975), pp. 10–11.

Vigor, P. H. and C. N. Donnelly. "The Soviet Threat to Europe," *Journal of the RUSI*, vol. 120 (March 1975), pp. 69–75.

Weller, Jac. "Middle East Tank Killers," *Journal of the RUSI*, vol. 119 (December 1974), pp. 28–35.

The USSR and Europe

Efremov, A. E. *Evropa i iadernoe oruzhie* (Moscow, 1972). This monograph is at once a history of, and commentary on, Western policies in relation to nuclear weapons in Europe.

Tomilin, Y. "Problem of Armed Forces Reduction in Europe," *International Affairs*, no. 4 (Moscow, 1973), pp. 37–42.

Ulam, Adam B. "The Destiny of Eastern Europe," and Robert Levgold, "The Problem of European Security," *Problems of Communism* (January-February 1974), pp. 1–12 and pp. 13–33.

Wolfe, Thomas W. *Soviet Power and Europe: 1945–1970* (Baltimore: Johns Hopkins Press, 1970).

Soviet Military Materials

Anureev, Major-General I. (Engineering Technical Services). "ASUV i dinamika boia," *Krasnaia Zvezda,* 5 March 1974.

Armii stran NATO; Voenno-politicheskii ocherk, ed. Lieutenant-General A. M. Shevchenko (Moscow: Voenizdat, 1974).

Belov, Colonel M. "Vertolety v bor'be s tankami," *Voennyi Vestnik,* no. 2 (1974), pp. 124–126. This is a review of "foreign opinion" on helicopter vs. tank and the tank-helicopter combination. "New Factors in the Development of Modern Armies," *Soviet Military Review,* no. 2 (1974), pp. 10–13. This article deals with air mobilization, automation, and radio-electronic warfare and the consequences for ground forces operations.

Biriukov, Major-General G. and Colonel G. Melnikov. *Antitank Warfare* (Moscow: Progress Publishing, 1972). Official translation of *Bor'ba s tankami.*

Cherednichenko, Major-General M. "Voenno-tekhnicheskii progress i taktika," *Voennyi Vestnik,* no. 5 (1972), pp. 12–17.

Konoplia, Colonel P. I. and N. A. Maikov. *Tankovyi batal' on v boiu,* 2nd ed. (Moscow: Voenizdat, 1972).

Larionov, Colonel V. V. "Razriadka napriazhennosti i printsip ravnoi bezopasnosti," *Krasnaia Zvezda,* 18 July 1974.

Liutov, Colonel I. S. and P. T. Sagaidak. *Motostrelkovyi batal' on v takticheskom vozdushnom desante* (Moscow: Voenizdat, 1969).

Loza, D. F. *Marsh i vstrechnyi boi* (Moscow: Voenizdat, 1968).

Lukashin, Colonel-General P. T. Under "Nashi interv'iu," *Znamenosets* (January 1974), p. 34. On career prospects of *praporshchik/michman.*

Nachal'nyi period voiny, ed. Army General S. P. Ivanov (Moscow: Voenizdat, 1974), especially pp. 343–353.

Nikitin, Colonel-General (Tank Troops) M. "Razvivat' iskusstvo vedeniia boia," *Voennyi Vestnik,* no. 10 (1968), pp. 8–13.

Novikov, Y. and F. Sverdlov. *Manoeuvre in Modern Land Warfare* (Moscow: Progress Publishing, 1972). Official translation of *Manevr v obshchevoiskovom boiu.*

Pavlovskii, General I. G. (Commander-in-Chief, Ground Forces). "Iskusstvo upravleniia sovremennym obshchevoiskovym boem," *Krasnaia Zvezda,* 6 March 1970.

Rotmistrov, Marshal P. A. *Vremia i tanki* (Moscow: Voenizdat, 1972), especially Chap. III.

Ryzhkov, Colonel A. "Bez primeneniia iadernogo oruzhiia," *Voennyi Vestnik,* no. 1 (1974), pp. 112–114. On Bundeswehr's view of conventional defense.

Savkin, Colonel V. E. "Cherty sovremennogo boia," *Voennyi Vestnik,* no. 3 (1974), pp. 24–28.

Savkin, Colonel V. E. *Osnovnye printsipy operativnogo iskusstva i taktiki* (Moscow: Voenizdat, 1972). "Manevr v boiu," *Voennyi Vestnik,* no. 4 (1972), pp. 22–27. See also *Voennyi Vestnik*, no. 8 (1972), pp. 30–33, which is a reply to Colonel Savkin. This polemical exchange concerning the significance of "maneuver" is both important and interesting. Colonel Savkin is at pains to point out that "movement" is not ipso facto "maneuver" in the fullest and most effective sense of the term.

Sidorenko, Colonel A. A. *Nastuplenie* (Moscow: Voenizdat, 1970). *Tanki i tankovye voiska*, ed. Marshal A. Kh. Babadzhanian (Moscow: Voenizdat, 1970). Part II deals with combat operations of tank troops.

Vinnikor, Colonel V. "O vstrechnom boe," *Voennyi Vestnik*, no. 1 (1973), pp. 20–26. Includes an editor's note that this article contains somewhat unorthodox views and that comments would be welcome.

Polish Military Materials

Ćwierdziński, Jan. *Taktyka na współczesnym polu walki* (Warsaw: MON, 1970).

Gołąb, Zdzislaw. *Początkowy okres wojny* (Warsaw: MON, 1972).

Gołąb, Zdzislaw and Stanislaw Kolcz. *Współczesne dowodzenie wojskami* (Warsaw: MON, 1974).

Ludowe Wojsko Polskie 1943–1973 (Warsaw: MON, 1974).

Nozko, Kazimierz. *Zagadnienia współczesnej sztuki wojennej* (Warsaw: MON, 1973). This is a significant Polish contribution on strategic ideas and operational forms.

Potencjał obronno-gospodarczy państw Układu Warszawskiego (Warsaw: MON, 1971).

Stankiewicz, Waclaw. *Ekonomika wojenna* (Warsaw: MON, 1971).

Technika wojskowa LWP; XXX lat rozwoju 1943–1973 (Warsaw: MON, 1973).

GDR Military Materials

Gać, Stanislaw. "Die Entwicklung der Polnischen Armee zu einer modernen Koalitionsarmee (1949–1970)," *Militärgeschichte*, no. 6 (GDR, 1972), pp. 651–661.

Höhn, Hans. "Zu den Ansichten über die Führung moderner Gefechtshandlungen der Landstreitkräfte in der NVA 1962–1965," *Militärgeschichte*, no. 1 (GDR, 1972), pp. 24–36.

Höhn, Hans and Ernst Stenzel, "Das sozialistische Militärbündnis als eine Verwirklichung der Lehren der Geschichte," *Militärgeschichte*, no. 1 (GDR, 1975), pp. 32–43.

Czechoslovak Materials

Bibliografie k problémům Evropské bezpečnosti (Praha: Ustav mezinárodniéh vztahu, 1971). Includes a listing of Soviet, Czechoslovak, Polish, and Bulgarian sources.

Part III
THE
ECONOMIC
DIMENSION

Soviet Economic Relations with Western Europe

PHILIP HANSON and MICHAEL KASER

SOVIET TRADE OBJECTIVES

"We plan imports and then export enough to pay for them."[1] This was the definition of foreign-trade policy by a distinguished Polish economist, Oskar Lange, when he had moved from a Chair of Economics at the University of Chicago to membership of the Central Committee of his country's ruling Communist party. A recent study has shown that such a policy of "imports first" planning remains in use in Poland, but may be less applicable today in the USSR to the extent that it has found stable export markets and adjusts its import bill to its earnings rather than vice versa.[2] Although the Soviet approach retains much of Stalin's inverted eighteenth-century mercantilism—exports being a necessary evil on the path to a paradise of autarky—the other Comecon countries whose scarcity of resources precludes self-sufficiency at least try to assess comparative costs at home in relation to those confronting them as export and import prices. The reform of systems of domestic and foreign-trade management has revised—albeit to a limited extent—the internal pricing practice of these nations, into which foreign price ratios have been guardedly admitted through applying coefficients to their arbitrary exchange rates differentiated by degree of convertibility.

[1] Cited by Peter Wiles, *Oxford Economic Papers,* no. 2 (1957), p. 201.
[2] C. W. Lawson, *Soviet Studies,* April 1974, p. 235.

In its simplest form the Soviet practice of foreign-trade planning has been that "an import plan is worked out on the basis of the production plan and an export plan on the basis of the import and production plans."[3] Any analysis of the intentions that Soviet policymakers formulate toward trade with industrialized capitalist countries must be founded on that planning procedure—that is, to define what elements in production plans, whether annual or longer term, require supplementation by imports and then to define the parallel Soviet dependence on exports in order to finance a determinate volume of purchases for convertible currencies. Somewhat different considerations apply to trade with developing countries and socialist states, although the Soviet-West European relationships may be affected by convertible currency earned or required in these other flows. The Soviet Union used to earn convertible currency, which it could spend in developing countries, by an excess of Soviet exports in Western Europe over purchases in those markets, but it now earns convertible currency from payments for its arms sales to the Middle East; even since 1973 it has sold little oil to developing countries.

Decisions on the products that the Soviet Union typically buys from Western Europe are intimately, though not necessarily, based on the use of material balances, that is, tables of availabilities and requirements of products, expressed as physical units, established by (or, centrally, on behalf of) producers with respect to every major user. At the level of aggregation operated by the State Planning Commission of the USSR (Gosplan), producers and users are industrial ministries and "industrial associations" (the *promyshlennye ob"edineniia* established in April 1973). In the simplest terms, these agencies, in allocating outputs to users, demonstrate shortfalls that are considered for inclusion in the import plan if domestic production or consumption cannot be rearranged to satisfy the implicit deficit. The same agencies are then inspected for "exportables," which are mobilized to quantities

[3]T. Liska and A. Marias, *Közgazdasági szemle*, no. 1 (1954), cited in *Economic Survey of Europe in 1954* (Geneva: United Nations, 1955), p. 133. See particularly Andrea Boltho, *Foreign Trade Criteria in Socialist Economies* (New York: Cambridge University Press, 1971), p. 52. The literature in the short time since he wrote is substantial, but we follow a survey of East European foreign-trade management by Harriet Matejka in H. H. Höhmann, M. C. Kaser, and K. C. Thalheim, eds., *The New Economic Systems of Eastern Europe* (London: C. Hurst, 1975).

needed to buy the imports. The Ministry of Foreign Trade participates in this iterative exploration of the economy, but as an intermediary or consultant, not as a principal. Enterprises, under directives from their supervising ministry or association, are allocated imports (for their use, if a productive enterprise; for sale, for example at retail, if a distribution unit) according to the import plan, and others are required to produce for export (rather than for delivery to other enterprises for use or retail sale) according to the export plan. They are protected from the price ratios attached to the purchase or sale abroad by the intervention of the foreign-trade corporation holding the monopoly of the product in question as an agency of the Ministry of Foreign Trade. Although the corporations are skilled and shrewd negotiators in their dealings abroad, their concern at home is primarily the procurement of exports and the disposal of imports rather than a comparison of domestic and foreign prices such as a market-oriented trader evaluates.

Decentralized Pressures to Trade with the West

To emphasize that this priority for import needs persists in Soviet trade is not to ignore the reforms that are now emerging, reforms that tend toward withdrawal of such priority in favor of comparative valuations of home and foreign prices and costs; but the USSR has gone very little of the way toward allowing market opportunities abroad, whether for purchase or for sale, to disrupt the essential pattern of plan formulation at home. Among those changes that could establish pressure groups to attenuate the trading authority of the Planning Committee involved in a process of physical allocation is, first, the establishment by Soviet ministries of their own specialized foreign-trade corporations and by a few Soviet production enterprises of foreign-trade departments. So far, these trade-oriented agents of producers have done little to question the procedures of the Ministry of Foreign Trade, whose own corporations remain few (only about fifty), in contrast to recent deconcentration in most other East European countries. Second, Western businessmen and bankers may now set up representative offices in Moscow and attract orders, or make offers, for trade other than through the Ministry's channels. The legal rights of such offices were significantly extended in July 1973. Third, foreign companies are encouraged to sign technical-cooperation agreements with industrial ministries or with the State Committee for Science and Technology, although the Ministry of Foreign Trade, and beyond it, Gosplan, retains the decisive voice on any transaction. A fourth channel, whereby consumer preferences can be expressed in foreign purchases and sales, as yet operates only with other Comecon partners—that is the allotment of foreign exchange to the Ministry of Retail Trade and the Consumer Cooperatives to buy abroad at their discretion. A fifth channel, one that is becoming ever more significant elsewhere in Eastern Europe, involves foreign manufacturers who arrange industrial cooperation with a specific state-run firm (for example, to supply components against technology or coordinated production with division of markets) and, in still a few instances, investing in the equity capital of that firm. Such export-promotion incentives as have been allowed the Soviet production enterprise mainly induce it to adhere to or overfulfill the Ministry of Trade's plan rather than to seek its own outlets. Even these are minimal: Since 1970 a Soviet firm producing for delivery abroad is granted from 1 to 6 percent of the foreign-exchange proceeds, which it may, however, invest only in export-expanding capacity. Industrial ministries are, by another recent regulation, permitted to have half the foreign-exchange earnings of their licenses at their disposal to buy technology (equipment or know-how) abroad.

It will probably take many years before interest groups such as industrial producers or retail trade organizations are permitted to choose abroad either their clients or their suppliers for current transactions, and still longer before they can allocate their capital expenditure between home and foreign projects. The central planning authorities will try to associate such groups with their own decisions, to make choice more rational, but even this involves changes in pricing policy of which as yet there is little sign. Some scope for admitting a "consumption-oriented approach" to Soviet planning may be perceived in the increasing application of programming and other mathematical techniques, because these permit different variants of production plans to be tested by computer before Gosplan or its agent takes the relevant decision.

Meanwhile, planning in the USSR begins from the production side and brings with it the "imports first" procedure for trade planning. The alternative of "exports first" seems long to have been tried in

China, where export capacity has first been established from production plans and imports tailored to the aggregate foreign exchange shown. In the Chinese case, aid deliveries to other developing countries seem to be the first commitment of the planners in defining exports, whereas for the USSR the aid allocation (to recipients in either the socialist or the capitalist category) is more like an addition to the export program after the import bill has been met.

Soviet Balances of Trade

Under an "imports first" policy, favorable balances of trade are required to furnish development aid, to pay for the net outlays on invisibles (also planned under the primacy of imports), and to constitute a minimum reserve for international liquidity. The "imports first" situation arises therefore in exchanges with trade groups or currency areas mainly for settlements in other groups and areas. The overall balance of trade after such transfers are netted out reflects the traditional deficit on invisible account (which is being whittled down as the Soviet merchant fleet grows) and is therefore positive except in years of exceptionally poor harvest, when foreign borrowing is substantial. Table 1 exhibits the typical pattern in 1971—earnings in Western Europe, purchases in other developed capitalist markets, and a positive balance overall mainly being applied to developing countries. In 1972 (and 1975), the buying of grain on a vast scale shifted the balance into a massive overall deficit, which, because the "aid" commitment to developing countries was almost exactly offset by a deficit tolerated by Eastern Europe, came from deficits with both Western Europe and North America.

In 1973 the USSR returned to a favorable balance of trade overall but continued to run a heavy deficit not only with the United States (which that year became its leading trade partner in the West) but also with major West European states, notably the Federal Republic of Germany. In the case of the latter, some special considerations apply in that substantial deliveries of steel pipe were being made in anticipation of long-term supplies of Soviet natural gas, which in fact began to flow during 1973. Indebtedness to the Federal Republic by the end of 1973, on this and on numerous other accounts, stood as high as DM 3 billion. Soviet turnover with all capitalist countries showed a particularly high

TABLE 1
**BALANCES OF TRADE (UNADJUSTED) OF EAST EURO-
PEAN COUNTRIES, 1971 AND 1972 (IN MILLION U.S. $)[a]**

Country	World	Soviet Union	Other East European countries	Asian planned economies	Western Europe	Overseas developed countries	Developing regions
Bulgaria							
1971	63	88	-10	12	-33	-13	19
1972	55	123	-61	14	-31	-6	16
Czechoslovakia							
1971	171	-35	148	22	-124	-1	161
1972	253	120	101	10	-80	-30	132
German Democratic Republic							
1971	95	43	227	38	-157	-93	37
1972	280	417	265	33	-394	-107	66
Hungary							
1971	-490	-148	-122	26	-192	-86	32
1972	137	94	77	34	0	-49	-19
Poland							
1971	-166	-38	-255	26	7	1	93
1972	-402	225	-338	-2	-285	-68	66
Romania							
1971	-2	82	-48	13	-55	-64	70
1972	-17	121	-59	33	-123	-69	80
Soviet Union							
1971	1,326	—	-18	466	243	-299	934
1972	-686	—	-1,159	384	-170	952	1,211

[a]At current prices and exchange rates.
Source: Economic Bulletin for Europe, vol. 25 (Geneva: United Nations, 1973), Part A, Table 16.

increment in 1973—27 percent in value terms and 16 percent in volume—but, the Federal Republic of Germany apart, the biggest share of the increment was outside Western Europe—that is, with the United States and Japan. In 1974 its surplus, due to the great improvement in its terms of trade, was $2570 million, of which, however, only $140 million was in convertible currency.

Table 2 adjusts East-West European trade for the costs of shipment so that values are those at the frontier. The Soviet Union has in the past earned balances in convertible currency, which it spent on invisibles (including a net outlay on freight and insurance and on purchases outside Europe). It ran down those positive earnings in 1968 (when it began making heavy purchases of consumer goods in Western Europe) into net outflows in 1969 and 1970 but resumed the more normal pattern in 1971. Eastern Europe, on the other hand, is regularly in deficit in trade with Western Europe, financing it by borrowing

TABLE 2
ADJUSTED TRADE BALANCES OF EAST EUROPEAN COUNTRIES WITH WESTERN EUROPE 1967–1971 (IN MILLION U.S. $)[a]

Country	1967[b]	1968	1969	1970	1971
Bulgaria	−145	−109	−81	−81	−78
Czechoslovakia	−3	−47	−16	−105	−151
German Democratic Republic	−44	−10	−161	−220	−178
Hungary	−60	−49	−16	−118	−191
Poland	−60	−51	−77	41	28
Romania	−242	−233	−205	−124	−111
Soviet Union	224	33	−138	−68	318
Total	−330	−466	−692	−675	−362

[a]At current prices and exchange rates.
[b]Excluding trade of the German Democratic Republic with the Federal Republic of Germany.

Sources: Economic Bulletin for Europe, vol. 21 (1969), no. 1, p. 34; vol. 22 (1970), no. 1, p. 33; vol. 24 (1972), no. 1, p. 33. Western Europe's imports are c.i.f. (cost, insurance, and freight) and are adjusted to allow for transport and insurance costs by a reduction of 10 percent to put them on approximately the same f.o.b. (free on board) basis as exports. The signs were then reversed to show an East European favorable balance as positive and an unfavorable balance as negative.

(commercial credits and Eurocurrency loans). The individual country figures indicate certain distinctive national trends. Bulgaria has been reducing its overspending after something of a crisis in the late 1960s when there seemed a danger, which was averted, that it might be unable to service and amortize previous loans; under the 1971–1975 plan it chose to reorientate its trade still more predominantly to Comecon markets (78 percent of both imports and exports in 1972), but it is likely to face further difficulties in the light of Soviet complaints about the quality of Bulgarian exports which Todor Zhivkov, the Party leader, revealed in March 1974. Czechoslovakia was increasing its deficit with Western Europe (after reaching balance on the eve of the abortive 1968 reforms) until 1971 but seems now to be decreasing it. Both the German Democratic Republic (GDR) and Hungary have been running up fairly substantial deficits, but Poland, on the contrary, has moved into modest surplus. Romania, which deliberately directed its trade toward the West in the 1960s, following its dispute with Comecon, like Bulgaria, reached a point of overcommitment at the end of the decade and has been reducing its deficit sharply as it resumes more relations with Comecon members.

These six East European countries made a major contribution to rescuing the USSR from the balance-of-trade consequences of the 1972 harvest. They held constant their purchases from the USSR[4] while continuing to increase their exports as the five-year bilateral agreements required. Of the $1.1 billion deficit that they thereby allowed the USSR to run up (see Table 1), the GDR contributed $0.4 billion, by far the biggest share within Comecon, while even Bulgaria and Rumania made small increases in their surpluses ($0.04 billion each). A step toward multilateralizing payments within Comecon, whereby planned surpluses in bilateral trade would be annually transferable into other Comecon currencies, was agreed by that body's executive in January 1975.

In the future, the Comecon group as a whole will have to finance somewhat more of their surpluses with developing countries in con-

---

[4]Soviet exports to Eastern Europe in 1972 were 3.2 percent above 1971 in value; because Hungarian unit-value imports from the socialist countries rose 2.2 percent that year and doubtless reflected the trend within Comecon, Soviet exports were probably constant in volume.

vertible currency, because both their "in-house" banks have made new provisions for credit to such countries. On 1 January 1974 the International Investment Bank (IIB) opened a fund that, with a first *tranche* paid up of $150 million, will reach $1.2 billion for credit to developing countries, while the International Bank for Economic Cooperation (IBEC) has made special provisions for use by developing countries of its collective currency, the transferable ruble. Comecon members' subscriptions to both institutions involve a modest convertible currency element. (The place of these institutions in relation to other international organizations is discussed on pp. 266–267 below.)

Intended Soviet Dependence

Although the USSR reverted in 1973 and 1974 to a favorable balance generally, the enlargement of its deficit with the Federal Republic of Germany may presage the end of the previous pattern—disturbed by the grain crises of 1972 and 1975—whereby the Soviet Union earned somewhat more in Western Europe than it spent. The excess partly paid for a deficit on invisibles with Western Europe, but also contributed to the deficit in the other regional balances just described. The recent pattern of import expansion implies that major increments will be bought in the United States and Japan and that significant increases are also to be expected from Western Europe. The increased receipts that the USSR is likely to derive from sales of oil, gas, and raw materials and from its armaments sales outside Europe would substantially be spent in Western Europe, chiefly on machinery, equipment, and technology.

As indicated above, the centrally planned demand for imports, especially those embodying a transfer of technology, will probably be the prime motivation for Soviet trade with the developed industrial countries. Although the strong Soviet penchant for a broad self-sufficiency (or Comecon self-sufficiency) in strategically important areas of production (including a 20 percent rise in grain production in 1976–1980 over 1971–1975 [which was a mere 8 percent above 1966–1970]) has been little modified, Soviet policymakers do seem to foresee a prolonged, and perhaps indefinite, period of increased Soviet involvement in the international transfer of technology. It must seem to them dangerous to remain on the sidelines.

Soviet "economic dependence" on Western Europe can scarcely be said to have been large. Nor has the desire to avoid such dependence been stilled. At the same time, however, there is a conflicting desire for negotiable technology transfer from the West. This does not seem to be a need that is felt in all or perhaps even most Soviet production activities, but it is nonetheless significant for Soviet foreign policy. It is hardly likely to disappear under any circumstances. It would be much reduced only if the Soviet domestic innovation process became much more dynamic and effective over a wider range of products and processes than it is at present, or conceivably, but not very plausibly, only if the effective acquisition and assimilation of an increased flow of Western technology were found to require an alteration of Soviet social management and control that was politically unacceptable.

Until its failure at the end of 1974 to secure MFN treatment in the United States, the latter seemed the increasing focus of Soviet interest in technology transfer in addition to Japan and Canada and away from Western Europe. But as long as the Western world retains a fair degree of political and economic cohesion, it is not obvious that this shift should greatly alter the influence of economic considerations on Soviet policy toward Western Europe. The relative independence and self-sufficiency of the Soviet economy in a strategic sense give it considerable freedom from economic constraints on foreign policy in the short run. The strong interest in technology transfer, however, seems likely to exert a persistent pressure for good commercial and political relations with Western Europe over a long period.

IMPORTANCE OF WEST EUROPEAN MACHINERY, EQUIPMENT, AND KNOW-HOW TO THE SOVIET ECONOMY

Aggregate Flows

As Table 3 demonstrates, throughout the entire post-Stalin period Western Europe has been the main, indeed the predominant, source of Western machinery supplies to the USSR. In the late 1950s, Western Europe was almost the sole source of such supplies. Even in 1972, after a substantial increase in Soviet-Japanese trade, and with the beginning of Soviet-U.S. détente and increased Soviet-American

TABLE 3
EXPORTS OF "WESTERN" MACHINERY TO THE USSR, 1955–1972

	1955	1960	1964	1965	1970	1971	1972
			Percent share of total exports				
Western Europe	99.7	92.5	75.2	82.2	83.7	78.1	76.1
North America	—[a]	1.5	1.2	3.2	4.9	8.0	6.3
United States	—[a]	1.5	1.0	1.4	4.9	7.5	5.6
Japan	0.3	6.0	23.6	14.6	11.4	13.9	17.6

[a]Less than 0.05 percent.

Sources: U.S. Department of Commerce, *Trade Between Free World and Communist Countries, Country-by-Commodity Series,* 1955; Office of Economic Cooperation and Development (OECD), *Trade by Commodities,* Series C, for other years.

trade, Western Europe (excluding Finland) accounted for more than three-quarters of Soviet imports of Western machinery. The West European share in this trade seems likely to decline in the face of further sharp increases in Soviet-U.S. trade but will almost certainly continue to be substantial in the foreseeable future. At the same time, the flow of machinery trade in the reverse direction—exports from the Soviet Union to Western Europe—remains pitifully small. In trade in machinery and transport equipment with what is now the enlarged European Community of the Nine, in 1972, for example, the Soviet trade returns showed the following (in million U.S. dollars, converted at the rate of $1.2135 to 1 ruble):

Soviet Exports	Soviet Imports (f.o.b.)	Balance
56.7	829.8	−773.1

The importance of Western Europe to the USSR, therefore, as a source of machinery, and equipment, and, more broadly, of advanced technology is a factor in Soviet-West European relations that deserves assessment. It is a commonplace of recent Western comment that the Soviet economy's growth rate has become critically dependent on imports of Western advanced machinery and know-how. The frequency with which something is said, however, is no sound guarantee of its truth. The question of recent and prospective Soviet "dependence" on technology transfer from the West deserves more careful consideration than it has on the whole received. The aim of this section of the paper is to assess past Soviet policies relating to the import of machinery and know-how from the West and particularly from Western Europe, from the mid-1950s through 1972, and to reach some conclusions, however conditional, on the importance of this import trade to the Soviet domestic economy; such an assessment should help provide an understanding of one—possibly major—influence on general Soviet policy toward Western Europe.

The discussion will be concerned mainly with technology transfer, because this seems to be of chief importance to the Soviet Union in its machinery trade with the West. The West has not hitherto been a large source of borrowing to finance the Soviet investment program. Nor has it provided, in aggregate terms, a major relief of pressure on investment-goods production capacity in the USSR (see the discussion in the notes to Table 6, pp. 236–238, below). The improvement of the Soviet terms of trade is likely to reduce Soviet demand for commercial credit still further, once the extraordinary grain purchases of 1975–1976 have been paid for, and the rates of interest now prevailing may eliminate it altogether.

Soviet Interest in Technology Transfer

The term "technology transfer" is a recently fashionable one in the West. The whole constellation of ideas and observations that have given it currency seem equally fashionable in the Soviet Union and in the Comecon group as a whole. Soviet writers and officials speak of the "scientific-technical revolution" as a matter of fundamental current economic and social importance, and they seem to have been putting increasing stress on it since the early 1960s. In the speeches of both Brezhnev and Kosygin at the XXIVth Party Congress in 1971, the view was clearly enunciated that more rapid technical progress was to be a central aim of the Ninth Five-Year Plan.

At the same Party Congress, attention was given to the need to acquire know-how from abroad. Subsequent speeches by the Soviet leadership and writings by Soviet officials, journalists, and academics have produced a swelling chorus in which the need to obtain more rapid technical change in the domestic economy, on the one hand, and the need for greater Soviet participation in the international diffusion of new scientific and technical advances, on the other hand, have both been recurring themes.

Mass publicity of this kind in the Soviet Union usually accompanies changes of policy. This one has been no exception. Thus, in a Soviet book on foreign trade in licenses, published in 1972, we find the following:

Beginning in 1970, the acquisition and use of [foreign] licenses has been conducted in accordance with special five-year and annual plans which are an integral part of the state plan for the development of the national economy of the USSR.[5]

[5]M. L. Gorodisskii, *Litsenzii vo vneshnei torgovle SSSR* (Moscow, 1972), p. 183.

The determination to implement this policy seems to have been a very real one. A *Pravda* lead story of 12 March 1974 berates Soviet domestic producers and research institutes for not making a greater effort to patent their own innovations and thus facilitate the sale of Soviet licenses abroad, to contribute to Soviet purchases of foreign licenses. It is specifically stated that the purchase of foreign know-how is of great importance to the Soviet economy and that Soviet partici-pation in world trade in patents, licenses, and know-how must be expected to increase. Some indication is given of the use so far made by the Soviet Union of licenses purchased abroad. Forty new processes and eighty new types of machinery and materials are said to have been introduced into the Soviet economy on the basis of license transactions between 1965 and the end of 1973. These figures appear to refer mainly, if not exclusively, to transactions with the West, and a large proportion would be transactions with Western Europe. More will be said below about the composition of this trade.

The priorities of the Ninth Five-Year Plan and the concurrent improvement in U.S.-Soviet relations have given particular promi-nence to the notion of technology transfer from the West to the USSR. The underlying change in Soviet official views and policies can, however, be traced back further and is by no means exclusively de-termined by the state of relations between the two superpowers. It is symbolized by the Soviet ratification in 1965 of the Paris Convention for the Protection of Industrial Property and more concretely demon-strated by the rapid growth of machinery imports from Western Europe in most of the post-Stalin period.

Before discussing this trade it is important to say briefly what is meant by international technology transfer (hereafter, simply "technology transfer"). For the purposes of this paper it is taken to mean any process by which innovations (new products and processes introduced into production for the first time anywhere) in one country are subsequently introduced into production in another country, not by a totally independent sequence of research, development, design, testing, and evaluation, but with some resort to the experience of the innovator in the originating country.

The ways in which the experience of the innovator may be used are varied. There might be some learning mainly from the applied research stage of the original innovation process; there might be some knowledge of the basic idea and some design features (as in the prison scientists' work on the telephone scrambler device in Solzhenitsyn's *First Circle*); or, by contrast, the use made of the innovator's experience might consist quite simply of the outright purchase of, say, a new machine.

A transfer of technology from one country to another, therefore, does not necessarily mean that the recipient country can subsequently reproduce the new product or process without further recourse to the original innovator. It may acquire the ability to do so, or it may acquire only the new machinery, say, and the ability to use it, with corresponding productivity gains, without the ability independently to replicate that machinery. One could perhaps speak of technology assimilation in the first case and technology acquisition in the second. Assimilation will often require a transfer of technology into the machine-building sector.

In neither case does technology transfer necessarily entail the achievement by the recipient country of a capacity to "catch up and overtake" in the area of technology in question. Its usefulness to the recipient country consists in the saving of resources (conventionally measured in development lead-times) that technology transfer offers compared to an independent reduplication of the entire research and development process of the original innovator. But it does not ensure that the recipient country develops the research and development experience and skills needed to move on to the "next stage" as quickly as the innovating firm or organization.

It seems important to distinguish, therefore, between technology transfer and the process (whatever it may be) whereby the "lead" in a particular area of technology may pass from one country to another. Sakharov's well-known metaphor for Soviet technological borrowing from the West—of the skier following in the tracks of another, trail-breaking skier—is apt. The skis (and perhaps the mental attitudes) of the follower may be suited to following but unsuited to breaking trail.

We do not live in a world in which information moves instantaneously and at no cost. Technology transfer typically takes time and requires resources. In a world of technical change and imperfect information, in other words, different national economies do not at any point in time operate with the same "given state of technology."

The position so far as basic scientific research results are concerned may be rather different, at any rate as between countries that have invested in some minimum basic across-the-board research effort. Basic research is by standard definition nonpatentable: It is usually quickly published, and the same major topics are usually being investigated simultaneously in many different national research establishments. Results reached first in one country can therefore quickly and perhaps at very low incremental cost be understood in other countries.

Specific applications, however—industrial processes, designs, prototypes, and so forth—can be patented or kept secret, and commonly are. There may also be elements of practical know-how acquired by individual technologists, technicians, and skilled workers in the development of a new product or process that cannot be readily transferred by documentary means but have to be learned directly from those who have them, in the setting of laboratory, pilot plant, or full-scale production, if they are not to be more slowly acquired in a substantially independent reduplication of the whole innovation process.[6]

The channels by which technology is transferred between countries may, however, vary considerably in the extent to which they depend on commercial transactions and require an atmosphere of political and commercial goodwill between the nations concerned. Some channels, which we may term "nonnegotiable," would seem to be almost as usable in an era of cold war and arm's-length dealing as in an era of relative relaxation and trust; the monitoring of technical journals, the one-time purchase of individual products that are then copied, and at least some industrial espionage would seem to come into this category. Other channels seem to depend more strongly on the state of international political and commercial relations and are hence "negotiable": From the purchase of licenses and know-how through the

[6]The importance of purely pragmatic or "empirical" innovation was probably much greater in the nineteenth century than it is now. Bernal has stressed this characteristic of technical change, particularly in an earlier period of history. He points out that the geographical spread of the industrial revolution was extremely slow; by the end of the nineteenth century the only centers rivaling those of the United Kingdom were those based on the Ruhr and in the Pennsylvania coalfields. J. D. Bernal, *Science and Industry in the Nineteenth Century* (Bloomington: Indiana University Press, 1970), p. 19.

large-scale purchase of machinery, including turnkey projects, and extending to continuing interenterprise cooperation agreements.

Negotiable technology transfer is greatly facilitated by medium- or long-term credits to the recipient country, by Most Favored Nation treatment of its exports, by the absence of an extensive strategic embargo, and, in general, by an atmosphere of some minimum political and commercial trust. A possible rationalization of the increased Soviet interest in machinery and technology trade with the West since the 1950s might be that technological change over the last fifteen or twenty years has tended to be such that the area has greatly increased in which negotiable technology transfer has become more cost-effective than nonnegotiable technology transfer. At all events, negotiable technology transfer would seem to be the form of technology transfer that is of operational political and commercial significance in international relations, and subsequent discussion will be confined to it.

Nothing in what follows is meant to suggest that technology transfer between Western Europe and the USSR has been, or must inevitably be, a one-way process, though the evidence is that the flow has been mainly from West to East. Nor is it suggested that the USSR has been, or will remain, necessarily more dependent on the import of foreign technology than any developed Western country. Overall technology transfer and its effects are at present beyond measurement. In any case, we live in a world of extensive technological interdependence. Even the United States, which is almost certainly the world leader in technology in a general sense, is on the receiving end of technology transfer in some areas and would lose some potential productivity gains on this account if it were isolated from the rest of the world. Recent Soviet policies have been designed precisely to reduce such isolation, and its costs, for the Soviet economy.

Soviet Machinery Imports from Western Europe

It follows from what has been said that machinery trade is an imperfect guide to technology transfer. The absence of substantial Soviet imports from the West of a particular kind of machine could mean that the Russians have no technology lag in that particular area. It could also mean a number of other things, however. It could mean that:

1. Western export controls prevent such machines being sold.

2. Soviet policy is to catch up by indigenous research and development.

3. Other channels of technology transfer are considered adequate.

4. There may be an indirect import of such technology via Eastern Europe.

5. A Soviet lag in this area is simply being accepted.

On the other hand, the presence in the trade statistics of substantial Soviet imports of machinery from the West is taken here to be a sign, usually, of technological borrowing. So, too, is know-how buying (to be dealt with below, pp. 248–251), but it is worth mentioning here that license and know-how trade is commonly linked with machinery purchases and is relatively small in value terms. In intra-OECD trade in 1963–1964 it was equivalent to about 3.5 percent of machinery trade.[7]

It seems reasonable to interpret all or most Soviet hard-currency machinery purchases as motivated by a desire to acquire or assimilate the technology that is embodied in them and that is not otherwise obtainable except with some delay. The following description of his work by Deputy Minister of Foreign Trade N. Smeliakov indicates the persistence of the traditional import-of-otherwise-unobtainable-items approach: "[my work] has been connected with the export of our goods and the acquisition by import of the necessary machines, equipment and so on."[8]

Mcre direct evidence on this point is provided by the product-group composition of Soviet machinery imports from the West. This indicates a highly selective purchasing policy, with a relatively high concentration on particular types of machinery, compared to the pattern of machinery imports (from all sources) of another large and relatively self-sufficient, but market-type, economy—that of the

[7]Derived from OECD, *Gaps in Technology, Comparisons between Member Countries* (Paris, 1970).

[8]N. Smeliakov, "Delovye vstrechi," *Novy mir*, no. 12 (1973), p. 203.

TABLE 4

PRODUCT-GROUP CONCENTRATION IN U.S. IMPORTS OF MACHINERY (SITC 7) FROM THE REST OF THE WORLD AND SOVIET IMPORTS OF MACHINERY (SITC 7) FROM "WESTERN" COUNTRIES, 1961 AND 1970

Shares of 4-digit groups within Section 7 (in percent)

	1961			1970		
	United States			United States		
	Including cars	Excluding cars[a]	USSR	Including cars	Excluding cars[a]	USSR
Largest 3	26.3	8.1	34.0	48.8	26.3	43.5
Largest 5	30.6	12.4	44.8	55.0	35.1	50.0
Largest 10	37.8	19.6	58.8	66.5	50.9	61.5

[a]Percentage of imports of SITC 7, *less* imports of cars (SITC 7321).

Source: OECD, *Trade by Commodities,* Series C, 1961 and 1970.

United States. If we take Section 7 of the Standard International Trade Classification (SITC), covering machinery and transport equipment, and look at its composition by 4-digit groups for both total U.S. machinery imports and Soviet imports of machinery from the West (derived from OECD, that is, from Western trade-partner export data, and with "West" signifying the United States, Canada, the European Economic Community [EEC], the European Free Trade Area [EF-TA], and Japan), we find markedly higher concentration ratios for Soviet than for U.S. imports in both 1961 and 1970—though in the latter year only if the very large U.S. imports of passenger cars are taken out (see Table 4).

This difference, together with the enumeration of the largest 4-digit groups in each country's machinery imports (Table 5), is consistent with the view expressed above of Soviet decision making. If the USSR systematically imported from the West whatever machinery was relatively cheap, regardless of whether or not Soviet industry could produce an equivalent machine, this would probably result in a less

TABLE 5
IDENTITIES OF LARGEST 4-DIGIT GROUPS IN U.S. AND SOVIET MACHINERY IMPORTS, 1961 AND 1970 (RANKED IN DESCENDING ORDER OF SIZE)

Rank	1961		1970	
	United States	USSR	United States	USSR
1	Passenger cars	Heating and cooling equipment	Passenger cars	Metal-working machine tools
2	Aircraft	Food-processing machinery	Motor car parts	Nonmilitary ships
3	Sewing machines	Textile machinery	Internal combustion parts	Heating and cooling equipment
4	Textile machinery	Metal-working machine tools	Radio receivers	Electrical measuring and control equipment

5	Agricultural tractors	Pumps and centrifuges	Motorcycles	Insulated wire and cable
6	Typewriters	Insulated wire and cable	Trucks	Agricultural tractors
7	Bicycles	Paper mill, etc., machinery	TV sets	Paper mill, etc., machinery
8	Electric power machinery	Mechanical handling equipment	Other tele-communications equipment	Pumps and centrifuges
9	Metal-working machine tools	Apparatus for electric circuits	Textile machinery	Other metal-working machinery
10	Printing and bookbinding machinery	Mineral-crushing equipment	Aircraft parts	Telecommunications equipment not elsewhere specified

Source: OECD, *Trade by Commodities*, Series C, 1961 and 1970.

"concentrated" pattern,[9] whereas if it bought lines which it had difficulty in producing (for example, chemical equipment), the pattern would be more "concentrated."

In other words, Soviet imports of Western machinery probably have, on the whole, a rather different significance for the Soviet domestic economy than do the imports of machinery by a Western country from other Western countries. In the Soviet case such imports are likely to be more exclusively related to the acquisition or assimilation of foreign technology.

At the same time, it is very important to be clear that Soviet imports of Western (mainly West European) machinery since the mid-1950s have been extremely small in relation to the Soviet domestic economy. Table 6 brings together Western data on Soviet machinery imports from North America, Western Europe, and Japan, on the one hand, and data on Soviet domestic investment in machinery and equipment, on the other. It shows, first of all (columns A and D), that Soviet imports of Western machinery in current prices have grown very rapidly. The growth of such imports from Western Europe alone has been somewhat slower—almost sevenfold between 1955 and 1972, as opposed to almost eightfold for machinery imports from the West in total.[10]

This growth has been constrained, of course, by the availability of hard currency. Variations in credit outstanding to the USSR, in Soviet gold sales, and in the Soviet hard-currency current invisible balance allow some flexibility in the relationship between export earnings and imports, but Column C shows that expenditure on Western machinery

[9]For comments on the large share of machine tools in Soviet imports of Western machinery in 1970, see p. 240 below. The observations made here about concentrations in these imports are consistent with, though not necessarily reinforced by, C. H. McMillan's finding that there is a relatively low level of intraindustry specialization in Soviet foreign trade in manufactures in general. His analysis is at a slightly more aggregative (SITC 3-digit) level, and he is concerned with both imports and exports, and the extent to which there are two-way flows in the 3-digit groupings. C. H. McMillan, "Soviet Specialization and Trade in Manufactures," *Soviet Studies*, April 1973, pp. 522–533.

[10]The countries that might be thought to be "developed Western economies" but that are excluded here are Finland, Australia, New Zealand, and Spain. The only one of these that has made more than negligible machinery sales to the USSR is Finland, whose machinery exports are commented on below.

has, between 1960 and 1972 at least, tended to account for something fairly close to two-fifths of the proceeds of previous-year export sales to the West less previous-year purchases of Western grain.[11] The importance of grain purchases as a prior demand on hard-currency resources is shown in Column B. The heavy grain purchases, as a result of poor harvests, in 1963–1966 stopped, and indeed reversed, for a time the growth of Soviet imports of Western machinery. This pattern is echoed, somewhat mutedly, in 1970–1971, but it was not repeated in 1972 and 1973, when both grain and machinery imports from the West rose sharply, apparently supported by a large increase in borrowing from the West and by substantial gold sales at historically high gold price levels.

For Western Europe, which has not been a major source of grain for the USSR, machinery has constituted a larger proportion of total exports to the USSR in most years than has been the case for the West as a whole. In 1972, on the basis of the Soviet trade returns, the share of machinery in Soviet imports from the nine present members of the EEC was 44.4 percent.

Column E of Table 6 shows that Soviet domestic equipment investment grew more steadily but also on the whole more slowly than Soviet imports of Western machinery, if the latter are considered in current prices. The Soviet "constant-price" equipment investment data probably include an element of concealed inflation in machinery prices. Nonetheless it seemed worthwhile to try to allow for the element of inflation in the prices of imported Western machinery (for details, see the notes to Table 6). When this is done the result is striking. Imports of Western machinery in "real" terms did not clearly and substantially outpace the growth of Soviet domestic equipment investment between 1956 and 1971, though their trend rate of growth was slightly higher. It seems that, in the entire period between Khrushchev's initial ascendency and the beginning of the U.S.-Soviet détente, the relative importance of imported Western machinery to

[11]The logic of this lag, at any rate for grain sales, is that in any given year grain imports are likely to be decided upon, negotiated for, and actually shipped within a short span of time, whereas machinery negotiated for in that year is more likely to enter the country (and trade statistics) in the following year. If so, machinery imports in year 2 are influenced by grain imports in year 1.

TABLE 6
USSR: IMPORTS OF MACHINERY AND TRANSPORT EQUIPMENT FROM THE DEVELOPED WEST (UNITED STATES, CANADA, EEC, EFTA, AND JAPAN), 1955–1973

Year	Imports of machinery, etc. (million U.S. $, f.o.b. current prices)[a] (Column A)	Column A as a percent of all imports (f.o.b.) from the "West"[b] (Column B)	Column A as a percent of Soviet previous-year exports to the West, less grain imports[c] (Column C)	Column A as index 1956 = 100 (Column D)	Soviet domestic equipment investment in 1969 prices—index 1956 = 100[d] (Column E)	Imports of Western machinery as a percent of Soviet domestic equipment investment following year[e] (Column F)
1955	104.4	38.0	—	75	—	1.0
1956	138.9	30.3	25.0	100	100	1.2
1957	128.3	27.0	21.9	92	108	0.9
1958	123.2	24.0	17.4	89	124	0.8
1959	177.2	33.8	26.0	128	134	1.1
1960	310.1	38.3	35.3	222	145	1.7
1961	389.5	43.2	38.4	280	163	1.8
1962	436.4	41.8	41.0	314	184	1.8
1963	401.9	37.2	35.4	289	204	1.4
1964	488.5	35.8	44.8	352	231	1.6
1965	366.0	33.4	44.2	264	246	1.1
1966	394.9	31.2	35.5	284	261	1.1
1967	456.7	33.7	35.5	329	280	1.2
1968	638.5	38.3	35.5	460	303	1.6
1969	888.5	39.0	44.7	640	317	1.9

1970	904.1	35.0	40.2	651	356	1.7
1971	840.0	32.5	37.2	605	375	1.4
1972	1,113.0	30.0	43.8	801	406	1.6
1973	1,566.0	27.1	75.7	1,131	420	—

[a]Imports from Finland are excluded both before and after its association with EFTA and inclusion (1969) in OECD trade statistics for EFTA. This was done because (1) Finland was excluded from OECD reporting-country data for most of the period and (2) it is not a hard-currency trade partner of the USSR. So far as can be determined, Finland is the only Western country excluded here whose machinery exports to the USSR were not negligible. The data are Western trade-partner data throughout, except that the 1960 through 1963 figures for machinery imports from Japan were obtained from Soviet trade returns. *Sources:* U.S. Dept. of Commerce, *Trade between Free World and Communist Countries, Country-by-Commodity Series* (annual), for 1955 through 1959; OECD, *Trade by Commodities,* Series C (annual), for 1960 through 1971; *Vneshniaia torgovlia SSSR za 1961g and 1963* (see above).

[b]Using a compilation of Western countries' total exports to USSR; these were for the same countries as in Column A except that Iceland's total exports are included throughout, and total exports of Finland were included for 1970 and 1971. The percentage figures for 1970-1973 are therefore not exactly comparable to those for earlier years. *Sources:* Same as for Column A, plus MITI (Japan), *Foreign Trade of Japan, 1964,* and OECD, *Overall Trade by Countries,* Series A.

[c]Using Soviet, not Western trade-partner, data for (1) total Soviet exports to all "industrially developed capitalist countries," (2) apparent grain imports from the same countries, derived as total reported grain exports less reported grain exports from soft-currency sources (Yugoslavia, Romania, Mongolia). The percentages are values for $Mk_t/(X_{t-1} - MG_{t-1})$ where MK is the Column A series and X and MG are Soviet exports to, and grain imports from, the West as defined above. Conversion to dollars is at official rates.

Regression equations for Soviet machinery imports from the West, 1955 through 1971 (annual data, current U.S. $ values)

symbols MK = machinery imports from the West (Column A, above)

X = Soviet exports to the "industrially developed capitalist countries" (Soviet trade returns)

MG = Soviet grain imports from the West (see note to Column C, above)

These are linear, least-squares estimates obtained with the use of a multiple regression program that gives final values after adjustment for first order autoregression. Bracketed figures under the coefficients are *t* statistics.

(Table notes continued on page 238)

TABLE 6 (Continued)

	R^2
(1) $MK_t = -49.839 + 0.336\,X_t$ $\qquad\qquad\ (0.444)\quad (5.185)$	0.863
(2) $MK_t = -52.050 + 0.348\,X_t - 0.108\,MG_t$ $\qquad\qquad\ (0.488)\quad (5.610)\quad (0.527)$	0.875
(3) $MK_t = -72.42 + 0.386\,X_t - 0.394\,MG_{t-1}$ $\qquad\qquad\ (0.934)\quad (8.086)\quad (2.502)$	0.916

In equation (3) the coefficients estimated for X_t and MG_{t-1} are both significant at the 1 percent level. *Sources: For X and MG: Vneshniaia torgovlia SSSR, statisticheskii sbornik 1918–1966* (Moscow, 1967), and annual *VT SSSR* for subsequent years.

[a] Derived from Soviet official "constant-price" equipment investment data; 1956–1960 data, originally given in 1955 prices, were converted to 1969 prices by chain-linking at 1961. *Sources: Narkhoz 1961*, pp. 538, 539; *Narkhoz 1922–1972*, p. 322.

[c] These are minimum estimates of the share of imported Western machinery, based on Boretskii's estimated ruble-dollar conversion rates for all engineering products, which do not allow for relative quality defects in Soviet machinery. Percentage figures twice as high as those given would be at least equally plausible. Broadly, the procedure used here is to take Boretskii's geometric mean purchasing power parity (ppp) for U.S. 1964 engineering-products prices in terms of Soviet 1955 prices, and adjust for (1) differences between Soviet 1955 and 1969 prices, (2) differences between U.S., West European, and Japanese machinery prices in 1964 (giving an "OECD" machinery ppp of $1.74 (1964) = 1 ruble (1969 estimate prices). This conversion rate to Soviet 1969 prices is adjusted, for years other than 1964, by applying to it a price index for OECD machinery exports to the USSR derived from West European wholesale price indices. A price index for Western machinery suppliers to the USSR was calculated from (1) wholesale machinery price indices for major European countries, 1955–1964, (2) wholesale machinery price indices for "manufactures" for all the fourteen countries considered here, 1964–1970 (in the absence of machinery price indices for this period). National price indices are aggregated into an overall index of machinery prices to the USSR using shares in Western machinery sales to the USSR as weights, as follows: for 1955 through 1959—shares in 1955–1956; for 1960 through 1964, average shares, 1960–1963; for 1965 through 1970 (where the index covered all suppliers but was based on a broad "manufactured" good wholesale price index for each country)—shares in 1964–1965. Individual national wholesale price indices were also adjusted to take account of parity changes with the U.S. dollar.

the Soviet investment effort did not, in any apparent and aggregate sense, greatly increase.

More important, perhaps, is the fact that the overall magnitude of such imports, at any time in the period under review, was extremely small in relation to Soviet domestic equipment investment (Column F of Table 6). The figures in Column F are almost certainly, it is true, somewhat too low, because the ruble-dollar conversion rate used to link dollar-value imports and domestic ruble-value investment data (at 1964) is derived from conventional Western comparisons of Soviet and Western machinery prices, which largely neglect differences in the reliability, maintenance cost, and service life of otherwise equivalent Soviet and Western machines. Western engineering assessments of Soviet machinery suggest that inferiority in these respects in Soviet machinery may be substantial and widespread.[12] A "true" ruble-dollar purchasing power parity for machinery in any year should be more favorable to the dollar than is implied here. Consequently, the real value of imports of Western machinery, relative to Soviet domestic equipment, should be higher than is suggested here. But even if figures twice as high were close to the truth, the aggregate, quantitative importance of such imports would still be small—not more than 4 percent of domestic equipment investment. A maximum estimate of the importance of machinery imports from Western Europe, in particular, would therefore be that they might in 1970, say, have constituted some 3 percent of total Soviet machinery investment in the following year.

In the light of journalistic statements about the key importance of such imports to the Soviet economy, figures of this order may seem remarkably low. But it would in fact be very odd if they came out much higher. We know, after all, that the Soviet economy is relatively autarkic in general, with total imports in recent years of the order of only 4 percent of GNP. We also know that Soviet trade with the West as a whole has in recent years been of the order of one-fifth to one-quarter of total Soviet foreign trade, and that trade with Western Europe has been around three-fifths of total Soviet trade with the West.

What is more interesting is the apparent implication that the

[12]M. R. Hill, "Aspects of Quality Control Regulation in the USSR," mimeographed (Loughborough, England, November 1973).

manifest Soviet interest in imports of Western machinery and know-how, especially since the early 1960s, in practice has not been translated, at least up to 1974, into a decisive increase in their importance. The major constraint, clearly, has been the availability of Soviet hard-currency earnings, with the emergency grain imports of the mid-1960s exerting a prior claim on those earnings. Inflation in the prices of Western machinery is a source of further difficulty. It was very slight up to the late 1960s, however, and of more significance only after 1969.

One indication of the importance of the balance-of-payments constraint in the period 1955–1971 is that Soviet earnings from exports to the West provide a moderately good "explanation," in a purely statistical sense, of machinery imports in the same year. The inclusion of imports of grain from the West as a further explanatory variable improves the "explanation," especially if grain imports are lagged by a year.

The statistical calculations underlying these remarks are given below. They should not be taken too seriously. They contain an element of spurious correlation because of the underlying upward trends of both export and machinery import figures. They do not, in any case, necessarily reflect patterns of Soviet foreign trade behavior that will persist in the future. Indeed the sharp increase in Soviet imports of both grain and machinery from the West in 1972 seems, as has already been said, to represent a major change in Soviet behavior. These calculations do, however, support the view that the balance-of-payments constraint on the Soviet import of technology has been an irksome one, and that if détente brings a relaxation of the 1974 Congressional limit on Eximbank lending to the USSR, the United States, as a major new partner particularly suited to certain large-scale cooperation projects would be all the more attractive.

Has the role of Western Europe, then, as a source of Western machinery and know-how for the USSR, been of only minor importance in the recent past?

To answer this question with any great confidence, we would need to know a great deal more than is at present known about the total economic effects of particular innovations and their diffusion in any economy, let alone in that of the USSR. We can say, however, that the importance of such imports to the USSR, considered merely with respect to their aggregate size, has indeed been minor. The Soviet policy, however, of relatively "concentrated" machinery imports, aimed at particular domestic production bottlenecks and technology gaps, makes a merely aggregate view unsatisfactory. It is necessary to discover what kinds of machinery have been imported, for what branches of the economy, in the pursuit of what particular objectives.

An examination of the composition of Soviet machinery imports suggests that they have been important in certain areas. Tables 7 and 8 draw on Soviet, rather than Western trade-partner, data on machinery imports from the "West" ("West" being still defined as in Table 6). The Soviet trade returns tend, for reasons that are unclear, to show somewhat higher values for imports of machinery from the West.[13] They do, however, have the advantage of subdividing machinery trade less on the basis of types of machines and more on that of the branch-user destination. This enables us to make some comparison (though not a comprehensive branch-by-branch comparison) of the patterns of machinery imports by user branch with domestic investment patterns. The main weakness of the Soviet trade data used in these tables is that they are not reported on a systematic basis.[14] The shares of different categories of machinery in total machinery imports from the West will tend to be slightly understated, by varying and unknown margins.

We can nonetheless see that there was a major concentration in 1960 on the import of equipment for the chemical industry, the next largest—and considerably smaller—priority going apparently to imports of ships and marine equipment. If we look at the corresponding branch shares of investment in the following year (an average one-year lag between the arrival of an imported machine and its incorporation in a Soviet investment project seems a plausible as-

[13]This is not explicable by a difference between c.i.f. and f.o.b. valuation, because Soviet import data are said to be f.o.b.

[14]For example, the reporting of trade flows in the country pages of the Soviet foreign-trade returns is not subject to any rule such as "for all 3-digit groups in the trade classification, all flows greater than X thousand rubles will be reported and all flows of X thousand rubles or less will not be reported." Inclusion and exclusion appear to be in some degree arbitrary. This is the main reason why Soviet data have not been used throughout this section.

242

TABLE 7

RELATIVE IMPORTANCE OF DIFFERENT KINDS OF MACHINERY IN TOTAL SOVIET MACHINERY IMPORTS FROM THE "WEST," 1960, AND RELATIVE IMPORTANCE OF CORRESPONDING INDUSTRY-BRANCH USER IN TOTAL SOVIET DOMESTIC INVESTMENT, 1961

ETN		Percentage share of all machinery imports from the "West" (1960)		Percentage share of corresponding branch user industry in "productive" investment (1961)[a]
100	Metal-cutting machine tools	2.2 } 3.3	MBMW[b]	8.3
101–3	Forging and pressing equipment	1.1 }		
110	Energy equipment	1.7	Electric power	6.6
111	Electrotechnical equipment[c]	1.7		—
120	Mining equipment	0.1	(Coal industry)[d]	(3.9)
125	Rolling-mill equipment	1.4	Ferrous metallurgy	8.3
128	Oil-drilling equipment	0.1	Oil and gas	8.0
13	Lifting equipment	0.2		—
140	Equipment for the food industry	7.8	Food industry	4.5
144	Equipment for light industry	6.7	Light industry	2.8

150	Equipment for the chemical industry	35.9	Chemical and petrochemical industry	4.1
151	Equipment for the timber, paper, and pulp industry	6.4	Timber, paper, and pulp industry	2.6
153	Equipment for the building-materials industry	1.5	(Building materials and construction)[e]	(8.8)
15924	Computers, etc.	0.1		—
170	Instruments[c]	2.2		—
191	Road-transport equipment	0.5		—
192	Ships	9.2	(Maritime shipping)[f]	(0.1)

[a]Total "productive" investment (*kapitalnye vlozheniia*) by state and cooperative organizations. This excludes investment in housing construction and social infrastructure.

[b]Machine-building and metalworking industry.

[c]These import product groups can probably be allocated, at least in large part, to the user branch MBMW.

[d]Investment in all mining must be a larger share of total investment than investment in coal mining only.

[e]Investment data for 1961 do not separate investment in the construction industry from investment in the building-materials industry. Each was probably equal to about half the total.

[f]Derived from year-to-year change in productive fixed capital of Ministry of Maritime Fleet, as given in R. E. Athay, *The Economics of Soviet Merchant Shipping Policy* (Chapel Hill: University of North Carolina Press, 1971), p. 29.

Sources: Trade data from *Vneshniaia torgovlia SSSR 1918–1966* (Moscow, 1967); and *Vneshniaia torgovlia SSSR za 1959–1963g* (Moscow, 1965). Investment data from *Narkhoz 1961*.

TABLE 8

RELATIVE IMPORTANCE OF DIFFERENT KINDS OF MACHINERY IN TOTAL SOVIET MACHINERY IMPORTS FROM THE "WEST," 1970, AND RELATIVE IMPORTANCE OF CORRESPONDING INDUSTRY-BRANCH USER IN TOTAL SOVIET DOMESTIC INVESTMENT, 1971

ETN		Percentage share of all machinery imports from the "West" (1970)		Percentage share of corresponding branch user industry in "productive" investment (1971)[a]
100–4	Metal-cutting machine tools and automatic lines	9.2 ⎫	MBMW[b]	10.8
101–3	Forging and pressing equipment	2.1 ⎭		
110	Energy equipment	0.1	Electric power	6.1
111	Electrotechnical equipment[c]	2.3	—	—
120	Mining equipment	0.4	(Coal industry)[d]	(2.8)
125	Rolling-mill equipment	1.7	Ferrous metallurgy	3.7
128	Oil-drilling equipment	0.8	Oil	4.6
129	Oil-refining equipment	0.9	—	—
13	Lifting equipment	0.4	—	—

140	Equipment for the food industry	1.9	Food industry	4.0
144	Equipment for the textile and light industry	3.5	Textile and light industry	2.3
150	Equipment for the chemical industry	8.7	Chemical industry	4.2
151	Equipment for the timber, paper, and pulp industry	4.2	Timber, paper, and pulp industry	0.6
153	Equipment for the building-materials industry	0.2	Building-materials industry	3.1
157	Equipment for the printing industry	2.0		—
15924	Computers, etc.	1.0		—
15965	Equipment for the motor industry	22.9		—
170–1	Instruments[c]	3.1		—
181	Agricultural machinery	0.5	Agriculture	27.5
192	Ships	12.2		—

[a] Total "productive" investment (*kapitalnye vlozheniia*) by state and cooperative organizations. This excludes investment in housing construction and social infrastructure.

[b] Machine-building and metalworking industry.

[c] These import product groups can probably be allocated, at least in large part, to the user branch MBMW.

[d] Investment in mining must be a larger share of total investment than investment in coal mining only.

Sources: Vneshniaia torgovlia SSSR za 1970g (Moscow, 1971); and *Narkhoz 1922–1972* (Moscow, 1972).

sumption), we can conclude that Khrushchev's "chemicalization" drive was relying to a substantial extent on imports of Western machinery (with embodied technology, as well as associated know-how purchases). We can also conclude that the situation in the less publicized development of the Soviet merchant marine was somewhat similar, though less marked. The development of the Soviet food and "light" industries (textiles, clothing, footwear, and so on) was also, though to a lesser extent again, Western-import intensive. West European supplies were predominant in each case.

Table 8 shows a similar selectivity and concentration in Soviet machinery imports from the West in 1970, but with the emphasis now passing from the chemical industry as a key customer to the large "machine-building and metalworking" (MBMW) branch itself. This emphasis seems to derive very largely from an emphasis on Western imports for the motor industry, as a subdivision of the MBMW branch; specifically, machinery for the Togliatti (Fiat) complex is a major ingredient.

The relatively large imports of Western metal-cutting machine tools may require some comment. Machine tools, after all, have had a semisacred status in Soviet industrialization, and it might be supposed that in machine tools, at least, the Russians should not need technology transfer from the West. The explanation seems to be that they have emphasized series production, in relatively large and specialized plants, of general-purpose machine tools. There is evidence, referred to earlier, that even these kinds of Soviet machine tools are prone to serious design and production defects. But the explanation of the imports seems to be, in large part, that the Russians, comparatively speaking, have neglected the development of specialized machine tools and automatic lines of machine tools such as are particularly suited to mass-production use in, especially, the motor industry. These specialized and relatively high-unit-value machines seem to constitute the bulk of Soviet machine-tool imports from the West.

West European suppliers still predominated in "import-priority" areas in 1970, with France the leading supplier of machine tools, West Germany, of forging and pressing equipment, and Italy, of equipment for the motor, food, and light industries. Finland, excluded here because of its special relationship (including soft-currency trade) with

TABLE 9
APPARENT DIFFERENCES IN DEPENDENCE ON
WESTERN MACHINERY IMPORTS OF INVESTMENT
IN SELECTED SOVIET INDUSTRIES, 1960–1961 AND
1970–1971

Degree of dependence	1960–1961	1970–1971
Relatively high (share in machinery imports clearly greater than share of user branch in investment in following year)	Food industry Light industry Chemical industry Timber, paper, and pulp industry Maritime shipping	MBMW Light industry Chemical industry Timber, paper, and pulp industry (Maritime shipping)[a] (Printing)[a]
Relatively low	MBMW Electric power Coal mining Ferrous metallurgy Oil and gas Building materials (Agriculture)[b]	Electric power Coal mining Ferrous metallurgy Oil and gas Food industry Building materials Agriculture

[a]1971 investment data for these industries are not available, but their shares in total investment must have been well below their machinery import shares.
[b]Information on imports from the West of agricultural machinery in 1960 is mostly lacking from *Vneshniaia torgovlia* 1960 country pages; data on total imports and imports from other Comecon countries preclude a large share for such imports in total imports of machinery from the West.

Source: Information in Tables 7 and 8.

the USSR, would have been the leading Western supplier both of ships and of equipment for the timber, woodworking, paper, and pulp industries if it had been included.

Table 9 lists Soviet industries according to their relatively "high" or "low" dependence on Western machinery imports. More precise measures of Western-import dependence by branch would require reliable information on relative Soviet and Western machinery prices by branch user, and a branch breakdown of investment between machinery and structures, neither of which is available. It should be stressed that even those industries classified as having a relatively "high" dependence on Western machinery imports will not be heavily dependent, so far as total Soviet availability goes, because a large amount of their newly installed machinery will have come from Soviet or other Comecon producers. Similarly, industries classified as having a "low" dependence may nonetheless contain subbranches or activities for which the import of Western machinery has been important.

Table 10 shows, for 1970, how the scale of imports of machinery from the West compares, in different product groups, with Soviet imports from all sources (the difference between "all" and "West" consisting very largely of Eastern Europe). Broadly speaking, those imports of Western machinery that seem to have been relatively important for the domestic economy tended in 1970 also to be relatively important compared to imports from other sources. A plausible interpretation of this would be that technology transfer was not being sought from the West in areas where equivalent technology was available from Eastern Europe.

Trade in Licenses and Know-How
The last subsection dealt with machinery imports, which, it is assumed, mostly embodied technology new to the USSR. It has also been open to the Russians to benefit from a different kind of negotiable technology transfer: the purchase of licenses and other forms of know-how (such as technical assistance in turnkey projects). This trade is poorly documented even between Western countries. The Soviet authorities, unlike those of some East European nations, release very little information about their know-how transactions. A recent Soviet statement that 120 foreign licenses were utilized in the Soviet economy in the period 1965–1973 has been cited above.[15] The purchase costs of these licenses, however, are not publicly known. Systematic Western

[15]The *Pravda* statement about license trade is a little vague. The period referred to is "the past eight years," which we have interpreted to mean the period ending at the end of 1973. Nor is it entirely clear whether the numbers given are for all license purchases within that period or only for those that have actually been utilized within the period in production. One suspects the former.

TABLE 10

APPARENT RELATIVE IMPORTANCE OF SOVIET IM-PORTS FROM THE WEST OF SELECTED TYPES OF MACHINERY, COMPARED WITH IMPORTS FROM ALL SOURCES, 1970

Relative importance	Soviet imports from the West
Unimportant (Less than 10.0 percent of all such imports)	Energy equipment Equipment for the building-materials industry Agricultural equipment
Some, but below average, importance (10.1 to 23.2 percent of all such imports)	Electrotechnical equipment Mining machinery Rolling-mill equipment Equipment for the food industry Ships[a]
Above average, but not preponderant, importance (23.3 to 50.0 percent of all such imports)	Forging and pressing equipment Oil-drilling equipment Oil-refining equipment Equipment for the textile and light industry Equipment for the timber, paper, and pulp industry[a] Printing machinery Equipment for the chemical industry
Preponderant importance (more than 50.0 percent of all such imports)	Computers Equipment for the motor industry

[a]These are the only machinery groups listed here for which the exclusion of Finland from the "West" appears to make a difference. If Finland is included in the "West," "ships" moves to the "above average" category, and "equipment for the timber, paper, and pulp industry" moves to the "preponderant" category.

Source: Derived from *Vneshniaia torgovlia SSSR za 1970g.*

trade-partner data seem to be lacking. License and other know-how sales are frequently, perhaps predominantly, part of package deals including machinery sales. Their valuation in any particular sale is treated by most Western sellers as confidential, and it would appear that such transactions are frequently inextricably imbedded in the visible trade returns. The presumption is that they are in total fairly small and in composition somewhat similar to the pattern of machinery sales.

Recent know-how trade between the USSR and the West has frequently been linked to industrial cooperation agreements (using that term in its microeconomic, rather than intergovernmental, sense). A rough indication of the likely branch distribution of Soviet know-how purchases is therefore the branch distribution of such agreements. The following tabulation is an estimate of that distribution, based on a sample survey:

Branch	Percentage Share
Chemical industry	31.8
Transport equipment	13.6
Machine tools	9.1
Other mechanical engineering	4.6
Electrical engineering, electronics	18.2
Other	22.7

Source: United Nations Economic Commission for Europe, E/ECE/844, 14 March 1973.

A culling of Western press reports of such agreements between 1966 and 1974 supports this general picture. It also gives the following (incomplete) picture of West European trade-partner composition:

Number of Agreements					
Austria	Belgium	(Finland)	France	Netherlands	Italy
7	5	(8)	36	4	23
Sweden	Denmark	Switzerland	UK	West Germany	
3	3	7	20	15	

Total: Western Europe 131

Because this total, for Western Europe alone, exceeds the declared number of Soviet license purchases in the slightly longer period 1965 through 1973, and because the same survey of press reports provides a further thirty agreements (with firms from the United States, Canada, and Japan), it appears that by no means all such agreements include (or have so far generated) license sales. It is quite likely, however, that there is an element of some other kind of know-how sale in at least some of those that do not include a license sale from the Western partner.

An arbitrary listing of some of the products, processes, and activities covered by such agreements will give an impression of the scope and variety of this kind of technology transfer from Western Europe in the late 1960s and early 1970s (though it need not follow from the existence of these agreements that Soviet enterprises have so far derived substantial gains under all of them):

paints and synthetic resins;
gasoline stations;
marine diesel engines;
recovery of unburnt converter gases;
color TV tubes;
adhesive-bonded foam-backed fabrics;
catalytic oil refining;
seismic equipment;
glass manufacture;
separating sulphur from natural gas;
telecommunications equipment;
numerically controlled machine tools;
refrigerators;
technical services for airports;
mobile compressors for gas pipeline testing in Siberia;
polymers;
soft drinks;
pharmaceuticals (cortico-steroids);
watchmaking;
ignition coils;
polyester fiber production; and
the manufacture of disc brakes.

Prospects

If the Soviet Union and the United States continue to "normalize" their commercial relations in the remainder of the 1970s, with the United States extending both Most Favored Nation tariff treatment and (more important) large export credits to the USSR, and in general giving more governmental support and encouragement to U.S. firms trading with the Soviet Union, the USSR will have much better direct access to U.S. technology and U.S. resources at large than it has had in the recent past.

Western Europe, which was already trading on a more "normal" basis in the 1960s, has been the main source of technology transfer to the USSR until now; no doubt it has often been an intermediary for technology originating in the United States, especially in the case of sales by European subsidiaries of U.S. companies. Its role is likely to decline in a relative, though not necessarily in an absolute, sense. Not only is the United States beginning in general to compete on a more equal footing, but it has particularly strong expertise in areas now regarded as of key importance by the Soviet leadership—oil and gas extraction under permafrost conditions; the motor industry; agricultural machinery; and computers.[16]

What the preceding analysis suggests is that, for balance-of-payments purposes if for no other reasons, the use made by the Russians of technology transfer from Western Europe has been limited, and has been concentrated on certain areas. In such basic activities as coal mining, iron and steel, electric power supply, and agriculture, for example, not to mention defense industries, dependence on the West has been extremely small, at least as far as negotiable technology transfer is concerned. And this list includes not only traditional priority branches in which Soviet technology might be expected to be relatively good, but one formerly neglected branch whose priority rose substantially during the period—agriculture.

---

[16]We are indebted to Dr. John P. Hardt for the perspective adopted here on Soviet-U.S. commercial relations, drawing both on Hardt and G. D. Holliday, *U.S.-Soviet Commercial Relations: The Interplay of Economics, Technology Transfer, and Diplomacy*, committee print for the Subcommittee on National Security Policy and Scientific Developments of the Committee on Foreign Affairs, U.S. House of Representatives (Washington, D.C., June 1973), and also on a talk given by Dr. Hardt at Carleton University, 22 March 1974.

It may not be overingenuous to detect, in the many statements by Brezhnev, Kosygin, and lesser Soviet spokesmen about the need for greater Soviet participation in the international development of technology, a sense of loss—a sense that the USSR had been to some extent left out of the increasingly rapid circulation of new technology in the Western world, channeled, among other means, through international corporations and linked with international investment as well as with trade.

Negotiable technology transfer from Western Europe has probably been of considerable importance in the development of certain previously neglected branches of the Soviet economy: chemicals, the motor industry, food processing, some branches of light industry, timber, paper, and pulp, as well as computers. But it would be hard, on the face of it, to argue that this has been a quantitatively large source of Soviet economic growth. Both for the recent past and for the foreseeable future, it seems more reasonable to say that the growth of domestic capital stock and labor force, home-grown technical change, and nonnegotiable technology transfer have been and will continue to be the main sources of Soviet economic growth.

The U.S.-Soviet détente opens up prospects for an increase in negotiable technology transfer from the West as a whole, particularly if some of the larger so-called "self-liquidating" cooperation projects take place. The hard-currency balance-of-payments constraint, however, will not simply disappear. It so happens, though, that it seems coincidentally likely to be somewhat relaxed as long as relatively high prices continue for certain major Soviet hard-currency earners, notably oil and gold. The recent improvement in Soviet hard-currency terms of trade (counting gold, for present purposes, in commodity trade) reduces the danger of an actual reduction of Soviet machinery imports from Western Europe to help finance a large deficit with the United States. This danger cannot, however, be entirely dismissed.

AGGREGATE REQUIREMENTS
BY EASTERN EUROPE
East European Interest in Technology Transfer

Eastern Europe taken as a whole exhibits the same priority for technology transfer as the Soviet Union by itself. Data for 1972 would

TABLE 11

COMMODITY COMPOSITION OF IMPORTS, EXPORTS, AND TRADE BALANCES (UNADJUSTED) OF OECD EUROPEAN COUNTRIES (INCLUDING YUGOSLAVIA) WITH EASTERN EUROPE AND THE SOVIET UNION, 1971

Commodity	OECD imports (c.i.f.)		OECD exports (f.o.b.)		Balance in million U.S. $ (unadjusted)
	Million U.S. $	Percent of total	Million U.S. $	Percent of total	
TOTAL	6,621	100	6,378	100	−243[a]
Food, beverages, tobacco	1,061	16	584	9	−477
Meat, meat products, live animals	525	8	105	2	−420
Crude materials (inedible)	1,045	16	375	6	−670
Wood, pulp, paper	505	8	95	2	−410
Mineral fuels and lubricants	1,514	23	67	1	−1,447
Coal and coke	498	8	19	—	−479

Petroleum and petroleum products	990	15	45	1	−945
Chemicals	382	6	806	13	424
Manufactured goods, classified by material	1,263	19	1,852	29	589
Textiles	169	3	382	6	213
Paper and paper products	41	1	246	4	205
Iron and steel	504	8	686	11	182
Nonferrous metals	283	4	194	3	−89
Machinery and transport equipment	736	11	2,200	35	1,464
Miscellaneous manufactured articles	465	7	464	7	−1
Clothing	190	3	157	3	−33
Footwear	39	1	94	2	55
Other	155	2	30	—	−125

[a]If imports of OECD countries were reduced by 10 percent (as in Table 2) to allow for transport costs, the OECD countries would have an export surplus.

Sources: OECD, *Trade by Commodities,* Series C, January–December 1971, vols. 1 and 2.

reflect the extraordinary grain imports of that year, but those for 1971, in Table 11, show that over one-third of East European imports from Western Europe (defined as OECD members in Europe, including Yugoslavia) comprised machinery and equipment. Comecon members other than the USSR have been still more active in seeking West European licenses and in gaining technology through joint ventures that have taken a number of forms. Not only are industrial-cooperation agreements more numerous, but three countries (Bulgaria, Hungary, and Romania) have legislation permitting foreign firms to invest in a minority shareholding in domestic enterprise. Poland has, however, now decided against a corresponding measure, and the GDR maintains commercial legislation that can, if desired by the government, permit foreigners to establish themselves.

Certain of the East European countries have developed a significant return flow of licensing, and to the extent that exchange of technology introduces more permanent elements into interfirm relations, this would imply still longer-term transfers of technology into Eastern Europe. Considerations of commercial tradition (notably with the Federal Republic of Germany but by no means insignificantly with Benelux, France, Italy, and the United Kingdom), geographical proximity (involving many factors from ease of commercial representation to speed in delivering spare parts and service) will militate in favor of an East European interest in deriving technology from Western Europe. Although Soviet deals in equipment supply and technology transfer are likely to include, as shown above, a higher proportion derived from North America and Japan, the relatively smaller countries of Eastern Europe can be expected to seek as large a share for themselves in Western Europe. The very magnitude of the potential for Soviet-U.S. and Soviet-Japanese arrangements on technology and equipment delivery has caused some concern in Eastern Europe lest the United States and Japan preempt the part expected for the relatively smaller Comecon members, who in consequence will seek to take up any potential for trade such a Soviet shift might provide.

Current Commodity Composition

A certain characteristic of technology transfer can also be discerned in East European purchases of manufactures other than engineering goods. Table 11 shows that 13 percent of 1971 imports were chemicals—mostly products which are capital- and research-intensive in their manufacture or are required in quantities small enough to deter any one purchasing country from starting the production process. East European countries differ among themselves not only in the structure and size of their chemicals industries but in the purchasing policies they adopt toward Western Europe. Thus while the GDR, which has the largest chemicals industry of Comecon in Europe, tends to buy short-term from the Federal Republic—to "shop around," as it were, on the current market—Hungary, which has, again proportionately, the smallest chemicals industry, prefers long-term contracts with major Western corporations. The development of Interchim, the Comecon international organization established at Halle (GDR),

TABLE 12

ACTUAL OUTPUT AND TARGETS FOR OUTPUT OF MAJOR CHEMICALS IN THE SOVIET UNION (THOUSAND TONS)

	Synthetic fibers	Plastics and synthetic resins	Mineral fertilizers
1963 actual output	310	580	20,000
1970 target (formulated in 1963)	1,350	3,500–4,000	80,000
1970 target (formulated in 1966)	780–830	2,100–2,300	62,000–65,000
1970 actual output	623	1,672	55,000
1973 target (formulated in 1971)	823	2,277	55,000
1973 actual output	830	2,300	72,000
1974 target (formulated in 1971)	911	2,759	80,200
1974 actual output	887	2,500	80,300
1975 target	1,068	3,533	90,000[a]

[a]1975 actual was 1.6 times 1970, *Pravda*, 14 December 1975, implying 88,000.

Sources: Plan documents and annual statistical abstracts (*Narkhoz*), except for 1970 target formulated in 1963, which is from Khrushchev's Report to the Central Committee of the CPSU, 9 December 1963, and 1973 output, which is from the 1973 Plan Fulfillment Report, *Pravda*, 26 January 1974, and 1974 output, which is from the same report for 1974, *Pravda*, 25 January 1975.

should suffice for arranging the cooperative production of small-volume chemicals, and the general increase in overall chemicals production should fill some of the deficits currently experienced.

The lag between target and fulfillment dates in expanding the chemicals industries of Comecon members suggests, however, a continuing substantial need for imports. Table 12 shows how over-ambitious the output plans for Soviet chemicals have proved to be in the past, although we see some possibility of better performance in the future (the decentralization to industrial associations and technical assistance from Western firms being among the reasons).

The phasing down of the targets after Khrushchev's dismissal cannot be attributed solely to the reduction in the investment program for chemicals, but it is true to say that, although the downward path of chemicals investment in the USSR (see Table 13) has been checked, the industry, at least in the USSR, no longer has the overriding priority it enjoyed in the first half of the 1960s. We can reasonably conclude that continuing reliance will be placed on imports of chemicals.

The decrease in 1972 of purchases in the United States by the USSR of those lines it previously purchased in substantial quantity (see Table 14) suggests a selectivity on the part of Soviet policymakers rather than any general ranking.

Western sales of pharmaceuticals are one specific group of research-intensive chemicals that should substantially expand (see Table 15). An earlier series of studies by the Stanford Research Institute, drafted by one of the authors of this paper, showed imports of

TABLE 13
SOVIET INVESTMENT IN THE CHEMICAL AND PETRO-CHEMICAL INDUSTRIES

Year	Million rubles in constant prices	Percent of all industrial investment
1960	1,056	7.0
1965	2,671	10.5
1970	2,415	8.4
1972	2,759	8.5

Source: Narkhoz 1972, pp. 480–481.

TABLE 14
SOVIET PURCHASES OF CHEMICALS FROM THE
UNITED STATES, 1971–1973

	1971	1972	1973
Plastics and materials for plastics (thousand rubles)	4,862	2,492	3,122
Pesticides (thousand tons)	6.6	1.7	4.9
All chemicals (million rubles)	8.7	8.9	11.3

Sources: Vneshniaia torgovlia za 1972g, pp. 102–103; za 1973g, pp. 103–104.

$35 million of these products in 1968, overwhelmingly from Western Europe. Some of the tripling or more that can be expected by 1980 may be taken up by U.S. firms, but licensing and other relationships are so well established with the major West European firms (CIBA/Geigy, ICI, Hoechst, and others) that reliance on Switzerland, the United

TABLE 15
ESTIMATES OF EAST EUROPEAN IMPORTS OF PHARMA-
CEUTICALS FROM THE INDUSTRIAL WEST (IN MILLION
U.S. $)[a]

	1968	1980
Soviet Union	17	80
Poland	8	16
Czechoslovakia	4	11
Hungary	3	4
Romania	2	4
Bulgaria	1	2
Total Eastern Europe	35	117

[a]At 1968 manufacturers' prices and exchange rates.

Source: Stanford Research Institute, Health Planning Research Program: Growth Opportunities in World Markets for Health Products, Reports nos. 11, 45, 80, 83, 87–89, Menlo Park, California, 1970–1971 (forthcoming in M. Kaser, Health Care in East Europe, London and Boulder, Colorado, 1976).

TABLE 16
EXAMPLES OF CUTBACKS IN SOVIET IMPORTS OF FOOT-
WEAR AND KNITWEAR FROM WESTERN EUROPE IN
1971–1973, SELECTED COUNTRIES

	Imports		
	1971	1972	1973
Leather footwear (million pairs)			
Austria	0.8	0.5	0.6
Italy	2.0	0.8	0.5
Switzerland	0.7	—ᵃ	—ᵃ
United Kingdom	1.6	0.4	0.3
Knitwear (million valuta rubles)			
Belgium	5.3	3.7	2.5
Italy	8.7	5.5	3.8
United Kingdom	7.4	2.5	2.5

ᵃNegligible.

Source: Vneshniaia torgovlia za 1972g, pp. 110–111, 119, 135; za 1973g, pp. 112, 120, 135.

Kingdom, the German Federal Republic, France, and Italy is likely to continue.

In addition to pharmaceuticals, textiles and footwear are the main consumer goods that Eastern Europe buys from Western Europe in greater quantities than it sells; the deficit is offset by some net West European purchases of ready-made clothing. The countries other than the USSR are generally balanced in their trade with Western Europe in these manufactures, the imports and the fluctuations therein being chiefly attributable to Soviet buying. Thus the EEC described as "staggering" the leap of 70 percent in 1967 in Soviet purchases of this group of "other manufactures";[17] it was followed by a further increase in 1968. In 1972 and 1973, on the other hand, severe cuts were imposed, as Table 16 shows, in the case of all countries listed in the Soviet trade abstract for 1972 except for France, whose footwear sales were increased (20.6 to 21.4 million pairs), but by much less than the cuts made with respect to other countries. An earlier experience of

[17]Economic Bulletin for Europe, vol. 21, no. 1 (1970), p. 40.

TABLE 17
PROJECTION OF COMECON'S TRADE IN MANUFACTURES (IN BILLION U.S.$)[a]

	Imports		Exports	
	1967 (actual)	1980 (projection)	1967 (actual)	1980 (projection)
Developed market economies	3.4	13.4	1.5	5.2
Comecon members in Europe	8.3	20.5	8.3	10.5
Developing countries	0.2	1.7	1.5	8.9
Total	11.9	35.6	11.3	24.6

[a]At 1967 prices and exchange rates.

Source: Economic Bulletin for Europe, vol. 24, no. 1 (1973), p. 56.

sharp expansion (in 1954) followed by cutbacks in Soviet orders for consumer goods (and, at that time, also equipment for the textile industries) indicates the variability of this group of products in terms of Soviet import priorities. Despite the enhanced place of personal consumption in Soviet domestic resource allocations over the ensuing two decades, we cannot consider the USSR as "dependent" on Western imports for consumer goods. As Table 11 shows, the overall balance of Eastern Europe with Western Europe for consumer goods is positive[18] because of the former's heavy exports of agricultural produce.

A sophisticated projection of world trade to 1980 made by the Secretariat of the Economic Commission for Europe may be cited (Table 17) as summarizing likely demand by Comecon members in Europe for imports of manufactured goods of all kinds; although pegged at 1967 prices and 1967 exchange rates of the U.S. dollar, the divergent movements of prices and exchange rates keep the magnitudes within the margin of error at 1972 prices. An entirely separate calculation by one of the authors of this paper at 1972 prices indicates

[18]Negative in the table, which shows the flows from the West European side.

that by 1980 the USSR would account for half of all Comecon's imports from the developed capitalist countries.[19]

PAYING FOR THE IMPORTS
Reliance on Commodity Exports

Eastern Europe's surplus with Western Europe in agricultural goods, just mentioned, is part of the surplus of primary products in general, with which it pays for its net deficit in machinery and equipment. As Table 11 shows for 1971, the unfavorable balance in machinery and equipment ($1.46 billion) was nearly exactly offset by the favorable balance in mineral fuels ($1.45 billion); the deficit on chemicals ($0.42 billion) was almost equal to the surplus on foodstuffs ($0.48 billion). The countries of Eastern Europe are dependent on such exports to the extent that they rely on imports from the West, with the USSR being in the special position of supplying the other members of Comecon with much the same type of materials as it also exports to the West. Posed with particular sharpness by the rapid price rises of oil after October 1973, the Soviet choice, in the decade during which its trade with the West has become significant for buying technology, has been between investing in resource exploitation for export to the West or for export to Comecon.

The issues within Comecon relevant to supplies for the West are two—on investment and on prices. The organization is currently engaged in identifying members' raw material needs to 1985. Experience of shortfalls in the current Five-Year Plans, to end in 1975, has led importing governments to seek firmer commitments for the next two five-year periods, which the USSR has to evaluate in the light of three interrelated factors: (1) the exploitation of Siberian resources is capital-intensive; (2) the incremental capital-to-output ratio for raw materials is higher than for Soviet manufacturing; and (3) although the payoff period is shorter than elsewhere in the USSR, there is an initially higher outlay at a time when the trend of Soviet capital productivity generally is downward and when consumer demands (and through them, agricultural demands) have higher ranking against investment than in any previous five-year plan.

[19]M. Kaser, "Comecon's Commerce," *Problems of Communism*, July-August 1973, pp. 1–15.

As we have indicated, the USSR is less anxious to have East European counterdeliveries—the strictures against Bulgaria underline the point—than to attract Western investment that would enable the raw materials exploited to be sold against equipment from the West. Even after successful negotiations, the lengthy preliminaries (exploration, formulating the technical plans, and putting in the infrastructure) mean that major projects can be expected to begin yielding only around 1980, and given the severe restriction of export-import financing in the interim (as decided by the U.S. Congress in the framework of the Trade Reform Act of January 1975), any cost-benefit analysis would come down on the side of sales to North America, Japan, and Western Europe.

The Soviet authorities have long complained that the capital-intensity of exploiting their raw material resources is inadequately recompensed by the prices paid by Comecon recipients in comparison with those paid by Western purchases. The escalation of world raw material prices since the October 1973 worldwide general inflation has exacerbated the divergence from intra-Comecon prices, which are fixed for intervals of at least five years. It is being run down only gradually under the 1976–1980 Five-Year Plans, when five-year rolling averages are to be annually applied (and additionally and exceptionally also in 1975). Thus against a quadrupling of world oil prices, the USSR is reported as having raised its oil prices for Comecon purchasers only 2.3 times.

Before the oil prices leaped in late 1973, one of the authors of this paper drew up the projection of the East European oil balance reproduced in Table 18; subsequent study by the Economist Intelligence Unit has independently yielded closely similar results. The estimates imply that on production plans and consumption expectations valid before the quadrupling of oil prices, the USSR would have in 1980 no more oil to export than it had actually sold a decade earlier. The increment in consumption by its Comecon customers over that period could be met almost entirely from external sources. If the USSR maintained its rate of supply to Comecon, to prevent the East European import deficit from going higher (and keep in capacity use the pipelines it and its Comecon allies have built from the Urals-Volga oilfields in Eastern Europe), therefore, it would have virtually no more to spare for sale elsewhere than it had in 1970.

TABLE 18

**1980 PROJECTIONS OF THE EAST EUROPEAN OIL BAL-
ANCE (IN MILLION TONS)**

	1970	1980
Soviet Union		
Crude production	353	607
less production and transport loss	−10	−17
plus imports	+4	—
less exports	−67	−70
Charge to refineries	280	520
less refining loss	−22	−40
plus production of synthetics	+4	+10
plus imports of refined products	+1	—
less exports of refined products	−29	−30
Consumption of refined products	234	460
Other East European Countries		
Crude production	16	24
less losses	−1	−2
plus imports (refined equivalent)		
other than from the USSR	+6	+50
from the USSR	+36	+40
Consumption of refined products	57	112

Sources: M. Kaser, "Technology and Oil in Comecon's External Relations," *Journal of Common Market Studies,* nos. 1–2 (1975); "Soviet Oil to
1980," London, *Economist Intelligence Unit,* QER Special, no. 14, shows
estimates close to these, except that 1980 Soviet output of oil is put at 640
million tons (the draft Soviet goal published on 14 December 1975 is 620–
640 million tons, but includes gas concentrates).

Nevertheless, that portion sold for convertible currency would—
allowing for some downturn in the world oil price (relative to other
prices) of the 1970s—be selling for triple the 1970 level, while, as
stated, the intra-Comecon price would have doubled.

The USSR can also bank on a terms-of-trade gain in its exports of
other primary commodities to the West, with perhaps the same ratio of
preference accorded to Comecon purchasers. No political reasons

need be advanced for the formal price differentials (interpreted here as ratios to foreign-traded manufactures) accorded by the USSR in its Comecon trade, because the "world-market" prices at which the USSR buys from Comecon members may be correspondingly preferential.

Other Soviet Sources of Finance

The price of gold has risen still faster than that of oil. At around $140 per fine ounce in January 1976, it was 3½ times that of 1971 and nearly that of the trough of summer 1973. Even when gold was at $90 an ounce in mid-1973, one of the authors of this paper estimated that sales were profitable in purely commodity terms, and production, in view of the much higher prices prevailing, can certainly be expanded. Estimates that gold output was 440 tons in 1975 seem possible.[20]

If Soviet imports of equipment increase at the rate shown by the recent trends discussed earlier, and if the volume of raw materials and bullion sales is expanded more slowly—because of the lead-time in opening up new deposits—the Soviet balance of payments needs either a compensating improvement in its terms of trade (as is already taking place) or must incur more foreign debt (as is also happening) or a combination of both. The prospects for each development are too uncertain at present for meaningful projection. In the more stable perspective of the summer of 1973, one of us published an estimate of the Soviet balance of payments during the 1970s,[21] showing the current balance in convertible currency in deficit of $2.2 billion by 1980, which, cumulated to preceding recourse to Western credit (commercial, joint-venture, and Eurocurrency), would have resulted in serious indebtedness, after allowance for the maximum likely export of gold from Soviet mines at $90 per ounce. Even in 1973 it was right to emphasize an option that is always open to the Soviet Union (on the likely assumption that it remains a command economy), that is, its ability to check for a year or two increased home consumption of domestically produced raw materials (though a cutback, as distinct from a leveling-off, such as occurred in 1972 on sales to Comecon would

[20]D. Dowie and M. Kaser, *A Methodological Study of the Production of Primary Gold by the Soviet Union,* Consolidated Gold Fields, London, 1975.

[21]M. Kaser, "The Soviet Balance of Payments," *International Currency Review,* July-August 1973, pp. 88–98.

be unlikely) and use the proceeds to reduce indebtedness sizably. Oil is one of the raw materials of which the rising curve of demand could not be held back seriously, unless reserve capacity had been built in by Western joint ventures, for the Soviet energy balance should already have reached during the 1975–1980 Plan the degree of reliance on liquid hydrocarbons that the EEC had in the early 1960s (namely, 43 to 44 percent), at perhaps a not incomparable industrial structure. But oil has become a major convertible-currency earner, and, until the perspective of future fuel and raw material prices is clearer, the degree to which the USSR can pay its way without borrowing cannot be determined.

The likely balance of trade for Eastern Europe as a whole with the industrialized West has been estimated for 1980 by the Secretariat of the EEC.[22] Imports in 1967 dollars (prices and exchange rates) exceed exports by $5.3 billion, but imports rise from $5.0 billion to $16.6 billion. Like the estimates of the Soviet balance, this must now be modified by the price changes of late 1973, but not yet quantifiable as far ahead as 1980.

Membership in International Organizations

The advantages to be gained in conditions of adverse current balances and a structural need for capital inflow from abroad suggest that the Comecon members as a group could value membership in the International Monetary Fund (IMF) in order to gain access to World Bank loans. Romania is already taking advantage of the facility of IMF drawing rights from the membership it was accorded in late 1972, although its indebtedness ($200 million in convertible currencies in 1974) seems to be leading it to shift back toward Comecon.[23]

If, as might well be possible in the next five years or so, all Comecon members joined both the IMF and the World Bank, their reliance on Western funds would be both increased and facilitated. If individual resumption of membership of those organizations (and the USSR was a founder of the Bretton Woods schemes) were not acceptable to the West, some working relationship that reduced or precluded one-way transfer of funds might be found through IBEC and IIB.

[22]*Economic Bulletin for Europe*, vol. 24, no. 2 (1973), Table A IX.
[23]M. Kaser, *The Guardian* (London), 14 March 1975, p. 18

In an article commemorating the tenth anniversary of IBEC, its chairman, K. Nasarkin, made an observation in this sense:

Time is working in the direction in which the states with different social systems, under the impact of world changes, are increasing their efforts to promote international cooperation.[24]

The general line, however (expressed in this case by M. Maiorov, head of the Chief Administration of Foreign Exchange, Ministry of Foreign Trade of the USSR), is that reform of the international monetary system will take a long time,[25] and, as the chairman of the IIB pointed out, that organization is undertaking only "business relations" with non-Comecon banks.[26]

Czechoslovakia, Poland, Hungary, and Romania are all members of General Agreement on Trade and Tariffs (GATT), as well as of Comecon (as is Yugoslavia as an observer on Comecon). The GDR with membership in the UN would now be able to join, and Bulgaria must be tempted not only by GATT preferences but even by the EEC, from which Romania in May 1973 gained the generalized preferences on manufactures applicable to a developing country. The position of the USSR on GATT remains detached but, because the Trade Reform Act signed by President Ford in January 1975 did not accord Most Favored Nation treatment to Soviet goods (as the treaty of October 1972 envisaged), it could well seek the same result through GATT (after the present round of tariff and nontariff negotiations).

Membership in international economic organizations would increase the dependence of East European states upon the West and, in the case of agreements with EEC, upon Western Europe, but because they would maintain their power to withdraw if the occasion demanded—as some of them did in Stalin's day—the effect would be unlike the more permanent trends of a relationship based on the need for Western technology.

[24]*Foreign Trade*, no. 11 (Moscow, 1973), p. 16.
[25]*Foreign Trade*, no. 8 (Moscow, 1973), p. 25.
[26]V. Vorobev, *Foreign Trade*, no. 8 (Moscow, 1973), p. 15.

West European Economic Relations with the Soviet Union

JOHN PINDER and PAULINE PINDER

The Comecon countries[1] accounted for about 7 percent of the external trade of the European Economic Community (EEC) in 1972. The Soviet Union's share amounted to only 2.5 percent. The Community's exports to this whole area accounted for well under 1 percent of the gross Community product and Community imports from the area for less than 1 percent of Community income. As Table 1 shows, the Community's trade with the rest of Western Europe was three to four times as important as its trade with Eastern Europe; its trade with the United States was more than twice as important; and its exports to Switzerland were greater than its exports to the whole Comecon group. Austria, Spain, Sweden, and Switzerland were each a larger trading partner for the Community than was the Soviet Union.

In general terms, therefore, the Community is certainly not economically dependent on the Soviet Union. But this does not dispose of the question. For dependence might arise in particular regions or sectors of the economy; and the growth of trade and cooperation might cause dependence to arise that was not there before. There are certainly those who fear that economic relations will provide the Soviet

[1]The Comecon countries referred to in this text are the European members of the Council for Mutual Economic Assistance (CMEA): Bulgaria, Czechoslovakia, the German Democratic Republic (GDR), Hungary, Poland, Romania, and the Soviet Union. These countries are also called "Eastern Europe," and the Soviet Union's six European partners are called "the smaller East European countries" or, in statistical tables, "other Eastern Europe."

TABLE 1

EXTERNAL TRADE OF THE EUROPEAN ECONOMIC COMMUNITY BY MAJOR TRADING PARTNERS, 1972

	Percent of community exports to nonmember countries	Percent of community imports from nonmember countries
Other Western Europe[a]	32.6	22.9
Switzerland	8.9	4.9
Sweden	6.0	6.2
United States	17.2	17.5
Japan	2.2	4.0
CMEA	7.3	7.0
Soviet Union	2.3	2.5
Other Eastern Europe[b]	5.0	4.5

[a]Austria, Finland, Greece, Iceland, Norway, Portugal, Spain, Sweden, Switzerland, and Turkey.
[b]Bulgaria, Czechoslovakia, GDR, Hungary, Poland, and Romania.

Union with levers to influence Western Europe. Thus the Institute for the Study of Conflict has written in a recent report:

The Soviet Government is already in a position to buy much Western European technology and know-how. The prospect of the resulting economic gain to individual enterprises, and so to the economy generally, has led West European countries to modify their policy towards the Soviet Union, in order to avoid alienating such an important potential customer. But such sales of technology, especially if paid for in hard currency, gold and other raw materials, do not yet involve the economies or the labour forces of Western Europe to any great extent. Soviet policy appears to envisage the development of exchanges to the point where large sectors of the West European economies, and the employment of an appreciable proportion of their labour forces, will depend on exports to the Soviet Union ... similarly, the advantages to the Soviet Government of increasing West European dependence on areas under Soviet control for essential raw materials, and more especially for petroleum products and other forms of energy, would give the Soviet Government a much more effective hold over the economy of Western Europe than Western

Europeans could exercise over the Soviet economy even if they could operate together.[2]

The Institute gives evidence neither of Soviet intentions to acquire a hold over the West European economies in this way nor of its possible capability to do so. But the Institute raises an important question, and it is the purpose of this paper to consider whether the scope for such Soviet influence exists now, or might come into being some time in the future.

The question is a difficult one to answer, because strangely little thought has been given to the subject of economic dependence. Those who are interested in diplomacy have usually concentrated upon *la haute politique*—that is, on issues of security rather than economics. Liberal economists have contented themselves with the belief that free trade leads to better political relations.[3] Marxists appear to believe that exploitation is inevitable under capitalism and impossible under socialism; which is an unpromising starting point for empirical research into interdependence or dependence as between directive and market economies. The analysis of dependence has, however, an unimpeachable liberal source in classical economic theory on monopolies; and the theory has been developed during this century in works on oligopolistic competition. Most economists had become more or less aware that oligopoly (domination of the market by only a few sellers) was no longer the isolated exception that the classical model had made it seem to be. But few were prepared for such a shattering lesson as the Organization of Petroleum Exporting Countries (OPEC) have recently given us that monopoly and oligopoly, so far from being the exception, are now among the international economy's most important rules.

With the behavior of monopolies and oligopolies as a starting point, then, one might define dependence as an economic relation in which one party can administer to another party important rewards or penalties through the use of market power—that is, by agreeing to or

[2]Institute for the Study of Conflict, *The Peace-Time Strategy of the Soviet Union*, London, February-March 1973, pp. 15, 16.

[3]An official West German publication recently quoted John Stuart Mill's famous dictum that trade is the principal guarantee of peace. J. Jahnke and R. Lucas, *Osthandel-Ostpolitik in der Praxis*, Bundesministerim für Wirtschaft and Finanzen, Bonn, October 1972, p. 41.

withholding economic transactions, or varying their terms. Such a definition is deliberately designed to cast the net wider than Wiles does in his analysis of economic warfare as practiced by the Soviet Union.[4] For Wiles places the emphasis of his analysis on deliberate economic damage to the other side. Yet political influence can be exerted also through granting economic benefits; dependence that results in un-intentional economic damage may be as uncomfortable as damage intentionally caused to an economic dependent; and dependence might develop to the point where substantial damage could be caused, without any harm having resulted up till then. Such, after all, was the case with respect to Western Europe's dependence on Middle East oil up to the autumn of 1973.

It seems more helpful, therefore, for understanding not only economic relations in general between the European Community and the Soviet Union but also the issue of economic dependence in par-ticular, to examine the phenomenon of market power: the scope it may offer for causing another party benefits or injuries, whether intended or not; and the possibility of its growth over time. To understand this subject, we need to step back from the arena of Community-Soviet relations and consider the nature of market power and the reasons for its growth in the world economy as a whole.

MARKET POWER

Oligopoly (we use the word to include the rarer case of monopoly) has grown enormously in the modern world economy because of the technical and organizational advantages of scale and specialization: The advantages of scale increasing a firm's share of a given market, and those of specialization breaking a market down into a number of smaller sectors, in each of which there are fewer firms to compete with one another. This has caused a very high degree of interdependence among the different economic agents within the economy of a nation-state. The automobile industry depends on the continuous supply of components from quite small plants and on the continuous working of a handful of men who paint the finished vehicles. An entire economy can

    [4]P. J. D. Wiles, *Communist International Economics* (Oxford: Blackwell, 1968), Chaps. 16 and 17.

be brought to a halt by a power failure or by the refusal of miners to work.

The advantages of scale and specialization are not, however, confined within the frontiers of nation-states. Interdependence and oligopoly have spread throughout the international economy. Traditionally, the links were mainly between the industrial economies and the producers of raw materials, with the latter dependent on the former. But after many years in the role of the dependent, the oil exporting countries have turned the tables and shown that the industrialized importers of oil are dependent upon them. Interdependence among the industrial economies, moreover, has become intense with the very rapid growth of their mutual trade. Thus the trade among the European Community's member countries amounts to about one-tenth of the gross Community product, and the proportion continues to grow. This means not only that a growing number of economic agents in one member country can exercise market power over economic agents in another member country, but also that general conjunctural trends in one member country are increasingly transmitted to the others. The stability or instability of each member economy is of growing interest to all, and so are the member governments' economic policies.

Interdependence within the European Community is intense. But it is not unique; and the economic forces that have caused it are likely to continue to work in the international economy as a whole. The usual conclusion drawn by the students of international relations is that the freedom of choice of nation-states is steadily and inevitably being reduced. This is not strictly correct, for the growth of interdependence can be prevented by a state that is willing to forego the benefits of international specialization. This has been the effect of the autarkic elements in the policies of the Soviet Union. It is also the implication of protectionist trends in the West. However, given that growing interdependence is usually accepted, national economies tend to become more dependent on the behavior of markets and governments abroad. Such dependence can be mitigated or removed in two ways: By collective choice on the part of a group of economies (such as those of the European Community) or by the ability of the more powerful to increase their own freedom of choice by constraining the choices of the weaker, or dependent, economies. The European Community has been accused by smaller European countries and by the developing countries of behaving in this way; Europeans have leveled the same charge at the U.S. government and multinational companies; and the Soviet Union has certainly at times constrained the economic choices of the smaller East European countries. It is the purpose of this paper to consider whether the Soviet Union might ever be in a position to do the same to the countries of the European Community.

THE SOVIET UNION AND ITS MARKET POWER

The economic forces that have caused interdependence to grow so rapidly in the West are also at work in relation to the Soviet Union and, more pressingly, the smaller East European countries. The keen interest in specialization and the international division of labor among the Comecon countries is witness to this; so are the massive projects put forward by the Soviet Union for economic cooperation with Western countries. The growth of East-West trade at rates faster than production in either half of Europe shows that similar forces are working in relations between the market economies and the directive ones. At the same time as the scope for exercising market power is growing, this may become a more important instrument in relations between Eastern and Western Europe insofar as international behavior comes to reflect the belief that the balance of terror has neutralized the use of strategic power in Europe.[5] There is, therefore, a stronger case than the bare figures given at the beginning of this paper might imply for examining the possible scope for the use of the Soviet Union's market power.

Soviet market power is exercised through fifty or so state trading corporations, which have the monopoly of buying goods from abroad or selling goods abroad for their respective sectors of the Soviet economy. Although this is no longer the case in all East European economies, the monopoly of the Soviet state trading corporations with respect to any trade involving Soviet sales or purchases is complete. But this is very far from implying a monopoly in the world market. The Soviet state

[5]Arguments for this proposition are to be found in R. O. Keohane and J. S. Nye, in C. F. Bergsten, *The Future of the International Economic Order: An Agenda for Research* (Lexington, Mass: D. C. Heath, 1973), pp. 119–121.

trading corporation usually accounts for only a small share of the world market for the product in which it trades—multinational companies will often account for larger shares—and the Soviet position is therefore usually at most that of a participant in an oligopoly or oligopsony (domination of the market by only a few buyers). The question we have to ask is whether this status could give the Soviet Union important market power over the European Community, "important" in the sense suggested by the Institute for the Study of Conflict, that it would be enough to effect changes in the political behavior of the European Community or its member states. Do any of the state trading corporations have important market power in relation to the European Community or to sectors of its economy? Could such power develop in the future? Could the combined power of the state trading corporations add up to substantial market power? Could the market power of the Comecon countries as a group be important, if the Soviet Union were to cause the other East European countries to follow a common line?

These questions are worth studying not only because a substantial degree of economic dependence could be dangerous for the political independence of the Community, but also because fear of dependence could, where it is unjustified, place an unnecessary brake on the development of relations between East and West. Quite apart from any fears of dependence, moreover, the growth of East-West trade and cooperation will make it necessary to improve the ways in which these relations are regulated. Increasingly, because of the trends that are discernible in the world economy (and not only because of the peculiar organization of the Soviet economy) this will become a question of the mutual control of market power. If the relations are well regulated, both sides will benefit because greater trade and cooperation will bring greater welfare and the experience of joint regulation should increase mutual confidence.

WAYS IN WHICH SOVIET MARKET POWER CAN BE USED

The ways in which Soviet state trading corporations use their market power are, for the most part, quite humdrum and similar to the ways in which market power is used by firms in the West—namely, to secure some advantage in the terms of a transaction, particularly in its price.

Although this may have been important in the Soviet relations with other East Europeans in the early postwar years, it is certainly of little importance to the European Community today. Even if the Soviet state trading corporations were to secure an advantage of 10 percent on the average transaction with firms in the Community, this would still amount to an oligopoly rent (the sum exacted from its trading partners by an enterprise using its oligopolistic market power) of only $200 million or so in a year, or 0.25 percent of the Community's total imports; and it is just as likely that the bargaining power and skill of Community firms are sufficient to ensure that any oligopoly rent is secured by the Community, not by the Soviet Union.

Although oligopoly rents may be unimportant in the Soviet Union's exports as a whole, it is worth considering whether there are particular commodities that are important or essential to the Community, and where the Soviet Union's market position is strong enough for it to extract a bigger advantage. In the case of oil, the Soviet Union's share of the Community and of the world market is small, and the Soviet Union has gained its recent price advantage by following the OPEC countries. It has been suggested in West Germany that the Russians went close to the edge of legitimate commercial practice and perhaps even beyond it in renegotiating the price under which their oil was supplied to Germany under contract, toward the end of 1973 when the contract provided for the price to be reviewed. But the Soviet Union acting on its own cannot exert more than a marginal influence on the market for oil. The Russians could exert substantial market power only if they were able to influence the policy of the OPEC countries.

In no important commodity does the Soviet Union appear to have anything approaching a monopoly. This means that the withholding of supplies, which is another instrument of monopoly power that was used most effectively by OPEC, is not usually available to the Soviet Union. Even the complete bans imposed on Soviet trade with Yugoslavia in 1948 and with Albania in 1961 failed to change the policies of these two countries, and the slowdown in trade with Yugoslavia in 1958 and with China in 1960 proved equally ineffective.

For most commodities, the Soviet Union will have to act in combination with other exporters in order to make a reduction of supplies effective. In the cases of transport and energy, however, it may be possible for the Soviet Union to squeeze a particular region of the Community. Thus the Berlin blockade in the late 1940s resulted when the Soviet Union and its East German ally blocked all ground transport services to West Berlin. West Germany's dependence on the supply of natural gas from the Soviet Union may put Bavaria in an exposed position. The Berlin blockade was, however, broken by the use of air transport, and it seems likely that means would be found to provide Bavaria with sufficient energy should Soviet supplies be withheld.

It is possible that, as a result of cooperation deals, some Western firms will become dependent on Soviet supplies of parts for industrial products. West German firms already have a significant turnover of subcontracting done for them by enterprises in the Soviet Union. Other East European countries have gone much further with both subcontracting and other forms of industrial cooperation. This reflects the worldwide trend toward specialization, but it is still relatively undeveloped as between East and West. Any substantial dependence of the European Community as a result of industrial cooperation with Eastern Europe is still a long way off, a subject for observation, not for immediate treatment. Meanwhile, it will be interesting to observe how far the industrial specialization and integration within Comecon provides the Soviet Union with a means of influencing the economies of the smaller East European countries.

A more likely possibility than the withholding of supplies is, perhaps, the favoring of friends by supplying them on advantageous terms. Thus, for over a year following the quadrupling of OPEC oil prices in late 1973, the other East European countries received their supplies of Soviet oil at prices far below the world market level. It is conceivable that such advantages could in the future be offered to friendly countries in Western Europe as an example of the benefits to be derived from participation in the socialist rather than the capitalist world market. The Soviet state trading corporations will, however, generally continue to behave like "economic man," getting the best price they can from the market.

It is equally unusual for the Soviet Union to sell so cheap as to disrupt world markets or the markets of trading partners, causing Western firms severe losses and Western workers unemployment.

Sales in the market economies are usually made at local market prices, and antidumping duties are a reasonably effective defense for the producers of Western countries where markets have been disrupted by lower-priced Soviet goods.

Wilczynski has listed the most publicized cases in which accusations were made in the West about socialist dumping during 1957–1968, and the list contains only twenty-one products with respect to which accusations were leveled against the Soviet Union.[6] The degree of undercutting in cases involving the Soviet Union did not usually exceed one-fifth or one-quarter. As Vernon says:

> Soviet officials... have learned the classic strategies of marginal suppliers who sell in oligopolistic markets: to cut the price only to the point at which retaliation will not be provoked, lest the reaction wipe out the oligopoly rent that was being shared by all the sellers.[7]

The Soviet Union has behaved as an orthodox oligopolist in selling not only industrial products but also commodities such as oil, diamonds, aluminum, tin, and other nonferrous metals. A few of the complaints have, however, concerned commodities such as tin, aluminum, and oil, but these related to a period in the late 1950s and early 1960s when the Soviet Union was less restrained or less sophisticated, against the background of widespread Soviet dumping in the 1920s and early 1930s when the world markets for grains, oil, timber, furs, flax, and coal were severely disrupted.[8]

During the last ten years the Soviet Union has kept to the role of the well-behaved oligopolist. Markets have not been disrupted by Soviet trading, until the inflation in world grain markets was triggered by the enormous Soviet wheat purchases in 1972. These purchases were intended to supply Soviet needs, not to disrupt world markets or to cause inflation in the West. But, despite the absence of premeditated malice, these Soviet purchases did give a sharp twist to the spiral

[6]J. Wilczynski, *The Economics and Politics of East-West Trade* (London: Macmillan, 1969), pp. 149–153.

[7]R. Vernon, "Apparatchiks and Entrepreneurs: U.S.-Soviet Economic Relations," *Foreign Affairs*, New York, January 1974, pp. 257–258.

[8]Wilczynski, *The Economics and Politics of East-West Trade*, p. 146.

of Western inflation, and the rise of wheat prices was a significant factor in causing social and political conflict in Britain in particular during the winter of 1973–1974.

This incident of the Soviet wheat purchases has led Vernon to question whether it is clear to Soviet policymakers "that their role as price takers rather than price makers can only continue so long as they are very junior partners in the markets of the West."[9] Where the Soviet Union is a predominant force in a market, will it know how to avoid disruption? The question seems more applicable to Soviet imports than to the exports, which we have considered up to now.

With respect to exports of commodities, Soviet behavior does not lead one to expect that the state trading corporations would forego large sums of money by heavy dumping in the world markets. A more likely problem for the Soviet Union's Western trading partners would be that the Russians might exact too big an oligopoly rent as their exports of commodities grow. But except for commodities where the Soviet Union may approach a monopoly position (and these seem to be very few), the oligopoly rent would by definition be shared with oligopolists elsewhere. These would probably be either private companies in the capitalist world or the governments of developing countries such as the oil exporters. The problem is, therefore, one of market power in general rather than its exploitation by the Soviet Union in particular.

For the Soviet Union's imports, as for its exports, the question of oligopoly rent seems unlikely to become a very important one, except as one case of the use of this type of market power in a world where its use is prevalent. Such use of Soviet bargaining power could, however, be important in relation to countries that cannot find other markets for their staple exports (for example, Iceland's fish) or that are also subject to other forms of Soviet pressure (for example, the other East Europeans).

At the limit, this form of market power can reach the point of withholding purchases, thus causing losses and unemployment. The trade boycott of Yugoslavia and Albania, already mentioned, applied to Soviet imports as well as exports, as did the slowing down of trade with

[9]Vernon, "Apparatchiks and Entrepreneurs," p. 258.

China and, again, with Yugoslavia. These boycotts and slowdowns were, it has been suggested, ineffective in securing changes of policy desired by the Soviet Union. In another case, the Soviet ban on imports of Australian wool from 1954 to 1959, the action was little more than a gesture. Soviet purchases are a small part of the world imports of wool; and the world wool market comes near to being a perfect one, so that the switch of Soviet purchases from Australia to South Africa was almost certainly compensated by other buyers switching in the reverse direction.

Wiles considers, however, that Soviet pressure on Finland in late 1958 was successful.[10] The Russians were annoyed that a Finnish cabinet had been formed including Conservatives after an election in which the Communists, who normally get about a quarter of the vote, had done rather better than usual. They canceled some contracts to purchase goods from Finland's high-cost engineering industry, which could not easily find markets elsewhere, and sectors of that industry were therefore placed on part-time employment. At the same time the Soviet Union refused to proceed with normal trade negotiations or with negotiations on Soviet credits and on transit rights through the Saimaa Canal. The result of these pressures was that a new cabinet was formed without Conservatives. But the Soviet Union does not appear to have repeated this demonstration of the use of its market power against Finland, and the Finns have maintained their previous political and economic equilibrium between East and West.

The guidelines and instructions issued by the Soviet authorities to the state trading corporations are not published, and so it is not usually possible to be sure whether the trend of Soviet trade with a particular partner is due to commercial or to political reasons. But it does seem likely that political motives were not absent when Soviet imports from Britain stagnated during the period of Heath's Conservative government, after it had caused over a hundred members of the staff of the Soviet Embassy in London to be returned to Russia. Commercial reasons have been adduced for the failure of Soviet imports from Britain to grow, but Britain's goods were found during this period to be sufficiently competitive by a number of other East European coun-

---

[10]Wiles, *Communist International Economics*, pp. 503–506.

tries, which rapidly increased their imports from Britain. If there was a political motive, however, there is no evidence that the action caused any change in British policies.

A more promising means of influence is the other side of the importer's coin, the making of purchases so as to cause employment and profit in friendly countries. Outstanding cases have been the purchase of Cuban sugar, thus underpinning the Cuban economy after the U.S. boycott, and Soviet purchases of fish from Iceland, which started in 1953 after a British embargo had been imposed on imports of fish from Iceland following the 1952 extension of Icelandic territorial waters. Soviet influence increased until, in 1956, a member of the Communist party joined the Icelandic cabinet and the Alting resolved that the U.S. military base should be shut down. Wiles suggests that the base would have been removed had it not been for the Soviet action in Hungary later in that year.[11]

It is not likely that Soviet purchases could have such a big impact on the diversified economies of the European Community countries. But Soviet buying can be very useful for sectors where there are surpluses or surplus capacity, such as oranges or ships, and for technologically advanced industries, such as the computer industry, where Europeans are trying to make headway against severe U.S. competition. The Soviet Union can also become a major factor in the sales of particular firms. The big European firms usually sell in many markets and have substantial market power so that they are less dependent on the Soviet Union, while smaller firms can become more dependent. But the big firms have more political influence and might therefore bring more effective pressure to bear on governments to adopt policies acceptable to the Soviet Union.

The more likely use of imports as an instrument of Soviet policy toward the European Community is, however, a more general one—increasing the amount of trade with countries whose attitudes are favorably regarded or which the Soviet Union wants to influence. It may well be that the rapid growth of trade with France was a consequence of the Gaullist opening to the East, and it is interesting to consider whether there is a political as well as a commercial motive in the recent

[11]Wiles, *Communist International Economics*, p. 518.

tremendous growth of Soviet economic transactions with the German Federal Republic.

Although it is fully plausible that the Soviet Union should use its buying power in the interest of favored countries, there is no reason to suppose that it has bought commodities with the intention of disrupting world markets. The effect of Soviet wheat purchases in 1973, however, has already been mentioned, together with the consequent boost to Western inflation. The inflexibility of the Soviet planning system and the highly centralized organization of its external trade make for lumpy and jerky behavior in world markets.

With regard to its major exports of commodities, the Soviet Union tends to be in the world market fairly continuously, so that it has an interest, like other oligopolists, in avoiding the depression of world prices. The wheat purchase showed, however, that the same constraint may not apply to Soviet imports, so there may be further unintentional disruption in commodity markets due to big Soviet purchases. Alternatively, the Russians may come to feel that they have an interest in long-term stability for commodities that they import, and become normal oligopsonists, just as they behave like normal oligopolists in relation to their exports. Nevertheless, they could, conceivably, use their buying power intentionally to damage Western economies through inflation generated in commodity markets.

One of the markets in which the Soviet Union now has a substantial impact is that of international finance. Not only is it today, as it always has been, a major supplier of gold—it is also one of the big borrowers in the Eurodollar market. By the end of 1974, the Comecon countries as a whole had borrowed not far short of $15 billion from the West. In addition to the normal export credits, this included some big loans raised directly from the international market. The servicing burden may by now have reached a point where at least some of the Comecon countries will not wish to add to their net borrowings, and current rates of interest are also a deterrent. Insofar as they do come to the market, however, they will have a significant influence in it. Just as in the commodity market, this influence is likely to be used in order to improve the terms of borrowing, not to disrupt the international financial system.

The Soviet Union has not made a habit of attacking the currencies of other countries as de Gaulle did in relation to the dollar and the pound.

With the acquisition of financial strength, however, it is possible that the Soviet Union could—not only as an important borrower but also as a major gold supplier—develop the capacity to manipulate the international money and currency markets to the detriment of Western countries. It is probable, moreover, that a Soviet Union endowed with considerable financial strength would use it to advance credits not only to developing countries but also to Western countries that may need them, particularly if, like the Finns, they are regarded as friendly.

Of all these ways in which market power can be used, the prevalent one employed by the Soviet Union has probably been the attempt to improve the terms of its transactions in order to earn a bit more money and to pay a bit less. Because of countervailing market power in the West, it is unlikely that the net effect has so far been important. The Soviet Union has also been prepared to allocate some advantages to countries that it favors and, less frequently, to cause losses to countries with which it has a quarrel. Such losses do not seem usually to have been great or to have effected political changes in the countries that were supposed to suffer them. Finland is perhaps a significant exception, and the Berlin blockade showed that the Soviet Union can cause significant damage, even if it does not change policies, by the withdrawal of essential goods or services.

The capability of the Soviet Union to use market power in order to extract a commercial advantage from the Community countries or to allocate rewards or penalties to them has, in the past, been generally modest, in line with the scope of Soviet economic relations with the West. The experience of the 1973 wheat purchases shows that the impact of Soviet market power can be great when Soviet relations with Western countries or markets become more important. Before examining how much market power the Soviet Union is likely to have, however, it is necessary to consider the other side of the question, namely, how much bargaining power the firms and governments of the Community have in their dealings with the Soviet Union.

THE SOVIET UNION
AND THE EUROPEAN COMMUNITY:
RELATIVE BARGAINING POWER

In economic transactions between the Soviet Union and the countries of the European Community, both sides usually have some market power, and it is no simple matter to determine which side has the advantage or how great that advantage may be. The answer depends partly on the Soviet Union's market power and partly on the ability of Community firms or governments to resist it. On the other hand, there are the elements of Soviet dependence on the European Community, involving the Community's market power and the Soviet Union's capacity to resist.

The ability of the Soviet Union to exercise market power depends on the importance of its contribution to a given sector or geographical area of the Community's economy. In considering the Soviet share of Community imports or exports of a given product, it is necessary to ask how essential this contribution is. Can the Soviet products be replaced by products of the same kind from another source, or can goods for export to the Soviet Union be sold to another country? Can the products be replaced by other products? Or are they essential and irreplaceable?

For a geographical area of the Community, it is necessary to consider the proportion of production and of consumption that depends on trade or cooperation with the Soviet Union. If a particular region appears to be exposed in relation to the Soviet Union, it is necessary to consider how far its interdependence with the rest of the national economy, together with help from the national government, can counteract any use of market power on the Soviet side. By the same token, the degree of interdependence between one member country and the rest of the Community and the extent to which official help and the collective bargaining power of the Community are likely to lend support to that member country will affect the extent to which it may be in any way dependent on the Soviet Union.

Broadly speaking, the Soviet Union is little dependent on the European Community. It sells raw materials to the Community countries in order to be able to buy the equipment and the participation of Community firms in Soviet projects. Although the role of this equipment in the Soviet economy is qualitatively important and the Soviet leadership seems to be strongly committed to the new policy of greater economic cooperation with the West, Community equipment accounts for only a tiny proportion of total Soviet investment, and the Soviet Union regards as normal a degree of autarky that is extremely high by international standards.

The other East European countries are, on the contrary, very dependent on the European Community as well as on the Soviet Union. About 8 percent of the Hungarian gross national product, for example, is exported to Western Europe, and trade with the West has reached about one-half of Polish as well as Romanian trade. The East Europeans other than the Soviet Union rely heavily on Community countries for the development of their technology, and the Community thus enables them to avoid complete dependence on the Russians.

Although the Community buys substantial quantities of raw materials from the Comecon group and significant proportions of some foodstuffs and manufactures from the smaller East European countries, its dependence in terms of imports of commodities or manufactures is still slight. Likewise, the exports, mostly manufactures, from each Community country to the Soviet Union and the other East Europeans comprise a very small fraction of each country's production. The Community countries are, moreover, in a strong position in their total trade with the East, as witness the size of the commercial debts of the Comecon countries and the softness of their currencies.

Before considering whether the general strength of the Community's position in its economic relations with the East contains any particular weaknesses or whether the general balance of advantage may change over time, it is necessary to examine how the bargaining power of each side is deployed and in particular how the decentralized economic systems within the Community, where power is divided between Community institutions and member governments and between governments and private firms, behave when faced with the concentration of economic power that is in the hands of the Soviet state.

HOW THE SOVIET UNION
AND THE EUROPEAN COMMUNITY
DEPLOY THEIR BARGAINING POWER

With the public ownership of the means of production and the monopoly of external trade in the state trading corporations, the Soviet authorities can deploy the resources of the Soviet economy in the interests of whatever economic or political aims they may have for their relations with foreign countries. This centralized apparatus has probably kept the level of Soviet external trade, and hence Soviet market power, well below what could be expected from a less centralized system. But the centralization at the same time gives the Soviet authorities a very powerful instrument when they wish to use it.

As has been noted, the trade of the other East European countries with the European Community is greater than that of the Soviet Union, and it is pertinent to ask how much this trade might be used so as to add to the Soviet Union's market power. Although the smaller East European countries usually conduct their trade with the European Community countries according to economic, not political, criteria, they did join the Soviet Union in its boycott of Yugoslavia in the late 1940s, and the GDR put a brake on its trade with the German Federal Republic during the Korean War and the dispute over Berlin in the early 1960s. But in 1961 the smaller East European countries failed to join the Soviet Union in its boycott of Albania, and since then they do not appear to have distorted their trade patterns for political reasons.

The Soviet Union could certainly force the other East Europeans to break their trade relations with the European Community in an extreme crisis, and integration in Comecon might enable the Soviet Union to guide the development of the external trade of the Comecon group. Unless and until the nature of integration in Comecon changes greatly, however, the Soviet Union is not likely to be able to deploy the market power of Comecon as a group except in times of great crisis.

On the side of the Community, most of the bargaining is carried out by the large number of firms who engage in trade or cooperation with Eastern Europe in pursuit of their own objectives rather than those of governments. They bargain according to normal business criteria, and, as already noted, they often deploy as much market power and bargaining skill as the state trading corporations. They are not, however, responsible for the economy as a whole nor do they bargain on behalf of it. That is left to the government.

The member governments of the Community do bargain with Eastern governments about some of the terms on which trade takes place generally, or in particular sectors, but there are severe limits to the aims they seek to achieve or the instruments they use in order to achieve them.

Thus, although the Eastern government bargains to improve its terms of trade by reducing the prices of its imports or increasing the prices of its exports, the government of a Community country seldom does this. On the contrary, it is more likely to bargain to worsen its terms of trade by asking the Eastern country not to sell its exports below local market prices. Tariffs do improve the terms of trade by reducing the payment to the exporter for the imported goods, but Community governments almost always reduce tariffs and hardly ever increase them.

On the export side, the terms of trade may be slightly improved where Community or international cooperation reduces the subsidization of export credits, but such cooperation does not prevent governments from granting subsidies at fairly high rates. Thus the attitude of Community governments toward the terms of trade is, generally, that they are a matter for the individual firm. Should the market power of the Soviet Union in the average transaction with firms in the Community countries come to exceed that of the Community firms, the Community governments would, on present form, have little idea how to rectify the imbalance.

Community governments are, on the other hand, quite effective in the use of quotas or antidumping duties to prevent unemployment or market disruption within their borders, but they share with the other Western governments an inability to control the world commodity markets when these are disrupted, even when, as in the case of wheat, the exports come mainly from countries in the Western group.

Apart from the defenses against local disruption or unemployment, the main aim of the Community governments in their dealings with the East has been to encourage the growth of trade and cooperation. There has been a continuous process of reducing tariffs, relaxing or removing quotas, and increasing the availability of credit. In recent years, joint commissions have been set up by individual Community and East European governments to consider ways of increasing trade and cooperation. Generally, the Community countries compete with each other in these measures to facilitate trade and cooperation with the East.

The Community governments have been quite successful in expanding economic relations with the East in these ways, as well as in preventing disruption of their local markets. In considering the possibilities of future dependence on Soviet exports of essential commodities such as oil and natural gas, it remains to be seen how the Community countries will guard themselves against possible abuses of Soviet market power. As regards disruption of world commodity markets, their behavior, like that of other Western governments, appears generally ineffective. Nor has their success in expanding trade relations been accompanied by any significant effort to influence the terms of that trade in their favor. In other words, apart from preventing the abuse of Soviet market power through undercutting in their countries' markets (or indeed the proper use of Soviet competitive strength in doing so!), the Community governments have done virtually nothing to control or countervail the use of Soviet market power. This market power has not in the past been great, nor has it been much abused, and so Community countries have not suffered substantially from their governments' passivity in this respect. The question now arises whether, as trade and cooperation with the Soviet Union grow, it will be necessary for the Community governments to adopt a more active attitude toward the effect of market power if they are to safeguard the welfare of their citizens.

One way in which the Community governments can do this is to avoid competing against each other in offering favors to the Soviet Union to worsen their terms of trade. This is one purpose of the Community's common commercial policy, which advanced a step on 1 January 1973 when the member governments ceased to have the right to make bilateral trade agreements. The Commission of the European Community claims that consultation about import quotas and export credit terms has already had this effect.[12] In the same document, the Commission proposes that the Community should adopt a similar procedure of consultation in relation to cooperation agreements; and the ministerial Council has since adopted this proposal.

Although the Community can, if it is effective, limit the competition among its member governments to expand their economic relations with the Soviet Union by worsening their terms of trade, it cannot

---

[12]*Communication on Problems Arising From Cooperation Agreements and Proposal for a Council Decision Establishing a Consultation Procedure for Cooperation Agreements Between Member States and Third Countries*, COM 73, 1275 Final, 13 October 1973.

prevent the Soviet Union from allocating trade among the member countries according to its political as well as economic priorities. Nor are Community tariffs or quotas likely to be important instruments in bargaining with the Soviet Union, unless the Soviet Union greatly expands its exports of manufactures that encounter the Community's common external tariff, or the Community places restraints on its imports of materials from the Soviet Union, which could become a live issue in the case of oil and natural gas.

As this brief analysis of the general bargaining power of the European Community and the smaller East European countries shows, however, the Community's tariffs on imports of manufactures and levies on imports of agricultural products are of no small importance to the Soviet Union's East European associates. Pressure on the smaller East European countries through use of these instruments of Community trade policy could be very effective, but its effect, mirroring the Soviet boycott of Yugoslavia, could well be to induce the East Europeans to forge a closer unity within Comecon with respect to their relations with the West. The smaller East European countries look with some alarm at the Community's bargaining power, and this power will have to be used with moderation if the Community is to remain a factor that enables the East Europeans to limit their economic dependence on the Soviet Union.

If Soviet exports of manufactures increase, as they probably will, reductions in the common external tariff for products of interest to the Russians will provide the Community with a significant bargaining counter. It is not a very substantial one, however, for the Community's tariff is low and, in the course of successive general trade negotiations, is always being reduced. If the Community were to provide itself with the means to offer collective finance for big cooperation deals with the Soviet Union, as has been tentatively suggested in the Commission's document,[13] this could be of major importance, since the West German reaction to some of the vast projects outlined by Brezhnev during his visit to the Federal Republic in 1973 was that they were too big for West Germany to handle alone. If the Community were to handle them collectively, this would not only be of considerable economic

---

[13]*Communication on Problems Arising from Cooperation Agreements.*

interest to the Soviet Union, but would also make the political point that the Community is an entity to be reckoned with.

It was noticeable that the Soviet attitude moved toward de facto recognition after the enlargement of the Community had taken place at the beginning of 1973. The Community has, since then, taken some steps to implement its common commercial policy and has acted as a cohesive group in the Conference on Security and Cooperation in Europe (CSCE). The more the Community comes to act as an effective unit, whether with respect to tariff negotiations, finance or cooperation deals, or other negotiations about the conditions on which trade and cooperation are to take place,the more will fears of any economic dependence of the Community on the Soviet Union be reduced, and political relations be placed on a basis of greater mutual respect.

GENERAL TRENDS AFFECTING THE BALANCE
OF MARKET POWER

An analysis of the Community's trade with Eastern Europe by product group does not show that the Soviet Union's market power has reached a point where the Community is approaching anything that could be called economic dependence on the Soviet Union. There are, however, some trends affecting the balance of market power between East and West that could tilt the balance in favor of the Soviet Union in the future.

One factor is the rise of the cooperation agreement. The Economic Commission for Europe defines industrial cooperation as an "economic relationship and activities arising from contracts extending over a number of years . . . which go beyond the straightforward sale or purchase of goods and services to include a set of complementary or reciprocally matching operations."[14] These arrangements include a number of elements that existed before. Thus goods and services are sold as in the case of normal trade, although in the case of cooperation they may be sold under contracts for a longer period. Licensing can be a part of cooperation. So can the provision of credit, as it often has been for normal exports.

[14]*Analytical Report on Industrial Cooperation Among ECE Countries*, Economic Commission for Europe, Geneva, 1973.

But there are new elements that tend to increase the inter-dependence between East and West. Thus the "complementary or reciprocally matching operations" often include the interlocking of the production of Eastern and Western partners, through specialization, coproduction, or subcontracting. This is, as was suggested earlier, some reflection of the forces that have caused the tremendous growth of interdependence among the Western economies. Although its scale is small as yet in East-West relations, it does create interdependence in a growing number of sectors, with varying balance of market power between the Eastern and Western partners.

The very big deals that have been put forward by the Soviet Union, amounting in some cases to between $5 billion and $10 billion for a particular project, are also a new element that has come with the development of the cooperation agreement. Their very size indicates that both parties to such deals must have substantial market power.

It may be argued that a small number of such massive deals together with a large number of smaller ones would offer a centralized economy such as that of the Soviet Union major new scope for the exercise of market power. This argument cannot be taken for granted, because the big projects will be undertaken by big companies on the Western side, and it is by no means certain that the Western partners will be inferior bargainers.

Industrial cooperation does, however, at least extend the field of research in a study of relative market power. It is also expected by some to change or even transform the commercial relations between East and West by radically improving the marketing of Eastern goods in Western markets. For cooperation in marketing, or the direct pur-chase by the Western partner of part of the Eastern partner's produc-tion, is an important feature in many cooperation projects.

The second factor, which will be influenced by the cooperation projects but is largely independent of them, is the rate of technological progress in the Soviet Union and in other East European countries. It has long been the Soviet aim to overtake the West in technology, and as far as production for military purposes is concerned, there is no reason to suppose that the Soviet Union is inferior. Soviet technology for other purposes tends to be discounted because the Soviet economic per-formance is still manifestly inferior to that of the West. Yet the Soviet effort in this direction is very great, as witness for example the number of qualified scientists and engineers working in the Soviet Union. There have been substantial achievements in particular industries, and the Soviet Union sells several thousand licenses each year to firms in the West. The weakness of the directive economies has lain in the application of technology to the production of marketable goods. The economic reforms that took place in all East European countries in the latter half of the 1960s were designed to improve performance in this respect, and it may well be that they are beginning to bear some fruit. The prospect that Soviet technology will overtake that of the European Community is certainly not an immediate one, and the odds perhaps are that it will never happen. But it would be unwise to discount it altogether.

If the East Europeans were to improve their technology and their marketing faster than they at present show signs of doing, they might be able to reduce their constant tendency to run deficits in their trade with the West and alleviate the endemic weakness of their currencies. A more powerful impulse for change in this direction would, however, be given if the Soviet Union expands its exports of raw materials and if world prices of those materials remain high. It has been suggested that, for the Soviet Union, "the big rise in prices of the resources in which it is so rich, like gold, oil, and timber, must have added immeasurably to its financial strength."[15] Even if the boot has not found its way quite so rapidly onto the other foot, the Soviet Union's enormous endowment of resources seems likely to strengthen the Soviet economy and balance of payments over the longer run; and its exports of oil and natural gas will strengthen its payments position over the medium term, and thus enhance the Soviet Union's bargaining power.

This leads to the possibility that the capability of the Soviet Union to assert its market power will grow because East-West trade is growing faster than it has in the past. There was certainly a sharp spurt in 1973 and 1974. Cautious forecasters have suggested that this would be short-lived, particularly in view of the mounting indebtedness of the Comecon group. But two of the factors already considered could cause this faster growth to be maintained: (1) continued strength in Soviet

[15]D. Lascelles, "Strengthening of East-West Ties," *The Financial Times,* London, 29 April 1974.

exports of energy products and (2) the continued improvement of Eastern technology and marketing. Perhaps neither of these will occur. But if either does, the Community's trade with the Comecon countries and with the Soviet Union in particular would come to occupy a weightier part in the Community's economy.

Although the growth of trade and cooperation between the European Community and the Soviet Union gives both sides the possibility of exercising greater market power, it is the bargaining power of the Soviet Union that has been increased by the emergence first of Japan, then of the United States, as major competitors of the Community countries in trade and cooperation with Eastern Europe. If Community firms or governments bargain too hard, the Soviet Union now has much greater opportunities to take its trade elsewhere.

Even if all these factors work at first to increase the Soviet Union's relative market power, and even if the countries of the European Community fail to make use of their opportunities to unite, it is still hard to envisage the Community becoming economically dependent on the Russians, provided that the Community countries continue to enjoy economic progress at a reasonable rate. The current inflation and the enormous oil deficit have, however, raised fears that Western countries may relapse into unemployment with continued inflation, and hence into a vicious international spiral of protection and depreciation. Should this happen, the stability of the Soviet Union's prices, trade, and employment, and the steady growth of its production, will begin to look impressive to those who are suffering the absence of these good things in the West. As in the 1930s, many people would in those circumstances conclude that the Soviet system was superior. This general point would, moreover, be powerfully reinforced by concrete offers of growing trade with the Soviet Union, for which the member countries of the European Community would compete fiercely among one another in order to reduce their unemployment and boost their ailing economies.

This leads to the general issue of the relative political strength of the European Community, the Soviet Union, and the other East European countries. This is not the subject of this paper, but political questions must be mentioned in order to assess the possibilities that the balance of market power will tend to make for dependence of the

European Community on the Soviet Union. For unless there is economic disaster in the Community, it does not seem at all likely that the
economic relationship with the Soviet Union will become sufficiently
intense to imply any general danger of dependence, unless Soviet
market power can be used along with other means of pressure. But
opportunities for other means of pressure are quite likely to occur. If
Britain continues to flounder in its sea of economic troubles, social
conflict might provide a favorable background for the use of economic
influence. The Soviet Union might obtain leverage in France and Italy
through the participation of their powerful Communist parties in
government, in the context, in Italy at least, of severe economic
difficulties. In West Germany, economic difficulties are not so severe,
but they are by no means absent. Nor is political instability out of the
question; and the Soviet Union could exercise a powerful attractive
force if improvements in the relationship with the GDR were in
prospect. Unless the behavior of the Federal Republic's principal
partners in the Community is to improve very substantially, moreover,
it will hardly be surprising if West German arguments in favor of
having a freer hand in relations with the East do not gather strength. In
short, even though economic pressure is not likely to change political
behavior unless it is accompanied by other instruments of influence,
such instruments are not likely to be entirely lacking in the years
ahead.

FUTURE TRENDS
Both sides would like to see East-West exchanges rise to a level
commensurate with the economic importance of Comecon, and each
sees great advantages for itself in bigger trade. For the East it is quicker
and cheaper to import technology and know-how than to invest in
research and development; the West has valuable market skills, and it
offers flexible supplies that can be used as reinsurance against planning
failures. In this respect the Federal Republic is most useful to the
GDR, particularly as trade between the two is little more cumbersome
than internal trade. For the Western countries, Eastern labor is a
welcome alternative to *Gastarbeiter* (migrant workers) and makes
possible production at unit costs lower than those of domestic plants,
and Eastern markets open attractive opportunities.

Whether performance will match expectations is, however, another matter, and estimates are particularly difficult where they have to take account of political factors, of the difficulties of reaching a *modus vivendi* between two very different economic systems, and of the spoken and unspoken reservations that each side may have about desirable levels of interdependence, as well as of more humdrum matters, such as the ability to pay for greater trade.

With the German treaties signed and the two Germanies recognized as independent states, the political factors seem at their least unfavorable for some time to the growth of East-West trade, and, so long as the Soviet Union needs Western help to develop its resources, there should be no reversion to general political action inimical to trade. However, particularly in trade with the USSR itself, Western Europe will have to fight hard against competition from U.S. and Japanese companies, which are often of a more appropriate size to undertake the projects for which the Soviet Union seeks Western tenders. Already the Russians have found that in the case of large-diameter pipes, for example, only West Germany among West European countries can supply the goods required, and some West German companies have been daunted by Soviet proposals and have excused themselves from tendering for projects that would tie up their entire resources for years ahead. This problem could, however, disappear if the Soviet Union adopted a clearer policy toward tendering by consortia.

There are some differences in the approach and prospects of the four major Western partners (West Germany, France, Italy, and the United Kingdom). Before the war, German firms had extensive business connections throughout the whole Comecon area, and these have provided a very useful base from which to build up and maintain a commanding position even in the face of political hostility and the absence of diplomatic relations or any elaborate framework for trade relations. West Germany and Eastern Europe are accustomed to regard each other as natural trading partners, and although German industry has less need of Eastern markets than most other West European industry, there is a will to expand sales; the only market in which no great increase in the volume of sales is envisaged is the GDR. In France there is no lack of organizational framework for East-West trade—indeed France was something of a pioneer in this field—and the French state is as anxious to promote trade with the East, as part of its general European policy, as is French industry, and it is better placed to do so than the governments of other Community countries. French industry, whether or not at official instigation, would appear to be much more willing than West German industry to accept Soviet machinery and Soviet help in French industrial development and to organize joint training of French and East European technicians, and it is anxious not to be left out of the exploitation of Soviet natural resources. Italy, too, is a buyer of Soviet machinery and licenses, and the USSR has offered to help financially and in other ways with Italian industrial development, particularly in the south. After a pioneering start with purchases of Soviet oil and the building of the Volga automobile plant, however, Italian trade with the USSR languished somewhat until the signature in 1973 of the ten-year cooperation agreement. The signing of a similar agreement in May 1974 between the United Kingdom and the USSR may open the way for larger British exports to the Soviet Union, for hitherto British businessmen on the whole have been much more conservative about trade with the East than their counterparts on the Continent and less willing to explore nonconventional channels of increasing exchanges.

The organizational structure needed to bridge the gulf between state-controlled and private trading systems has been much strengthened recently. To the Eastern partners it is indispensable, and to Western traders less adept at selling goods than the West Germans it seems a necessary concomitant to greater business. Trade agreements between Comecon countries and individual members of the Community ended in 1974 (which should make little difference to the volume of trade); but during 1973 and 1974 there was a proliferation of cooperation agreements of one kind or another between East and West. The governments of the four larger members of the Community have all signed ten-year agreements on industrial, economic, and scientific and technical cooperation with the USSR, and many such agreements have also been signed with the smaller East European countries. These provide a general framework within which governments can discuss ways of improving economic relations and within which more specific agreements are negotiated. They are regarded by the Soviet Union as a substitute for national trade agreements and by the Western partners as a means of ensuring that national interests do not get overlooked. It is generally assumed that opportunities will be given to any country to tender for international contracts in the sectors in which it has declared a particular interest.

In addition to intergovernmental accords, agreements between Western firms and Eastern organizations are multiplying as never before. The Russian State Committee for Science and Technology, for example, has agreements for scientific and technical cooperation with a dozen or so West German firms (including AEG-Telefunken, Bayer Leverkusen, and Schering AG), with SNIA Viscosa, with Rank-Xerox, and with a number of others. Techmasheksport has an agreement on technical cooperation with a French firm on textiles, and technicians are to be exchanged between the two countries.

West Germany has a five-year agreement with the USSR on cooperation in building machine tools, and greater cooperation is in prospect between British and Soviet machine-tool makers. Another five-year West German-Soviet agreement provides for joint research into coal industry problems; contact between German and Soviet agricultural institutes has been agreed upon; and an Italian firm is to cooperate with the Soviet Ministry of Agriculture on livestock breeding. A similar network of contacts is being established with the other East European countries.

To some extent these agreements generate more rhetoric than trade and increase the cost of doing business with the East, but they have the useful side effect of disseminating information, the lack of which has been a deterrent to trade in the past. On the Western side, this has tended to concentrate business with the USSR in particular in the hands of a few large companies that can afford the time, men, and money to explore and cultivate the Soviet market. Now, however, some positive steps are being taken to draw medium- and small-sized firms into the business. For example, with Soviet blessing, the West German Embassy in Moscow has a special section to help them sort out their problems, and Vice Minister Komarov told the Italian-Soviet Chamber of Commerce that the USSR was prepared to supply credit on favorable terms to small Italian firms to buy Soviet machinery for expansion and modernization (particularly to those firms located in the south). Another factor in Soviet-West European relations is that more and more foreign companies are being allowed to open effective (and not merely hotel-based) offices in Moscow. A Soviet report early in 1974 claimed that fifty-five had already done so, among which are ten or so from West Germany and a handful from other Community members. Western banks, too, are now well represented. The Soviet state trading corporations still have a strong attachment to official channels and obstinately underestimate the importance of market forces in capitalist economies, but even they are extending their joint sales companies in the West. Their greater success in selling machinery to France than to West Germany is perhaps in part due to the fact that Gisofra (a joint Soviet-French project to promote trade cooperation) has been working since 1971, whereas in West Germany the first joint company was not set up until 1973 (Neotype, to sell Soviet printing machinery).

Hitherto, Eastern Europe's limited ability to pay for Western goods has imposed a ceiling on exchanges, but there are indications that it may be a less restrictive factor in the future. In the very long term, East-West trade is self-generating in that it will result in a wider and more acceptable range of goods being available from Eastern Europe, but there are other factors whose effects will be felt much more quickly. The availability of credit does not appear as yet to impose much restraint—indeed credit was largely responsible for the surge in trade with the smaller East Europeans in 1973 and 1974—but its price may be a sticking point, and some countries will have to watch their debt-repayment burden carefully. All the West Europeans are willing to lend to the East, and some current lines are on offer at well below market rates. If West Germany had its way, this would not continue; it can sell as much as it wants without extending cheap credit and will do so only if forced to by internecine competition among West European suppliers.

In addition the East is becoming increasingly active in Western capital markets. Comecon's International Investment Bank (IIB) has sought long-term money in the Eurodollar market to finance the exploitation of copper deposits in Siberia and for other major projects. At the same time, increased earnings from sales of gold and raw materials at 1974's rising prices, and bigger sales of arms to the Middle

East, meant that there was short-term money available to take advantage of the very favorable interest rates in London and elsewhere. This unexpected liquidity also enabled the Russians to offer cash down to the West German consortium for the first stage of the giant Kursk steel plant.

Even more promising for the future of East-West exchanges are, perhaps, the new types of cooperative trade that are playing an increasingly important part in East-West exchanges. Licensing agreements have been common in East-West trade for many years, although it is generally felt that the possibilities are far from exhausted, particularly from the standpoint of Western imports of Eastern licenses. Subcontracting and contract-processing have been undertaken for some years and are particularly important in trade with the smaller East European countries. For example, in 1972, DM 100 million worth of West Germany's total imports from Poland of DM 972 million were processed goods[16] as were DM 125 million of total imports of some DM 650 million from Hungary. This type of business may be less rewarding for the East European partner than are some of the more highly developed forms of cooperation. From these narrow foundations, however, an extensive network of cooperation, coproduction, joint innovation, and joint marketing ventures between East and West is being built up. So far, even in Hungary and Poland, where they started some years ago, their effect on trade is judged to be small—although not easily identifiable—but the indications are that they will become increasingly important, particularly in the engineering sector. The agreements take many different forms and, at their most developed, involve joint production (sometimes split among three or four partners), joint research and development, joint tendering, and marketing sharing arrangements. Little cash need change hands and rarely does so. Moreover, in many of the large turnkey and other projects that the West is undertaking for Comecon countries, it is stipulated that Western equipment will be paid for by deliveries of the resultant product. Lastly, although this is on a very much smaller scale as yet, arrangements for leasing machinery to East European producers are being promoted by both French and British banks.

[16]The term used in German trade statistics is *Einführ nach Veredelung.*

So much innovation should help to maintain the buoyancy of East-West trade for the time being, although it is not to be expected that all the experiments at present on trial will form a satisfactory basis for longer-term relations, and growth may well be uneven. Any change in the composition of exchanges will be gradual. In the long term it may approach the pattern common among industrialized nations, particularly so in the case of trade with the smaller East European countries. Raw materials and fuels seem likely to provide an important share of Soviet exports for some time to come, although the volume of manufactured exports will also rise. Little can yet be said about what new raw materials Western Europe will buy from the USSR and in what quantities, because many major resources remain to be exploited, but it is already clear that more Soviet energy will be bought, and, because this is the one sector in which Western Europe has openly expressed fears of becoming dependent on Comecon, it is worth examining current plans. There was a gentleman's agreement among the continental EEC members to keep oil supplies from Comecon below 10 percent of imports; and the West Germans intend to limit energy imports from and via the East to 20 percent of total energy imports.

At present, oil does not appear likely to provide any problems. Western Europe as a whole imports about 50 million tons of crude from Comecon, and the quantities taken by any of the major countries are tiny in relation to total demand: about 3 million tons in 1973 for Western Germany, a reported record 5.3 million tons for France, and 7.6 million tons for Italy. Only Finland is dependent on Soviet crude; in 1973 and 1974 it got 6.5 million tons. Although the major West European countries would like to raise their purchases somewhat, the USSR holds out few hopes of being able to increase supplies above their present level. There are desultory discussions about Soviet offers of help in building refineries to process Russian crude. The French state-controlled ELF-ERAP turned down one such proposal on profitability grounds, although the matter has been taken up by a small independent company, and in the summer of 1973 the idea was discussed in respect to North Hesse. Sweden is to build a refinery for Poland at Gdansk to handle 10 million tons of crude per year; half the resultant product will be taken by Sweden. Completion is set for 1978.

Unlike oil, natural gas is a growth sector. Hitherto, Western purchases have been negligible—a few thousand tons a year of liquefied gas—except in the case of Austria, which imports somewhat less than half of its total consumption from the Soviet group. Writing before the 1973 oil crisis, ECE[17] estimated that by 1980 Western Europe would satisfy its primary energy needs by solid fuels, liquid fuels, natural gas, and hydro and nuclear power in the following proportions: 20:63:12:5; it was further stated that imports would provide about 10 percent of gas consumption. It is now thought possible, however, that the share of natural gas may rise to as high as a quarter of total consumption, and that for the Community, one-third of this will be supplied by imports, perhaps up to one-third of these coming from the USSR—in total a not very burdensome dependence, but supplies are likely to be concentrated in certain areas rather than spread throughout the economy.

With the completion of pipelines, Soviet gas started flowing in October 1973 to Bavaria and in January 1974 to southeast Finland; it reached Italy in the summer of 1974 and France in 1975, when the new links between existing distribution networks were completed. The gas is bought under twenty-year contracts and in most instances is in payment for pipes and other material required to build the pipelines. After a run-in period, supplies to Bavaria will reach 10 billion cubic meters a year; to France, 2.5 billion; and to Finland, 1.4 billion, which total may be raised to 3 billion in the 1980s, particularly if Sweden eventually decides to import Soviet gas, because this will mean extending the line through southeast Finland (at present Soviet-Swedish discussions seem to be making little progress). In 1974, Austria hoped to get 1.9 billion cubic meters of Soviet gas, compared with 1.4 billion in 1973, and was pressing for a doubling of supplies. In general, it seems probable that the amounts passing through Soviet and East European pipelines by the 1980s will be substantially in excess of those foreseen at present, particularly because the USSR has agreed to participate in deliveries of Iranian natural gas to West Germany and, at the end of 1973, signed a protocol in Teheran for the building of

[17]*Preliminary Report on Some Medium- and Long-Term Problems of the Energy Economy in the ECE Region*, E/ECE/847, 14 March 1973.

a 700-mile, $1-billion, 13-to-16-billion-cubic-meter-capacity pipeline to parallel the present one from the Iranian fields to the Soviet border. The USSR will take a transit fee either in hard currency or gas. (This line would not, incidentally, carry all West German purchases of Iranian gas. Some might come in liquefied form via Turkish ports.) In addition to providing piping, West European countries are also providing desulfurization and other plant equipment, and France has a project for the joint design of domestic gas appliances with the USSR.

As regards electric power, the prospects are rather less clear-cut at present, and technical difficulties with respect to transmission over long distances as well as cost factors loom large in discussions. There is also an ideological gap to be overcome. The Western side would prefer a network of small connections between existing Eastern and Western grids, whereas Brezhnev is enthralled with the prospect of a single gigantic high-tension line from Siberia to some central distribution point in the West, but the technology is not yet sufficiently developed to fulfill his hopes. Of more immediate practical interest are the proposals that West Germany should build four atomic power stations near Kaliningrad. Combined capacity would be 4,800 megawatts and the plants would take six to ten years to complete. Equipment would be supplied by Germany, and repayment would be in electric current. When the German chancellor visited Moscow in October 1974, agreement was reached in principle to build one station, with the proviso that transmission lines to the Federal Republic should pass through West Berlin, which is expected to exhaust its present power capacity in the late 1970s. At the time of writing—March 1975—East Germany had not yet publicly signified its agreement to this condition, nor apparently had certain Anglo-American reservations to the sale of nuclear technology to the USSR been overcome, and work on the project had not begun. In West Germany itself the security aspects of the deal were by no means ignored, and had it not been for the problem of supplying West Berlin, Bonn would have preferred the cheaper alternative of importing French power.

At present, the USSR is helping Finland to extend its Loviisa atomic stations, and there is a fair amount of joint East-West research, particularly between France and the USSR, on the peaceful uses of atomic energy. In addition, most West European countries have turned to the USSR as an alternative to the United States for supplies of enriched uranium. The matter has been discussed by the Community, and France, Germany, Italy, and Belgium have all signed contracts. Italy plans to meet nearly half its requirements from this source; the Belgian Fynatrom has signed for 1,300 tons of Soviet enriched uranium for the period 1979–1985; and various German atomic power stations have made similar arrangements to meet part or all of their needs. Sweden, too, has an agreement for 300 tons to be delivered in 1979, and there is an option to increase the scope of the accord later.

Even with the substantial proportion of West European imports of solid fuel provided from Poland and the USSR, all this does not look like adding up to an undue dependence on Eastern sources of energy. It is, rather, a situation worth watching. Because energy is the sector in which the possibility of an uncomfortable degree of West European dependence on the Soviet Union is least remote, no more can be said of the idea of such dependence in the field of economics as a whole. The control of market power, on the other hand, in the sense of preventing the extraction by the Soviet Union of oligopoly or oligopsony rents from its Western partners, is a theme that is likely to grow in importance, along with the expected growth of East-West trade and cooperation.

Index

Warsaw Pact and Russian capabilities vs
NATO (Continued)
fenses, 147; data base for, 131; dynamic
equilibrium of, 156–157; Eastern
European contributions, 148–149; geographic imbalances, 135, 138–139,
149, 149n; qualitative appraisal of
ground forces, 139–142; 157; quantitative comparisons, 133–139, 177, 181,
182, 202, 203; Russian theater-warfare
doctrine and, 149–152; subjective factors of, 139, 157; technology and materiel factors, 142–145
Warsaw Pact and Warsaw Pact countries,
73, 88, 94, 97, 105, 107, 109, 122, 130,
173, 174, 175; integration with Russia
of economic and military life, 123–124,
148, 149, 150, 202; military capabilities
and exercises, 35, 148–149, 201–205,
206–207
Warsaw Pact Declaration at Carlsbad, 73
Wehner, Herbert, 93
Wehrkeis No. III, 203–204
Western Europe, 28; Communist parties
in, 57–58, 67, 82–84, 92, 102; creating
dependency on Russia and Comecon,
23–24, 29, 37, 39, 161, 269–270, 271–
303; détente in, 82, 84–94, 160, 162;
economy of, 16, 24, 167; energy needs
of, 37, 100, 101, 272, 276, 288, 289,
300–303; future of, and Russian policy,
109; military troops in, U.S., 30, 31,
138, 165, 166, 200; political security in,
97, 167; premeditated attack on, by
Russia, 160–163; Russian interest in,
14, 22, 29–32, 57, 75–77, 90; "security
pact" to replace NATO in, 30, 31, 82,
96, 129–130, 160, 200; trade with Russia and Eastern Europe, 124, 213–262,
269–303; see also Common Market
(EEC); NATO

West German Christian Democratic
Union (CDU), 69, 76
West German Federation of Labor, 39
West Germany, 32, 37, 41, 41n, 64, 68,
69, 70, 76–77, 84, 109, 112, 121, 122,
129, 177, 183, 200, 203; alliance with
England and France, 23, 166;
Brezhnev visit to, 72, 93, 94, 289;
France and, 78; integration of West
Berlin, 89; NATO troops, 165; natural
gas and, 301, 302; nuclear energy and,
302, 303; Oder-Neisse border, 86–87,
110; oil and, 300; recognition of GDR,
42; Russia and, 72–75, 76, 93, 94, 96,
98, 99, 101, 204, 289, 294, 296, 299;
trade with Eastern Europe, 256, 257,
260, 286, 295, 299; trade with Russia,
217, 219, 221, 246, 250, 276, 277, 297,
298; U.S. and, 94
White Russia, 113–114
Wilczynski, J., 278
Wiles, P. J. D., 272, 280, 281
Wolfe, Thomas W., 172, 191
World Bank, 266
World War II, 55, 57, 92, 98, 111, 113,
126, 129; Russian military elite and,
11n

Young Socialists, 72
Yugoslavia, 40, 98, 111, 113, 114, 115,
117, 203, 237n, 267; defection from
Russia, 107; Russia's efforts to regain
influence in, 125–126, 159, 159n, 175,
189–190, 199, 204; trade and, 254–255,
256, 276, 279, 280, 286, 289

Zhivkov, Todor, 220
Zhukov, Marshal Georgi Konstan-
tinovich, 55, 125